DERRICKS' BRIDGEHEAD

The 597th Field Artillery Battalion, 92nd Division, and the
Leadership Legacy of Colonel Wendell T. Derricks

LT. COL. MAJOR CLARK

Edited by

VIVIAN CLARK-ADAMS, PhD *and* WENONA CLARK, MBA

CASEMATE

Philadelphia & Oxford

Published in the United States of America and Great Britain in 2023 by
CASEMATE PUBLISHERS
1950 Lawrence Road, Havertown, PA 19083, USA
and
The Old Music Hall, 106–108 Cowley Road, Oxford OX4 1JE, UK

Hardcover Edition: ISBN 978-1-63624-271-2
Digital Edition: ISBN 978-1-63624-272-9

A CIP record for this book is available from the British Library

Printed and bound in the United Kingdom by CPI Group (UK) Ltd, Croydon, CR0 4YY
Typeset in India by DiTech Publishing Services

For a complete list of Casemate titles, please contact:

CASEMATE PUBLISHERS (US)
Telephone (610) 853-9131
Fax (610) 853-9146
Email: casemate@casematepublishers.com
www.casematepublishers.com

CASEMATE PUBLISHERS (UK)
Telephone (0)1226 734350
Email: casemate-uk@casematepublishers.co.uk
www.casematepublishers.co.uk

Cover image credit: Oklahoma Historical Society (OHS), Major Clark Collection

Contents

Editors' Introduction

Derricks' Bridgehead has been almost 80 years in the making. My father, Lt. Col. Major Clark, was the troop historian for the Buffalo Division, 597th Field Artillery Battalion. He began his diary during World War II. His commitment and promise to his commanding officer, Lt. Col. Wendell Derricks, and battalion members was to publish an accurate account of the experiences and performance of the 597th during World War II.

The 597th is unique and important because:

1. It was the first all-black unit in a combat division and, together with the 600th Field Artillery Battalion, constituted the only all-black units in any combat division.
2. It was the first all-black battalion of field artillery to enter combat as a complete battalion.
3. The 597th was the only former all-black officered color bearing ground combat unit restored to active status.
4. When the 597th AFA Bn was integrated in 1952, it became the first and only integrated unit perpetuating the history, traditions, campaign participation credits and unit decorations earned by an all-black officered unit in combat operations during a previous war.

My father, along with many African American military men, knew that, due to racism institutionalized in the military at that time, the accounts of African American military units would likely be omitted, denigrated, inaccurate, or slanted. This is one of the main reasons I believe this book should be published. My father explains in his introduction how the official history of the 597th was "grossly inadequate." In addition, the documentation in regard to black units covers only black units commanded by white officers, omitting the significant contribution of Lt. Col. Wendell Derricks as a Black commanding officer, despite his unique status in the history of the U.S. Army. No full history of the unit has ever been published, nor has a biography of Derricks ever been written.

The title *Derricks' Bridgehead* refers to the unique and essential role played by Lt. Col. Derricks in commanding this unit as he and the unit achieved many historical firsts. Due to Derricks' "bridgehead" (protection, advancement), the 597th provided combat training and experience, by rotation in key positions, to more "senior" black field artillery officers (captains and above) than in any other unit in the Army during World War II. He was preparing his officers for the final offensive—the refutation of the myth of black inferiority. Many former 597th officers would go on to excel in the Army, and many became outstanding achievers in other fields of endeavor. This success includes the author, Lt. Col. Clark, whose Army career culminated at the Pentagon from 1956 to 1960.

In order to write this full history of the 597th, he gathered a unique collection of first-hand accounts from those first black officers to serve in key command and staff positions in the field artillery during combat operations, including the combat diary of Derricks himself.

My father passed in 1999. He had been working on the book and other projects since 1945. Many of his friends believed he had already completed the book and told me to "kidnap" the manuscript and send it to a publisher. However, my father assured me the book was not ready. Nevertheless, after my father passed, we did find this manuscript which appeared to be complete.

Yet, it took another 22 years to send it to a publisher. Most of that delay rests with me. I honestly was overwhelmed with the extensive documents, newspaper clippings, papers and letters, maps, photos, slides, film strips, 8mm reels, and medals in my father's collection. I thank the Oklahoma Historical Society (OHS) for accepting his collection and preserving the items. I thank two people in particular for bringing this book to publication. One is retired Lt. Col. Lester McCants, the last surviving member of the 597th. Lt. Col. McCants regularly called, consulted, and encouraged me to get the book published. He would be 103 or 104 (in 2022), and I have not been able to reach him, but he was extremely instrumental. The other person is my niece, Wenona Clark. This young woman told me it was time to take the next step and offered to help me. With her help, *Derricks' Bridgehead* was accepted for publication by Casemate Publishers.

My goal has been to make sure my father's book is true to what he wanted to say. Wenona and I did a light edit to check for any misspellings and transitions; two pages were missing and we had to add a few sentences for a smooth flow. Also, I chose a few pictures from my father's collection at OHS to be included in the book. I wrote the epilogue, "A Distinguished Journey"; all other parts of the text are my father's words.

This book is important for African American history, American history, and military history. It is so interesting to follow the day-to-day activities and experiences of the battalion members. A little romance is included with letters between my mother and father. It highlights Lt. Col. Wendell T. Derricks, another African American "Hidden Figure." It is well documented and unique in the annals of military history.

Dr. Vivian Clark-Adams

As a young child, I vividly remember visiting my paternal grandfather and seeing him step away sporadically to type in a spare bedroom. I don't recall what I thought him to be working on other than "a book". However, I do remember his focus, the many periodicals and books surrounding him, and his devotion to his project. Decades later, when I read the manuscript for the first time, I was taken to Army bases across the United States and parts of Italy with a tremendous level of specificity.

There are elements of the book that are notably unique to the World War II era. However, there are some elements that are familiar to modern day. My interest in editing the book was to ensure it remained true to the vision and intent of the author, which my aunt was committed to as well. Thus, our light edit prioritized purism as it relates to the manuscript.

My hope is that the readers are transported to the settings of the book and understand an increased appreciation for the sacrifice of soldiers, the value of silent heroes, and more importantly, the contributions of American troops of African ancestry who put their lives on the line at a time where their lives were less valued on American soil. This book will highly appeal to those with an interest in American military history, African American history, and American history alike.

Wenona Clark

Author's Preface

I had several reasons for writing this book: it fulfills a commitment I made more than 40 years ago to members of the 597th Field Artillery Battalion; it fills some significant gaps in published material concerning the participation of black military personnel in World War II combat operations; it corrects a significant deliberate omission from official published material; it recounts in detail, for the first time, certain actions that had a significant effect on future events; and the account is unique in several other important characteristics.

I did not become the official historian of the 597th until January 1945, when Colonel Derricks transferred me from commanding a firing battery to his staff as Battalion Intelligence Officer. However, I had been preparing for that task since October 1942, when I was the first black officer to join the newly activated battalion. When I left the 597th in October 1945, a few weeks before it was inactivated, my three years of service with the battalion was twice as long as that of any other officer then assigned.

In the summer of 1945, I had submitted a draft history of the 597th to the Historical Committee of the 92nd Infantry Division, as directed, for use by that committee as source material for the division history. When the division history was published, the coverage given to the 597th was grossly inadequate and the name of our battalion commander, Lieutenant Colonel Wendell T. Derricks, was not even mentioned. As a result, I made a personal commitment that, someday, I would prepare a detailed history of our unit, the only all-black-officered direct support field artillery battalion committed to combat in the history of the U.S. Army.

***

In the four decades since World War II, many historians have authored books concerning the problems in connection with the participation of black military personnel in World War II. These problems reflected the culmination of the direct and residual effects of the unfavorable treatment of blacks as a matter of public policy, during two-and-a-half centuries of slavery and three-quarters of a century of segregation, discrimination, and deprivation of basic rights as citizens. On the one hand, these problems had, in some cases, resulted in ineffective combat forces. On the other hand, despite all of the difficulties, thousands of black individuals and a few black units had performed in an outstanding manner in combat.

Unfortunately, the documentation in regard to black units covers only black units commanded by white officers; and even in such units, there is little detailed documentation by blacks who saw war "at close quarters."

In this connection, during the period from the end of the Civil War until the end of World War II, 39 regiments and separate battalions with black enlisted personnel participated in ground combat operations carried out by the U.S. Army. These included cavalry and infantry units during the Indian Wars, the War with Spain and the Philippine Insurrection; cavalry units during the

Lt. Col. Major Clark in his dress uniform in his later years. (Oklahoma Historical Society)

Mexican Punitive Expedition; infantry and artillery units during World War I; and infantry, artillery, tank, and tank destroyer units during World War II. In addition, a coastal artillery battalion (the 49th) served as field artillery for several months during World War II; and an antiaircraft automatic weapons battalion (the 370th) served briefly as infantry.

Thirty-five of the 39 units had white commanders. Their officer complements varied from all-white (except the chaplain) on one end of the scale, to a mixture of black and white officers (with blacks in the majority, but junior in grade to any of the white officers assigned to the same unit) on the other end of the scale.

Only four of these units were completely staffed with black officers: the 366th Infantry, the 597th, and 600th Field Artillery Battalions, all serving in Italy during World War II; and the 870th Antiaircraft Artillery Automatic Weapons Battalion, which served in the Pacific Theater during the war. To date, no general distribution has been made of detailed histories of three of these units, for the following reasons:

- The 366th Infantry was withdrawn from combat before the end of World War II and converted to the 224th and 226th Engineer General Service Regiments.
- The World War II commander of the 600th indicated that he did not consider it necessary to publish a detailed history of the battalion.

- No general distribution has been made of the combat history of the 870th, although a summary of the history has been distributed in publications of the 369th Veterans Association.[1]

Accordingly, it appears that only the history of the 597th, among the all-black-officered units, will be documented in detail.

***

Notwithstanding the fact that the existing documentation is concerned with black units commanded by white officers, it is difficult to explain the omission of the names of many of the black officers who had a significant role in the history of World War II. The most obvious and inexplicable case concerns the exclusion of the name of the ranking black officer in command of troops participating in ground combat operations during World War II. That officer was Colonel Derricks, who had one of the most significant roles in the history of blacks in the field artillery. Colonel Derricks' presence on the stage of the United States military history took place during a particularly sordid chapter when, because of the requirements incident to maintaining a justification for segregation, the Army was making determined efforts to prevent black officers from realizing their potential. However, because blacks wanted to remove all excuses for their continued treatment as second-class citizens, they were determined to realize their potential despite those efforts (Barbeau and Henri, 1974: vi), and Colonel Derricks helped to make this possible.

Although a great deal of the subsequent progress made by black field artillery officers was the direct or indirect result of Colonel Derricks having opened the windows of opportunity during World War II, he has been ignored by military historians, and his name has been omitted in the books published concerning black participation in that war. This was done in spite of the fact that his status was unique in the history of the U.S. Army as:

1. the ranking black officer to command ground combat troops during World War II;
2. the first black officer in U.S. Army history—and the only one during World War II—to command a direct support field artillery battalion; and
3. the first black officer to command a field artillery battalion with white officers assigned (1946).

Colonel Derricks' contributions are not recognized in *The Employment of Negro Troops* by Ulysses Lee, a volume of more than 700 pages published in 1966 and one of the "Special Studies" sub-series in the "Office of Military Multi Volume Series, United States Army in World War II". This book, which is used as the official history of black troops during World War II, includes the names of over 300 individuals,

90 of these being military personnel in the rank of lieutenant colonel or below, but it omits the name of Colonel Derricks.

It is difficult to believe that Colonel Derricks' name was omitted inadvertently or because it lacked significance or was not pertinent to the subject of the book. Indeed, I believe that his experiences with black troops during World War II were as significant as those of any individual of his rank named in the book. For a period of almost five years, beginning on January 6, 1941, when he was called to active duty as the Commanding Officer, 2nd Battalion, 184th Field Artillery, and continuing without significant interruption until the 597th Field Artillery Battalion was inactivated on November 24, 1945, Colonel Derricks carried out the heavy responsibilities of a commander of more than 500 black military personnel, including the command of an all-black-officered unit in combat. No other officer in the entire U.S. Army could surpass or even equal this record.

***

This book documents the fact that Colonel Derricks had the foresight to plan for the day when the Army would be less race-conscious and black and white officers would be required to compete directly on the basis of merit. Taking advantage of the fact that the 597th had a greater potential than any other unit in the U.S. Army to provide combat experience for black officers in key command and staff positions, Colonel Derricks established a "bridgehead" and periodically rotated his officers in such positions, as they exhibited the necessary potential. Accordingly, more black field artillery officers were permitted to gain such training and experience in the 597th than in any other unit in the Army, in my opinion.

It documents the establishment of Derricks' bridgehead. Because of a February 23, 1944 speech he made in Congress, the Honorable Hamilton Fish was the individual, next to Colonel Derricks, who had most to do with making the event possible. He served in the U.S. House of Representatives (R–New York) from 1920 until 1945. His ninety-eighth birthday was December 7, 1986. Following are excerpts from a September 9, 1986 letter from former Congressman Fish to me after a telephone conversation and correspondence concerning the event:

> …Naturally I'm pleased that you are giving credit for certain speeches I made in Congress …
>
> It might interest you to know that when I first went to Congress in 1920 after the end of World War I, there were no Black members of Congress for the next ten years and I led every fight for civil rights and equal rights for what we called our colored citizens.
>
> I want to tell you that you are absolutely right in writing and publishing your truthful book … I wish you every success... and I will be very happy if you send me a copy of it…

As a result of Colonel Derricks' foresight, officers who remained in the Army following the war were able to serve and compete successfully with white officers during and after the transition to a desegregated military establishment.

Many former 597th officers who left the Army became outstanding achievers in other fields of endeavor. Eight officers who served in the 597th have been inducted into the Field Artillery Officer Candidate School Hall of Fame at Fort Sill, Oklahoma, more than the combined total of those from all of the other black World War II field artillery battalions.

This book also documents the fact that, in spite of the recommendations of the four successive echelons of commands closest to the action, Colonel Derricks' contributions to the U.S. Army during World War II should be recognized with an award of the Legion of Merit since the Army failed to do so in 1945. The Army also failed to approve a request for a posthumous award of the Legion of Merit to Colonel Derricks that was submitted in 1983.

It is a history based upon the accounts, contemporary with the events, of the personal experiences of the first black officers in history to serve in key command and staff positions in the field artillery during combat operations—the combat diary of Colonel Derricks, and the diary of then Captain Hondon B. Hargrove, who served as a battery commander and staff officer in the 597th. Hargrove is the author of *Buffalo Soldiers in Italy*. (McFarland, 1985)

Mrs. Derricks, who remarried and became Mrs. Baber, explained her decision to donate Colonel Derricks' diary to Moorland-Springarn Research Center: "When Colonel Derricks started keeping the diary, he wrote on the flyleaf: 'These notes are kept so that a fairly accurate account of my overseas service can be related to my dear wife, Elvira, if and when I see her again.' He gave me the diary when he returned from Italy after World War II, but I did not discuss many of the details with him because I did not want, inadvertently, to get into matters that might have been confidential. My decision to make the diary available to the public was influenced to a great extent by events that took place in 1975 at Fort Huachuca, Arizona."

As Mrs. Baber went on to explain, "I made my first visit to Fort Huachuca in 1944, a few weeks before the 597th left for combat service in Italy. I made my second visit in June 1975, to attend a troop reunion as part of the 597th family, to commemorate the Army's 200th birthday. It was a great pleasure for me to return on that occasion and enjoy the comradeship of many old friends who had been members of the 597th with Colonel Derricks ... Altogether, our group of former members of the 597th was larger than that of any other battalion represented at the reunion."

She noted that two presentations during the program particularly stood out. Mr. H. Minton Francis, Deputy Assistant Secretary of Defense for Equal Opportunity, "reminded us that, although great progress had been made since 1948 when President Truman ordered that equality of opportunity be provided for all persons in the Army without regard to race, color, religion or national origin, we could not be sure that progress would always be made. The clock could be turned back. And he showed us pictures of the way we were from the Revolutionary War to World War II." The second was a film, "*The Way It Was*," that I prepared and narrated, about the 92nd Division during World War II. Mrs. Baber explained "The film stirred up memories of things that had happened to us so many years ago."

After showing the film I explained the work I had done over twenty months to plan and prepare for the reunion, including reviewing all existing published histories about black combat units, from the Civil War until World War II. I had found the coverage of the World War II 92nd Division to be especially inadequate and in many cases to be inaccurate, distorted and biased. Furthermore, I explained how Colonel Derricks' name had been omitted from "The Employment of Negro Troops," published in 1966, the official U.S. Army special history about blacks in World War II. Mrs. Baber noted that this "seemed absolutely incredible to all of us. ... Since it was inconceivable to us that Colonel Derricks'[s] status during World War II could not have been determined by any competent military historian, we had to conclude that the omission was intentional."

As one of the reunion coordinators, I explained that I had suggested to the Army that time be provided in the reunion program for the affected units, including the 597th, to discuss, publicly, the inadequacies of their coverage in official World War II histories. But the Army had rejected the suggestion with the statement: "we are not seeking to rewrite history or to prove anything—simply to reunite, talk about old times and have a pleasant and memorable occasion." I also explained my determination to document the important part played by black military personnel in the life of this country and to clarify the omissions, inadequacies, inaccuracies and distortions in published histories.

Further to the reunion, Mrs. Baber generously agreed to let me prepare Colonel Derricks['s] diary for public release. The original copy was deposited in the Manuscript Department of the Moorland-Spingarn Research Center. Her hope was "that the diary will be of some use to historians who seek to clarify the record of the performance of black combat troops during World War II, a record that has been clouded by distortions, inaccuracies and omissions."

On March 22, 1985, Colonel Derricks' diary and six transcripts of taped oral history memoirs of selected veterans of the 366th Infantry Tuskegee Airmen were installed in a special ceremony in the Armour J. Blackburn University Center Auditorium, Moorland-Spingarn Research Center, Howard University, Washington, D.C. Participating in the ceremony were Clifford L. Muse, Jr., Acting Director of Moorland-Spingarn Research Center; Dr. Michael R. Winston, Vice President for Academic Affairs, Howard University; Dr. Thomas C. Battle, Curator of Manuscripts, Moorland-Spingarn Research Center; H. Minton Francis, Director, Office of University Planning; Mrs. Elvira M. Baber, Colonel Derricks' widow; Dr. Elinor Des Verney Sinnette, Head, Oral History Department, Moorland-Spingarn Research Center; Colonel John Thomas Martin, Chairman, Black Military History Advisory Group; and Brigadier General George B. Price, U.S. Army (Retired). The taped oral history memoirs were presented by the Black Military Oral History Project at

Moorland-Springarn Research Center. Among the World War II artillery veterans present at the ceremony were Colonel (Ret.) Marcus H. Ray, who had commanded the 600th Field Artillery Battalion, and five former members of Colonel Derricks' 597th Field Artillery Battalion: William G. Dix, Colonel (Ret.) Leonard L. Jackson, Lieutenant Colonel (Ret.) Walter L. Macklin, Lieutenant Colonel (Ret.) Lester McCants, and Major (Ret.) William Y. Rose.

***

My research on this book was made less difficult because I had prepared for the task since October 1942 and I was one of the most fortunate beneficiaries of Colonel Derricks' efforts on behalf of black field artillery officers. As a result, I was involved as a participant/observer in most of the significant progress made by blacks in the field artillery of the U.S. Army from 1940 until I retired in 1960. Thereafter, I was involved as a close observer until the mid-70s, by which time integration of the Armed Forces had succeeded to the point that tracking black progress became difficult and perhaps unnecessary.

In addition to the traditional types of research, a great deal of my investigation involved documents in my files, which were contemporaneous with the events, including personal correspondence, that I began to accumulate soon after I entered the Army. The files became rather extensive after I was appointed as the official historian of the 597th in 1945. Recently, these files have been supplemented by additional personal correspondence and interviews with some of the personnel involved.

A few years ago, I requested from the National Archives all the historical material on file there concerning the 597th. When I received that material, I discovered that it bore my signature as battalion historian and consisted of the periodic summaries of the battalion history that I had submitted during the war.

My overall research was conducted in five general areas:

1. To document the period when blacks were excluded from field artillery, Dr. Morris J. McGregor of the Office of Military History furnished me pertinent excerpts from the *Documents of Freedom* (McGregor & Nalty). I obtained other documents, including the 1907 Army War College Study and records of the 167th Field Artillery Brigade, from the National Archives and Record Services. I obtained the out-of-print *Scott's Official History of the American Negro in the World War* by Emmett J. Scott through an interlibrary loan in 1982 from the Cameron State University Library at Lawton, Oklahoma, to Tulsa Central Library, Tulsa, Oklahoma.

2. Based on my own documented experiences, supplemented by personal correspondence and other personal files, Congressional Records, interviews with personnel involved, newspaper articles, and official and unofficial

published histories, I documented the end of exclusion and the beginning of limited progress in the field artillery:

  (a) from the perspective of a black enlisted man in an organization with all white and no black officers (except the chaplain); and then

  (b) from the perspective of a black junior officer whose promotion and assignment opportunities in a field artillery battalion were severely limited because the battalion was commanded by a white officer and all positions of the grade of captain and above were reserved for white officers.

3. The establishment of Derricks' Bridgehead and the opening of the window of opportunity for the beginning of real progress for black field artillery officers was based on my own documented experiences, personal files, newspaper clippings, Congressional Records, and interviews with other personnel involved. I also consulted Derricks' diary, Hargrove's diary, historical reports from higher and adjacent headquarters, and items from the division newspaper. Goodman's "A Fragment of Victory" was obtained through an interlibrary loan from the U.S. Army Historical Research Collection and Library, Carlisle Barracks, Pennsylvania, to Tulsa Central Library, Tulsa, Oklahoma.

4. The part-title "After Derricks' Bridgehead" indicates some of the direct and indirect effects of the bridgehead on future progress. It includes a summary of the history of the 597th AFA Bn., which perpetuated the history and traditions of the World War II 597th, based on 597th AFA Bn. Command Reports, interviews with personnel involved, a summary of its history, and extracts from a 19-page personal letter from retired Major General Charles Rogers, who was assigned to the battalion as a junior officer and was still assigned after the battalion was integrated in 1952. Former members of the 597th AFA were contacted through the "Locator Files" in the *Army Times* dated May 6, 1985 and the "Reader Exchange" in *The Retired Officer* dated October 1985. It also includes the status of some former members of the 597th after World War II based on my personal files, correspondence, and interviews with personnel involved, and an overview of the situation from my own perspective in 1960 and again in 1986. This is based on my personal files from my Pentagon years, official and unofficial publications, newspaper clippings, and personal interviews and correspondence.

I would like to extend my grateful acknowledgment to the persons listed below, whose time and talents made writing this book possible. Readers' Review Panel: General Colin L. Powell, USA, Chairman, Joint Chiefs of Staff; Maj. General Albert Edmonds, USAF, Assistant Chief of Staff Systems for Command, Control,

Communications and Computers; Brig. General Sherian Cadoria, USA (Ret.), U.S. Total Army Personnel Command; Brig. General Lester L. Lyles, USAF, DCS Requirements, HQ Air Force Systems Command; RADM Walter David, USN, Commander, Naval District of Washington; The Honorable John W. Shannon, Under Secretary of the Army; Mrs. Joan M. MacKenzie, Staff Assistant to the Deputy Commissioner, Immigration & Naturalization; Dr. Meredith A. Neizer, DACOWITS Chairperson; Mr. Claiborne D. Haughton Jr., Direct of Civilian Equal Opportunity Policy; Mr. Walter R. Somerville, Chief, Office of Civil Rights. Col. William Walton, Director, Military Equal Opportunity Policy, (Civilian Personnel Policy/Equal Opportunity); Lt. Col. James E. Love, Deputy Director, Training & Research, Military Equal Opportunity Policy, (Civilian Personnel Policy/ Equal Opportunity); Lt. Col. Thomas L. Bain, Military Assistant to the Deputy Assistant Secretary Of Defense, (Civilian Personnel Policy/Equal Opportunity); Mr. Therman Jones (reprint permission); Mr. Mason Carl, Deputy Director, WHS Presentations; Colonel John Silvera, US Army (Retired), Tuskegee Airman; Mr. Jim Lawrence (photographs); Mr. Harry Wilson (halftones and contact prints); Ms. Avis Dillon (layout/design/typesetting); Dr. Leroy L. Ramsey (research/writing/editing); Mrs. Felecia H. Clark (Assistant Editor); Lt. Col. Lester McCants (review); Ms. Ingrid Brown (review); Ms. Rita Duncan (typing/review); and Mr. Franklin Clark (maps).

Lt. Col. Major Clark (ret.)
Summer 1987

Chronology

Aug. 1, 1940	349th Field Artillery activated at Fort Sill, Oklahoma
Aug. 15, 1940	Enlistment opened for 349th
Nov. 1940	349th fires first round from its 155mm guns
Dec. 13, 1940–Jan. 5, 1941	Key officers from 184th Field Artillery leave their unit in Chicago for supplemental training with 349th at Fort Sill
Jan. 1941	349th conducts cadre training
Feb. 10, 1941	46th Field Artillery Brigade activated at Camp Livingston, Louisiana; cadres furnished by 349th
Dec. 8, 1941	United States declares war on Japan and three days later, declares war on Germany and Italy
May 5, 1942	597th Field Artillery Battalion (597th RA Bn) constituted
Jul. 14, 1942	FA OCS Class #33 begins
Oct. 8, 1942	Three black graduates of FA OCS Class #33 commissioned as second lieutenants and assigned to 597th FA Bn
Oct. 15, 1942	92nd Infantry Division activated with major elements at four widely separated locations; 597th Field Artillery Battalion activated at Camp Atterbury, Indiana
Apr. 29–May 3, 1943	597th moves to Fort Huachuca, Arizona
Jun. 27, 1943	597th wins Division Artillery athletic competition
Late Jun.–early Jul., 1943	Battery B, 597th makes second highest battery test score in 92nd Division Artillery
Aug. 16–Dec. 23, 1943	597th participates in combined training program
Nov. 11, 1943	Battery B participates in the Armistice Day parade in Tucson
Dec. 3–23, 1943	597th participates in division exercises
Jan. 1–27, 1944	92nd Division prepares for Louisiana Maneuvers
Oct. 20, 1942	First black officers, graduates of FA OCS Class No. 33, report to 597th

late Nov. to early Dec., 1942	First fillers arrive
mid-Dec., 1942	597th begins individual training program
Jan. 15, 1943	597th fires howitzers for the first time, in a problem requiring overhead artillery fire for the infantry
Mar. 10, 1943	597th leaves Camp Atterbury, Indiana
Mar. 13, 1943	597th arrives at Camp Robinson, Arkansas
Apr. 3, 1943	Major C. W. Crockett relieves Major Workizer as 597th FA Bn. commander
Apr. 18, 1943	President Roosevelt visits Camp Robinson
Apr. 29, 1943	597th leaves Camp Robinson by rail for Fort Huachuca, Arizona
Jan. 28–Feb. 3, 1944	597th moves from Fort Huachuca to Louisiana Maneuvers area
Feb. 6–Apr. 2, 1944	597th participates in Louisiana Maneuvers
Mar. 15–Apr. 3, 1944	Lt. Col. Wendell T. Derricks and a number of other black former members of Illinois National Guard Field artillery units join the 597th as observers
Apr. 3–8, 1944	597th moves from Louisiana Maneuvers area back to Fort Huachuca.
Apr. 13, 1944	Lt. Col. Wendell T. Derricks assumes command of the 597th
Apr., 1944	Beginning of a three-month period when 92nd Division was visited by a large number of high-ranking civilians and generals
Jun. 5, 1944	Window of opportunity opened in 597th when, for the first time, a member of the original group of black 92nd Division Artillery officers is assigned to command a firing battery (Battery A)
Jun. 1 & 2, 1944	Battery firing tests completed in weeks
Jul, 25, 1944	597th completes Battalion firing tests
1st week Sep., 44	597th loads equipment on trains for shipment to port of embarkation
Sep. 5, 1944	597th leaves Fort Huachuca, Arizona, by rail for staging area at Camp Patrick Henry, VA
Sep. 8, 1944	597th arrives at staging area
Sep. 19, 1944	597th travels from staging area to Hampton Roads Port of Embarkation and boards USAT SS *Colombie*
Sep. 20, 1944	*Colombie* joins convoy and begins voyage across the Atlantic to Italy
Oct. 1, 1944	Convoy passes through Strait of Gibraltar
Oct. 4, 1944	Convoy docks in Naples harbor

Oct. 5, 1944	*Colombie* and one escort vessel proceed up west coast of Italy to Leghorn
Oct. 5, 1944	*Colombie* enters Leghorn harbor; 597th debarks and travels by truck to PBS Forward Staging Area near Pisa. Remains there until November 10, processing organizational equipment and checking personnel
Oct. 10–15, 1944	Key battalion personnel visit front-line U.S. Fifth Army artillery units for battle indoctrination
Nov. 10, 1944	597th moves up to assembly area south of Viareggio for final checks of personnel and equipment before moving to first combat position
Nov. 15, 1944	597th, led by Battery A, occupies its first combat position
Nov. 16, 1944	Battery B fires first rounds in combat
Nov. 17, 1944	365th Inf. Cannon Co. attached to 597th
Nov. 18, 1944	597th supports attack by 371st Inf. against German positions
Nov. 22, 1944	Colonel Marston, 92nd Div. Arty. Exec., leaves for 33rd Gen. Hosp. General Derricks becomes second ranking officer assigned to Div. Arty. and seventh ranking officer in division
Nov. 23, 1944	Advance party from 366th Inf. arrives in staging area
Nov. 26, 1944	Main body of 366th Inf. arrives
Nov. 28, 1944	366th Inf. attached to 92nd Div.
Dec. 1, 1944	597th notified of change in assignment and mission; attached to 88th Div. on Bologna front
Dec. 2, 1944	Colonel Derricks travels to the 88th Div. on recon. for new positions
Dec. 3, 1944	597th leaves coastal sector for the Bologna front
Dec. 4, 1944	597th arrives in the new area and goes into position in Idice River Valley
Dec. 11, 1944	Heaviest one day's shelling of the war; three men in 597th wounded
Dec. 20, 1944	Colonel Derricks attends parade and ceremony in Viareggio in honor of Lt. Gen. Truscott, the new Fifth Army commander
Dec. 26, 1944	Germans attack in the Serchio Valley
Dec. 29, 1944	365th assumes responsibility for the sector of the 349th Inf.; 597th resumes mission of direct support of the 365th
Jan. 6, 1945	597th moves from Bologna front to Serchio Valley sector of the 92nd Division

Jan. 7, 1945	597th occupies position—attached to 10 AGRA; continues mission of direct support of 365th Inf
Jan. 9, 1945	Cannon Companies, 365th and 366th, attached to 597th
Jan. 18, 1945	Colonel Derricks visits Bagni di Lucca
Jan. 31, 1945	92nd Division Artillery wins basketball championship; 597th has five men on a team of 10
Feb. 4, 1945	Diversionary attack for Operation *Fourth Term* launched in Serchio Valley
Feb. 5, 1945	597th supports 365th Inf. in attack on Lama di Sotto
Feb. 6, 1945	597th assigned additional mission of supporting 1st and 2nd Battalions, 366th Inf.
Feb. 7–11, 1945	597th continues to support attack by 365th and 366th Inf.
Feb. 14, 1945	General Marshall, Chief of Staff, U.S. Army, visits 92nd Division coastal sector
Feb. 17, 1945	First fatal casualties in 597th
Feb. 26–Mar. 1, 1945	365th and 366th Infantry move out of sector; replaced by 473rd Infantry; 597th assumes mission of direct support of 473rd
Mar. 1, 1945	Truman Gibson, Civilian Aide to the Secretary of War, visits 92nd Division
Mar. 2, 1945	597th CP moves to Fornaci
Mar. 4, 1945	Truman Gibson visits 597th
Mar. 7, 1945	Colonel Derricks leaves for Rome
Mar. 12, 1945	Captain White killed when his jeep overturned while he was en route between Fornaci and Barga
Mar. 13, 1945	Colonel Derricks returns from Rome
Mar. 14, 1945	597th's mission changed from direct support of 473rd to general support, reinforcing the 111th Field Regiment (British)
Mar. 23, 1945	597th starts to move out of Serchio Valley sector back to coastal sector
Apr. 5–8, 1945	597th in general support of 92nd Div., reinforcing 598th in support of 370th Inf.; fire in support of attacks on key terrain features east of Highway 1 from the same positions west of Pietrasanta
Apr. 9–11, 1945	597th moves forward to positions between the Cinquale Canal and the Frigido River and supports attacks which clear Massa and Marina di Massa
Apr. 12, 1945	597th moves to position north of Massa

Apr. 14, 1945	597th in direct support of 758th Tank Bn., which was responsible for the coastal plain; continues to reinforce 598th
Apr. 16, 1945	597th moves to a position northwest of Carrara where it supports 758th in its continued drive up Highway 1; provides fire support for attacks on Nicola, Ortanova, and Castelnuova di Magra.
Apr. 20–23, 1945	597th moves to position southwest of Castelnuova di Magra where mission changes from direct support of 758th and reinforcing 598th to reinforcing 599th in support of 442nd Inf. However, before all movements of liaison and forward observer personnel are completed to carry out mission, new mission places the 597th in direct support of 2nd Bn., 370th Inf., then enroute from the Mount Folgorito ridge through Gragnola to join its parent unit. 597th supports attacks on Sarzana and Fosdinova.
Apr. 24, 1945	92nd Div. placed under the control of the 15th Army Group and directed to take Genoa and block Cisa and Cerretta passes; 370th Inf.—with 597th attached and in direct support—assigned latter mission.
Apr. 24–25, 1945	597th moves to Isola; 442nd Inf. takes Aulla; 379th Inf. takes Pontremoli
Apr. 26–27, 1945	597th moves to position south of Pontremoli; fires last mission on enemy moving out of Pontremoli
Apr. 29, 1945	Battery A makes short forward movement to new position
Apr. 30, 1945	Battery C moves up to position in Montelunga, just south of Cisa pass
May 1, 1945	597th begins move from Pontremoli to Genova
May 2, 1945	Victory parade and decoration ceremony held in Genova; Derricks awarded Bronze Medal
May 3, 1945	597th moves to Bolzanetto
May 19, 1945	597th moves to Varazze
May 20, 1945	597th personnel conduct inventory of battlefield
Jun.1, 1945	Brig. Gen. W. H. Colbern, CO 92nd Div. Arty., leaves division for reassignment; Colonel Robert C. C. Ross assumes command
Jun. 2, 1945	Battery C, 597th, moves back to area south of Viareggio
Jun. 6, 1945	597th participates in 92nd Division parade ceremony to return Columbus's ashes to the city of Genoa

May 28, 1945	Sector patrol directive issued by 92nd Division
May 30, 1945	Operations instructions issued by 92nd Division Arty
May 31, 1945	597th organizes and operates first sector patrol
Jun. 4, 1945	Sector patrol contacted by Mrs. Frederic de Billier, expatriate American citizen, and her Italian family
Jun. 10, 1945	Members of the family are guests of 597th at special dinner in Varazze
Jun. 13, 1945	Last ceremony at Varazze
Jun. 16, 1945	Remainder of 597th moves back to the area south of Viareggio; begins training for redeployment to the Pacific
Jul. 5, 1945	597th's contribution of $2,177.00 to United Negro College Fund was largest contribution by any battalion in 92nd Division
Jul. 18, 1945	American Red Cross building in Varazze destroyed by mine explosion; one 597th man killed
Aug. 1, 1945	597th conducts first service practice on Montcatini Redeployment Training Area Firing Range
Aug. 6, 1945	597th conducts last service practice; first atomic bomb dropped on Hiroshima, Japan
Aug. 9, 1945	Second atomic bomb dropped on Nagasaki, Japan
Aug. 14, 1945	Japan surrenders; training for redeployment ended
Aug. 16, 1945	152 men transferred out of 597th
Aug. 31–Sep. 4, 1945	Derricks in 64th General Hospital
Sep. 24, 1945	Derricks refuses to accept Oak Leaf Cluster to Bronze Star in lieu of Legion of Merit
Oct. 1, 1945	123 personnel from 598th and 272 personnel from 600th transferred to 597th
Oct. 11, 1945	Derricks awarded Italian Military Cross for Valor by Crown Prince Victor Emmanuel
Oct. 6, 1945	597th boards ship for return to the United States
Nov. 23, 1945	597th disembarks at Boston, Mass.
Nov. 24, 1945	597th is inactivated at Camp Myles Standish, Massachusetts
Nov. 28, 1945	92nd Division is inactivated at Newport News, Virginia

Introduction

There are few occasions in the life of a career military officer more memorable and appropriate for reminiscing than the day he retires after completing a long tour of active military duty. I celebrated that occasion on September 30, 1960 after completing over 20 years of active duty, which included combat service as an officer in two wars and service on the Army Staff in the Pentagon.

The occasion of my retirement was especially memorable because the events associated with it took place at the Pentagon, where I had been assigned for almost five years. I began my reminiscing while waiting for the beginning of the final ceremonies which would bring an end to my active military service.

Major Clark after retirement from the Army, working at McDonnell Douglas, Tulsa, Oklahoma.

I recalled some of the events that had taken place during the 1,679 days since I had reported to the Pentagon in February 1956 to serve on the Army Staff. During that time, I had walked thousands of miles along the 17½ miles of corridors and up and down the stairways. I had spent more than a thousand 10-hour work days, dozens of 16-hour work days, and many 24-hour work days to ensure that my performance would not give aid and comfort to those who wanted to continue to perpetuate the myth of inherent racial inferiority. I had been a participant-observer in the making of a great deal of history in a place unsurpassed in providing an opportunity to accomplish an overview of the status of blacks in the field artillery from the "Big Picture" perspective; to evaluate our progress in terms of how far we had come and how far we still had to go.

For most of the history of our nation, the progress of blacks in the military had been impeded by the same considerations that hampered the progress of blacks in other phases of society: the myth of inherent racial inferiority. Because of the technical requirements associated with field artillery, the myth had been particularly adverse to blacks who aspired to be field artillerymen and had been responsible for excluding them, for several decades, from service in that branch. As a result, the first Regular Army field artillery unit had not been activated until August 1, 1940, three-quarters of a century after black infantry and cavalry units had been made a part of the Regular Army immediately following the Civil War.

In 1960, over nine decades after the end of the Civil War, certain areas in the United States were still resisting the granting of voting rights to blacks, the desegregation of public schools, and the desegregation of public accommodation. However, for more than a decade, the Armed Forces had been in the process of changing the old policies, which had perpetuated segregation and discrimination, to new policies, which had resulted in desegregation and would lead to eventual integration and equal opportunity.

I concluded that, although we still had a long way to go to gain full access to the mainstream, blacks had made remarkable progress in the field artillery in the 20 years since 1940. There were some unmistakable signs that the myth of inherent inferiority had finally lost some of its adverse effects because, during those twenty years, I had progressed from an assignment in August 1940 as a field artillery trainee in the first black Regular Army field artillery unit, to an assignment from 1956–60 with the Army Staff in the Pentagon, where I was responsible for the coordination of all Army training pertaining to artillery, missiles, and related nuclear weapons.

***

For almost 350 years, American whites had been divided in their attitudes concerning the treatment of blacks. Though some whites advocated favorable treatment of blacks from the outset, unfortunately those endorsing less favorable treatment had exercised the dominant political influence. Accordingly, in this, "the land of the free and the home of the brave," whose Declaration of Independence holds that "all men are created equal," overwhelming obstacles were placed in the way of many generations of black Americans to impede them in their struggle to gain access to the mainstream of American life. These obstacles were maintained in part by a massive exercise in psychological warfare which perpetuated the myth of inherent racial inferiority.[1]

Prior to the Civil War, the myth that blacks were subhuman and inherently inferior was used to justify the institution of slavery. Following the passage of the 13th, 14th, and 15th Amendments to the United States Constitution, the same myth was used to justify the denial of first-class citizenship to blacks.

To facilitate perpetuation of the myth, blacks and whites were segregated by law in many states, and in the U.S. Army, to prevent most whites from discovering that blacks were human. In addition, a black male stereotype was perpetuated that exemplified a combination of the worst characteristics of the worst individuals of the race. Furthermore, only that information was published about blacks that conformed to the image of the stereotype.

This is one of the clearest examples of the obstacles faced by black Americans—the struggle to be permitted to serve to the full extent of their capabilities in the field artillery of the U.S. Army.

Complete Exclusion before World War I

In 1866, Senator Henry Wilson of Massachusetts, Chairman of the Committee on Military Affairs of the U.S. Senate, introduced a bill for reorganization of the post-Civil War Army. In addition to providing for the inclusion of black infantry and cavalry units, the bill included a provision for one regiment of field artillery "to be composed of colored persons." However, General Ulysses Grant, the Commanding General of the Army, in his letter responding to a request for his comments on the bill, stated: "I am not in favor of a colored artillery regiment." (McGregor & Nalty, 1977) The provision for the black artillery regiment was deleted from the final bill.

Another significant attempt was made by Emmett J. Scott, Assistant to Booker T. Washington at the Tuskegee Institute, in a letter to President Theodore Roosevelt (NA RG 165, 4483, Scott):

> I have the honor to ask you to issue an order that six batteries of field Artillery … be recruited with colored men …
>
> … There has never been in the regular army a company of colored artillery, and as only men of superior intelligence are enlisted for that branch of service, our most intelligent men deserve a chance to prove their ability and serve their country in the artillery branch of the service the same as white soldiers of similar qualifications do.
>
> I have been informed that the War Department has been of the opinion that colored men with sufficient intelligence to make good artillery men cannot be found. This was doubtless

true in the 1860s and in the period immediately following, but does not hold good now as a trial, I am sure, will show.

Although the opinion cited by Scott was not the official position of the War Department at that time, it was held by a large and influential group of staff officers, as indicated in an excerpt from the minority report (NA RG 165,4483, Wilcox) to the Army War College Study made in response to Scott's letter: "From our knowledge of the Negro, from his evident mental inferiority, it is fairly to be concluded that he is not fitted for the modern artillery service." Scott's request was not approved and blacks were not admitted into the field artillery until the 167th Field Artillery Brigade of the 92nd Division was organized during World War I.

***

In all of the states of the deep South, segregation had been a matter of public policy since the end of Reconstruction following the Civil War. One of the stated objectives of this policy was to maintain white supremacy "forever," keeping blacks subservient and preventing the development of their self-esteem. For blacks who lived during that period, the reality of American life was a government system based on racism, justified by the assumption of the inherent inferiority of blacks. It was a system with the objective of forcing blacks to continue to exist in their inferior status; a system that was in and of itself the ultimate manifestation of racial bias, that mandated a predisposition for whites and against blacks in every social, political, and economic consideration that involved blacks and affected whites. It was also a system that was, in theory, benign when blacks stayed within their assigned space and accepted their inferior status; but in actual practice, it provided a protected environment in which any white—no matter what his station in life—could inflate his ego, if so inclined, by attempting to degrade any black—no matter what his station in life—and, if not satisfied with the results, could take any action of revenge or intimidation without fear of consequences to himself.

World War I

Conditions for black soldiers and officers became more difficult following the Spanish—American War. By the beginning of World War I, the whites exercising the dominant political and military influence perceived that black military personnel, especially officers, posed a potential threat to their way of life. The existence of a black officer group during wartime was a critical problem for segregationists in maintaining the status quo, because the achievement of the status of an officer by a black man was inconsistent with the myth of inherent inferiority. It had the potential of refuting the contention that all black males conformed to the image of the black male stereotype. Moreover, the uniform was a symbol of authority which provided blacks with a status completely unacceptable in certain sections of the United States.

The extent to which white American soldiers attempted to indoctrinate the French concerning black American troops is indicated in a document dated August 7, 1918 and attributed to the French Military Mission, stationed with the American Army.[2] The document, "Subject: Secret Information Concerning Black American Troops," states among other things:

> It is important for French officers who have been called upon to exercise command over black American troops, or to live in close contact with them, to have an exact idea of the position occupied by Negroes in the United States ... Although a citizen of the United States, the black man is regarded by the white American as an inferior being with whom relations of business or service only are possible. The black is constantly being censured for his want of intelligence and discretion, his lack of civic and professional conscience and for his tendency toward undue familiarity.
>
> The vices of the Negro are a constant menace to the American who has to repress them sternly ...
>
> ... We must prevent the rise of any pronounced degree of intimacy between French officers and black officers. We must be courteous with these last, but we cannot deal with them on the same plane as with the white American officers without deeply wounding the latter. We must not eat with them, must not shake hands or seek to talk with them outside of the requirements of military service.
>
> We must not commend too highly the black American troops, particularly in the presence of [white] Americans ...
>
> Make a point of keeping the native cantonment population from "spoiling" the Negroes. [White] Americans become greatly incensed at any public expression of intimacy between white women and black men.

Black Field Artillery Officers during World War I

Although political considerations had dictated that black officers would be commissioned to fill some of the officer positions in the firing batteries of the 167th Field Artillery Brigade, their assignment and promotion opportunities were severely limited from the very beginning. The instructions of the Secretary of War dated October 20, 1917, at the time the 92nd Division was being organized, specified (Scott, 1919, 437) that "All officers of General or Field Rank" and "All Captains of the Field Artillery Brigade" must be white.

This turned out not to be the major problem faced by black officers. It was apparent, from the results obtained, that no real effort was made in planning to give the black officers a fair chance for success. It seemed that the intent was just the opposite and that the black officers were being programmed for failure. For example, since there were no black artillery officers in any component of the Army, all of the black officers assigned to the 167th were provided from those commissioned as a result of three months of infantry training at the segregated Fort De Moines Officers Training Camp.

In white artillery regiments of the National Army—the term used for the conscript and volunteer force raised in 1917 to fight in World War I—only those officers who had already received artillery training were assigned to duty with troops. However, the black officers assigned to the 167th Brigade had no previous artillery training (NA RG 165, 8142–125). Furthermore, these officers were assigned without consulting their desires (NA RG 165, 8142–152) and without undergoing elimination on the ground of mental or other incapacity for artillery work (NA RG 165, 8142–125). Finally, about 24 of them considered to be the most advanced were sent to the School of Fire at Fort Sill, Oklahoma, but only five finished the course (NA RG 165, 8142–152).

This is only a brief summary of the problems encountered by black field artillery officers during World War I. As a result of these and numerous other problems, Major General Frank McIntyre, former artillery officer for the American Expeditionary Forces, made a proposal in a memo to the Chief of Staff that sought to avoid such problems in the future (NA RG 165, 8142–179):

> In order to prevent a recurrence of cases of this nature, it would seem advisable not to commission colored men in the Field Artillery as the number of men of that race who have the mental qualifications to come up to the standards of efficiency of the Field Artillery officers is so small that the few isolated cases might be better handled in other branches.

Enlisted Men during World War I

When the 167th Field Artillery Brigade was organized during World War I, it was doubted whether an artillery brigade of Negro soldiers (NA RG 165, 8142–125) "could be developed in the technique of artillery to make an effective fighting artillery unit." Since the draft did not furnish enough technically qualified men, many of the troops for the 167th FA Brigade were secured through canvassing from Tuskegee Institute and from the high schools of Baltimore, Pittsburgh, and other cities. (Scott, 1919)

The units of the 167th Brigade were plagued with serious problems in training, both before and after arriving in France, and participated in combat only during the last few weeks of the war. However, as a result of their performance they were praised by several high-level commanders, including the commander of the American Expeditionary Forces, General John J. Pershing. Also, on the basis of the performance of the brigade, it was believed that in future wars (Lee, 1966, 121): "Negroes could be employed profitably in supporting artillery units, especially in the heavier types where contact with the enemy would be least likely."

***

Black artillery units fought briefly during World War I, and although black enlisted men earned a conditional acceptance for use in future wars on the basis of their performance, black officers did not. Despite the performance of the brigade as a whole, it was inactivated within six months of the war ending.

Between World War I and World War II

The summer of 1919 became known as the "Red Summer" because there were more than 20 race riots in the United States in a six-month period, in which a large number of individuals were killed and hundreds injured. The worst riots took place in Washington, D.C. on July 19 and in Chicago on July 27.

Although thousands of blacks had risked their lives and many had died in combat during World War I, the military hierarchy waged a propaganda effort following the war to discount black achievements and began to develop policies that would ensure victory in the propaganda battle that would be waged against blacks during the next war.

These policies were developed at the Army War College during the 1920s at a time when racist thought in the United States had reached its zenith and "the Negro was established in his place." During that period, the future World War II commanders were in the important middle period of their military career development and participated in and absorbed the material from a number of anti-black studies at the Army War College that included the following assertions (*The Army War College Studies Black Soldiers,* 1925):

> Blacks were inferior to whites. The black man is physically unqualified for combat duty; is by nature subservient, mentally inferior and believed himself inferior to the white man; could not control himself in the face of danger and did not have the initiative and resourcefulness of the white man.

To keep the black officer in his place, the studies held that:

> No Negro officer should command a white man. Negro officers not only lacked the mental capacity to command but courage as well. Their interest was seen as not to fight for their country but solely to advance their racial interests. Worst of all, the Negro soldier utterly lacked confidence in his colored officer. The Negro officer was still a Negro with all of the weaknesses of character inherent to the Negro race, exaggerated by the fact that he wore an officer's uniform.

Getting Ready

In March 1919, when I was 15 months old, the three regiments of the 167th Brigade were inactivated, beginning a period of 21 years before blacks would again be permitted to serve in the field artillery of the U.S. Army. Although it was not even remotely anticipated at that time, events were taking place which would have a significant effect on my subsequent preparation to take advantage of the next such opportunity.

***

My grandfather had been born into slavery in Alabama in the late 1840s. Following the Civil War, his former master (who was also his father) gave him a substantial amount of land. My father was subsequently born in 1880. After he married my mother in 1905, 40 acres of the land was given to him by my grandfather.

According to a family legend, my grandfather operated a country store in a room attached to his house, and for several years competed successfully with a prosperous white merchant for the trade of the blacks in the area. Eventually, the store began to attract so many customers that it was difficult to properly serve them in its limited space, so he decided to expand it.

There was a group of hooded night riders in the community, patterned after the temporarily dormant Klan and dedicated to use any means necessary—including intimidation, force and violence—to maintain white supremacy and keep "biggety niggers in their place." One night in the early spring of 1908, they evidently concluded that my grandfather had become "a biggety nigger." Several night riders took my grandfather from his home by force, carried him several hundred yards away and draped him across a large log in preparation for a lecture and a whipping.

As they were taking my grandfather away, my grandmother—who was over 50 years of age—ran 300 yards to my father's house and told him what had happened, including the direction the night riders had taken. Although my father did not want to leave my mother, who was expecting the birth of their first child within a week, he decided that he could not let the night riders get away with what they obviously intended to do to his father. Accordingly, he selected a shotgun from his gun rack and ran in the direction the night riders had taken. He soon saw the outline of the white sheets as the night riders gathered around my grandfather, and from the noise they were making he concluded they were still in the lecture phase and had not begun the whipping.

My father, an experienced hunter, moved forward until the group was just within the maximum range of his shotgun—where the buckshot would be primarily irritating and not lethal. When he fired in the general direction of the white sheets, the group of night riders dispersed quickly, leaving my grandfather without further harm.

Since the night riders concealed their identities with sheets and hoods when they carried out their nocturnal missions, blacks had not been absolutely sure of the identification of individual members of the group, although they assumed that they were whites who lived in the community. After the incident with my grandfather, blacks were satisfied that they had identified some members of the group when they heard via the grapevine the names of whites who were recovering from minor buckshot wounds.

When my father's brothers and the other black men in the community heard about the incident, they organized an armed security group, taking turns each night for the next several weeks to guard my father's house.

***

The economic conditions in the South had been extremely poor for black farmers since about 1914 because of their worn-out land, the boll weevils, floods, the price of cotton, and exploitation by whites. In an attempt to solve his cash flow problem, my father "went north" late in 1916 and worked in Newark, New Jersey, for several months, leaving his family in Alabama. After he returned, the problem worsened and, in the fall of 1919, his cash-flow problem became critical. He borrowed $542.72, securing the loan with a mortgage which pledged his 40 acres of farm land along with his entire crop of cotton, corn, cotton seed, fodder, cane, peas, potatoes, turpentine, and other produce raised during the years 1919, 1920, 1921, and 1922; all rents coming to him in 1919, 1920, 1921, and 1922; two mules, each 12 years old; and one two-horse wagon and harness.

Eventually, my father had to dispose of his farm to satisfy the debt. Then, in the fall of 1924, he moved our family to a farm about 50 miles southeast of Tulsa, in the border state of Oklahoma, because he had heard that, unlike Alabama, Oklahoma was a "land of opportunity."

Although he did find that the segregated public schools in Oklahoma were better than those in Alabama, he also discovered that the "Jim Crow Codes" were essentially the same, requiring segregation of public education, transportation, and other public places. It was also a matter of public policy within the state to attempt to deny blacks the opportunity to vote, despite the fact that such denial was illegal according to state law.

The original Oklahoma state constitution had complied with the Oklahoma Enabling Act of 1908, which had permitted Oklahoma to become a state in 1907. This act had required that the constitution guarantee the right to vote regardless of race and previous condition of servitude, and President Theodore Roosevelt had indicated that he would not give his approval unless such provisions were included.

However, after Oklahoma became a state, the legislature began to amend the constitution to pattern its segregation laws after those of states of the deep South. An attempt was made to nullify the guarantee of the right of blacks to vote by providing that no person could be registered for voting unless he passed an examination demonstrating his ability to read and write various portions of the constitution. Exempted from the examination provisions under the "grandfather clause" were the lineal descendants of persons eligible to vote on January 1, 1866.

After that amendment was declared invalid by the federal courts in 1916, the constitution was amended to include another restrictive device. This consisted of setting an extremely brief registration period for voters not already eligible, which included most blacks. In addition, some registrars still used the invalid "grandfather clause" to deny blacks the right to vote, disregarding any who claimed the right because of ancestry (lineal descendant of a white man), and even disqualifying college graduates because of their alleged inability to read a section of the state constitution.

For the most part, blacks who voted in Oklahoma during that period were able to do so only as a result of federal court injunctions enforced by U.S. Marshals. (Gibson, 1965, 328, 343, 347, 353; Teall, 1971, 215–224)

Thus, the system of segregation was the same as it had been in Alabama, and there were other significant residual adverse effects to the self-esteem of blacks still remaining from the Tulsa Race Riot of 1921, during which hundreds of individuals were killed or injured.

Before our family could recover completely from the economic results of the move from Alabama to Oklahoma, the Great Depression began to affect Oklahoma and eventually the entire United States.

***

As one result of my family's move from Alabama to Oklahoma, I missed my first half-year of school. Thereafter, beginning at midterm during the 1924–25 school year, I continued until I graduated in 1935. I attended school in and around Haskell, Oklahoma, a typical small, agriculturally oriented town about 40 miles by road southeast of Tulsa. Soon after I entered the segregated school system at the age of 7, I began to acquire a reputation as an outstanding achiever. In my pre-teen years, I enjoyed reading, arithmetic, history, and geography. Accordingly, achieving required no special effort on my part. My parents encouraged but did not pressure me, and the widespread attention I received was just an added bonus.

When I was 13 and began high school, the attention I was receiving due to my academic prowess became a drag on my social life. I found that nothing caused me to lose friends more surely, except at examination time, than being continuously extolled by the teachers and the principal as an example of a perfect student.

In many ways I was a typical teenager, and because I disliked being a noncon-formist I set out to change my image. Among other things, I became involved in electrical, electronic, and mechanical projects and almost eliminated my study time after school. However, in spite of the fact that most of my high school teachers were "no-nonsense" graders, I was not entirely successful in changing my image. Out of 21 high school subjects with 31 recorded grades, I earned 22 As (11 of which were in English and math); four at B+, four Bs, and one C+ (for public speaking).

Major Clark and his classmates, Haskell, Oklahoma.

Because of my reputation as an outstanding achiever, the members of the white power structure (bankers, merchants, school superintendent, etc.) competed for my services as a part-time worker around their homes and businesses. Most of the work was of the type considered during that period to be suitable for teenagers, but some of it required an outstanding degree of trustworthiness.

Accordingly, my first direct contact with whites was in a favorable environment, involving white personnel of above-average intelligence who did not feel threatened by blacks in general, or me in particular. This permitted me to avoid the no-win confrontations with whites of less-than-average intelligence who were constantly looking for confrontations designed to keep blacks in their place.

My success in dealing with above-average white achievers made me confident that I had the potential as an individual to help disprove the myth of the inherent inferiority of blacks, if only I could gain access to a suitable forum.

Sometime in the mid-30s, an event took place which helped me to later select that forum. One day, while mowing the yard of a prominent citizen, I noticed three books on top of some discarded items which were quite different from those I had seen before. Because of the possibility that the books had been discarded unintentionally, I recovered them and brought them to the attention of my employer. He pointed out that, since they were more than 15 years old and out of date, they had been discarded intentionally, but if I wanted them, I could have them. I accepted the books with thanks. All of them were about field artillery[3] and I accepted them with gratitude!

One was a 1917 book about field artillery fire control equipment. The second was a 1918 book about the French 75mm Model 1897 gun, while the third was a 1919 book about field artillery survey, *Topography for Field Artillery*.[4] Since I was a "straight-A" student in high school math, I understood the book about surveying methods, but my lack of "hands on" access to artillery fire control equipment and guns limited my understanding of the other books.

However, the books did motivate me to observe with greater interest the activities around the National Guard Armory, which was across the street from one of the lawns that I tended. The armory housed the equipment and guns of Battery E, 160th Field Artillery, Oklahoma National Guard. Unfortunately, the only time I saw the entire battery with its equipment was twice a year, when they were either leaving for or returning from Summer Camp.

I noticed that there were no blacks in the unit—but there were several whites who impressed me as being of no more than average intelligence. I was confident that I could be as good a field artillery man as any of them if I had the opportunity to do so. It turned out that I was to have that opportunity in the near future as a result of the war in Europe.

Part I

The End of Exclusion

CHAPTER ONE

A Limited Opportunity

By the end of 1939, the continued escalation of the perilous international tensions had convinced many black Americans that another world war was inevitable. But the overwhelming majority, like other Americans, wanted the United States to stay out of the war, if possible. Many recalled a statement attributed to General William Tecumseh Sherman, who had commanded the Union Army during the Civil War: "I am tired and sick of war. Its glory is all moonshine. It is only those who have neither fired a shot nor heard the shrieks and groans of the wounded who cry aloud for blood, more vengeance, more desolation. WAR IS HELL."

In preparation for the coming war, the United States embarked on a large expansion of its armed forces during the summer of 1940, designed to protect the nation and the rest of the Western hemisphere against the hostile forces that might be unleashed by Hitler and his aggressive fellow dictators. (Matloff, 1973, 418–19) A bill was passed by the 76th Congress on July 2, 1940, authorizing an increase in the Regular Army by 95,000 to a strength of 375,000. (Marshall, 1943, 52) Under the provisions of the bill, the Army began to organize additional Regular Army units for blacks. One of the new Regular Army units, the 349th Field Artillery, was activated at Fort Sill, Oklahoma on August 1, 1940. (Lee, 1966, 68–69)[1]

As no blacks had been permitted to serve in the field artillery since 1919, it was necessary to provide the enlisted cadre for the 349th from existing infantry and cavalry units. These personnel were not familiar with field artillery, and time was needed to prepare them for their task of establishing and training a field artillery unit. This caused a delay of 15 days after activation of the 349th before enlistments could begin.

When enlistment was opened for the 349th on August 15, it had a cadre of 15 white Regular Army officers and a cadre of 150 black enlisted men from the 9th and 10th Cavalry, 24th and 25th Infantry, and the Colored Detachment of the Field Artillery School. (349A Hist)

In spite of Sherman's admonition, a large number of blacks from Oklahoma, Texas, and adjacent states took advantage of the opportunity to become field artillerymen by enlisting in the U.S. Army for assignment to the newly activated 349th. They did so in pursuance of several objectives: $21.00 per month of economic security;[2] and a chance to prove that they were entitled to first-class citizenship by fulfilling their patriotic duty. At the same time, they wanted to meet head on the myth of inherent racial inferiority that had impeded the progress of blacks for so many generations. It was the same myth that had caused blacks to be excluded from the field artillery for 72 of the 74 years between the Civil War and 1940.

***

On October 6, 1940, another black field artillery unit was organized when the all-black 8th Infantry, Illinois National Guard, was converted and re-designated as the 184th Field Artillery.[3] Since there were no black field artillery officers in the Army, the initial officer requirements for the 184th were provided by the transfer of black National Guard infantry officers to the field artillery branch. Key officers from the unit were sent to Fort Sill during the period December 13, 1940–January 5, 1941 for supplemental training with the 349th.

As in the case of the 349th Field Artillery, there were no black field artillerymen available for the enlisted cadre. Accordingly, it was necessary to use National Guard infantry personnel for that purpose.

I completed requirements for enlistment in the US Army during the last week in August 1940, and on the 31st was assigned to the 349th Field Artillery at Fort Sill, Oklahoma. When I arrived at Fort Sill, the men of the 349th were quartered in a tent camp, where we remained until just before Thanksgiving, then moved into our new barracks.[4]

Battery A, 597th Field Artillery Battalion, at Fort Huachuca, Arizona, 1944. First Lieutenant Major Clark as CO sits in the center, front row. Many of the other men have signed the photo, which was sent as a souvenir to Major's wife.

Fort Sill had been established in 1869 by General Philip H. Sheridan. It was built by the Tenth Cavalry and named for Brigadier General Joshua W. Sill, a Military Academy classmate of General Sheridan.

The 349th consisted of a Regimental Headquarters and Headquarters Battery and two battalions. Each battalion consisted of a Battalion Headquarters and Headquarters Battery, a Service Battery, and three firing batteries designated by letters of the alphabet (A, B, and C and D, E, and F). I was assigned to Battery A, which had an authorized enlisted strength of 137 men.

Since I intended to keep a record of my military experiences, I bought a pocket notebook from the Post Exchange (PX) on September 24, at the front of which I wrote: "Sept. 24, 1040. To Whom It May Concern. This Book is the Property of Private Major Clark 18020347, Battery A, 349th Field Artillery, Battery No. 128." A few days later, I made a notation concerning some of the articles purchased with my first military pay: Sept. 30, 1940—First Day. ARTICLES NEEDED: Shoe Brush; Tooth Powder—10 cents; Soap—25 cents; Soap Case—20 cents; Comb—15 cents; Stamps—15 cents; Envelopes—10 cents."

I found that the pace of training was too rapid to permit time for any systematic recording of my experiences, and although I bought and used several notebooks while I was assigned to the 349th, most of the information I recorded pertained to my training activities. Unfortunately, I failed to record anything about two of my most significant experiences as a new solder: in November, when we fired our big guns for the first time; and in December, when the black officers from the newly organized 184th Field Artillery of the Illinois National Guard participated in the first service practice.[5]

Selective Service and Training Act of 1940

The Selective Service and Training Act of 1940 (Public Law 783, 76th Congress), the first compulsory military training law in the history of the United States, was signed by President Roosevelt on September 16. Republican Congressman Hamilton Fish of New York,[6] in spite of the opposition of many Southern Democrats, had been successful in obtaining the approval of antidiscrimination language in the act which read: "That in the selection and training of men under this act, and in the interpretation and execution of the provisions of this act, there shall be no discrimination against any person on account of race or color."

By the end of September, the regiment had received most of the 77 additional officers and 1,100 recruits to bring the total assigned strength of the 349th to over 90 officers and 1,250 enlisted men. (349A Hist) All of the officers except the chaplain were white.

Late in September, Battery A received four big guns, 155mm Model 1918 GPF (Grande Puissance Filloux) field guns designed and used by the French during World War I.[7]

At the start of individual training, I was assigned to one of the gun sections, first as a cannoneer and then as a driver of the section's tractor. I was awed by the power of the tractor, which was several orders of magnitude greater than any vehicle that I had driven before. However, I did not remain in either assignment very long. After the battery commander had reviewed my records and test scores, and determined that I had some proficiency in math and electronics, he reassigned me from the gun section to the battery detail section.[8] Although I trained for all the various jobs in the section, I was assigned specifically as an instrument operator, my duties requiring me to work as a member of the survey party and in the service practice support group at the battery observation post.

First Promotion

Two months after I enlisted, I was promoted to private first class, specialist fourth class:[9]

Under the provisions of AR 615–5 the following appointments is [*sic*] hereby announced:

TO BE PRIVATE FIRST CLASS

Private Major Clark   18020347

Under the provisions of AR 615–10

TO BE SPECIALIST 4TH CLASS

…Pvt. 1cl. Major Clark   18020347

(349A/A/BO6/11–01–40)

I was present at the gun position when, after several weeks of drill and training, actual service practice firing of live ammunition was begun, and the first round was fired from the 349th's 155mm guns. "This was the first time most of the personnel of the regiment, both officers and men, had ever seen a gun of this size in action". (349A Hist) The crews serving the guns on that day were then firing one of the largest guns in the Army after receiving only two months' training. Master Sergeant Hansen Outley was awarded the honor of pulling the lanyard to fire the first round, having done so to fire the last round fired by the 349th during World War I. (349A Hist)

One old soldier (cadreman) warned me to expect the loudest noise I had ever heard and to prepare for it by stopping up both of my ears just before the gun fired. I took all the recommended precautions, but in spite of the warning, the noise of the gun firing was much greater than I expected and there was a "ringing in my ears" for a short while afterwards. During the next 20 years I had many other significant "first-time experiences" with noise, including the explosion of an atomic bomb when I was an atomic test observer in Nevada in 1953. However, not even the atomic bomb explosion made a greater impression on me than did the first firing of the 155mm gun.

***

On November 19, 1940, *New York Times* reporter Hanson W. Baldwin visited Fort Sill as one of 17 newspapermen participating in a special War Department tour of defense installations. In an article published in the *New York Times* of November 20, Baldwin noted that the 349th Field Artillery, which passed in review during the visit, marched well for a unit only three months old.[10]

The last three paragraphs of the article provided an excellent encapsulation of the then current status of black field artillery in the United States Army:

> Although the peace-time Army had Negro infantry and cavalry regiments, the 349th, which was reactivated on 15 August, is the first peace-time Negro field artillery regiment. Its officers are white but its men are mostly recruits from the Texas and Oklahoma open spaces, but it had a cadre of trained non-commissioned officers, drawn chiefly from the army's regular Negro cavalry regiments.
>
> One of them, Sergeant Hansen Outley, fired on Nov. 11, 1918, the regiment's last shot fired during the World War. The regiment is armed with the wartime 155-millimeter G.P.F. guns, towed by Diesel-driven tractors, with a total weight gun and tractor of about 57,500 pounds. In a few months when trainees are inducted in quantity, the newly formed regiment will be split into four parts. Three of them will leave for other posts to form cadres for three more regiments of Negro field artillery. (*NYT* 11/20/40. Copyright 1940 by the New York Times Company. Reprinted by permission.)

Black National Guard Artillery Officers

Late in December, 10 black officers arrived at the observation post, where I was serving as instrument operator, to fire their first artillery service practice. These officers had been recently transferred from the infantry to the artillery in the conversion of the 8th Infantry, Illinois National Guard, to the 184th Field Artillery, which was scheduled for induction into the Federal Service on January 6, 1941.

The officers were attached to the 349th for their preliminary artillery training because there was insufficient time remaining before the scheduled induction of their unit for them to complete Field Artillery School courses.

The highest-ranking officer was January Anderson F. Pitts, who, as a colonel, would later command the 184th. There was also Captain Wendell T. Derricks, who, as a lieutenant colonel, would be a battalion commander in the 184th, then of the 930th FA Bn., later of the 597th FA Bn., and finally, after World War II, of the 349th FA Bn., the successor to the 1st Bn. of the old 349th Field Artillery Regiment. Five other officers who would later be assigned to the 92nd Division or the 366th Infantry were: Captain Marcus H. Ray, who, as a lieutenant colonel, would command the 600th FA Bn.; Captain Oscar Randall, who, as a lieutenant colonel, would command the 3rd Bn., 366th Inf.; First Lieutenant Raymond Watkins, who, as a major, would serve on special duty with the 92nd Division staff and, after World War II, as a brigadier general in the Illinois National Guard; First Lieutenant Ed Wimp, who, as a major, would serve as Executive Officer, 600th FA Bn.; and Second Lieutenant Orion Page, who, as a major, would serve as Executive Officer, 597th FA Bn.

CHAPTER TWO

The Opportunity Expands

At the beginning of 1941, the 349th Field Artillery was engaged in a program to train selected personnel to serve as cadres for the next black field artillery units to be activated. Accordingly, in February 1941, when the brigade headquarters and the three field artillery regiments of the 46th Field Artillery Brigade were activated at Camp Livingston, Louisiana, trained enlisted cadres from the 349th were available for those units. (46A Hist)

After the United States entered the war against Germany and Japan late in 1941, a program was initiated by the Army to increase the number of qualified blacks applying to attend officer candidate schools. (Lee, 1968, 202, 211, 270; MacGregor, 1981, 47–51)[1] Although the Field Artillery Officer Candidate School (OCS) at Fort Still attained an output rate in 1942 of one graduating class per week, the classes contained only a small number of black graduates. For example, FA OCS Class #33 (my class) began on July 14, 1942 with approximately 600 white and six black officer candidates, ending on October 8, 1942 with the commissioning of approximately 400 white and only three black graduates. (MC/POR)[2]

As a member of the battery detail section, I was just as qualified as any of my contemporaries, on the basis of artillery training and experience, to compete for the assignment as the (three stripes) sergeant in charge of the section. However, a cadre was being formed for a new black field artillery brigade to be activated at Camp Livingston, Louisiana in February 1941, and I was selected to do on-the-job training in the supply room for the position of supply sergeant for the new brigade headquarters battery. Since a promotion to staff (four stripes) sergeant was possible in the proposed assignment—one more stripe than I could get in the position I had been competing for in Battery A—I started the new year of 1941 with enthusiasm.

During January, the 349th received a large number of draftees and additional volunteers. These were used to replace the 440 cadre being transferred out of the 349th to activate the field artillery brigade at Camp Livingston, Louisiana, along with the replacement training centers at Fort Sill, Oklahoma and Fort Bragg, North Carolina. One of the draftees was Roscoe C. "Rock" Cartwright, who, 30 years later, became the first black field artilleryman to attain general officer rank in the Regular Army.

On February 19, our cadre for the 46th Field Artillery Brigade left Fort Sill in a special 12-car train and arrived the next day at Camp Livingston, several miles north of Alexandria.

A few days later, I wrote a letter to my mother describing our move: "There were 437 of us ... [on the 12-car special train] from Fort Sill. At Camp Livingston we are 14 miles from Alexandria. It costs 20 cents on the bus to go there." (MC/EC/2-28-41)

When we arrived at our destination, we found an officer-cadre of 56 Regular Army officers. Within the next two months, they would be joined by 172 reserve officers to bring the total officer strength to 232. All of the officers were white, except the chaplains. (46A Hist)[3]

During the latter part of April, the first increment of the 3,800 black draftees arrived at Camp Livingston to begin filling the brigade headquarters and three field artillery regiments. They came from Forts Benning and Bragg and Camp Shelby after being inducted from the Carolinas, Florida, Georgia, Alabama, Mississippi, Louisiana, Tennessee, Kentucky, and Texas. (46A Hist) After the fillers arrived, the personnel strength of each regiment was about 1,400 and the 46th Brigade became the largest black field artillery organization in the U.S. Army. (46A Hist)

The 350th and 351st were issued with 155mm "box-trail" howitzers, towed by 4-ton trucks and classified as medium artillery. Although they fired the same size ammunition as the 155mm gun, they could only shoot about two-thirds as far.

The 353rd was issued with 155mm guns, towed by tractors, and was classified as a heavy artillery regiment, the same as the 349th.

Although about 125 men were eventually assigned to the 46th Brigade Headquarters Battery, only the cadremen were present during the short period of my assignment there as supply sergeant, and during that period our supply operations were combined with those of the 351st.

On March 16, less than a month after assuming my new duties, I was promoted from private first class to sergeant, skipping the grade of corporal. Shortly thereafter, a vacancy occurred in the 351st for a battalion supply sergeant. A technical (five stripes) sergeant was authorized for the position.

I wrote to my mother concerning my impending transfer to the 351st and subsequent promotion:

> To be transferred to the 351st F.A. to be Battalion Supply sergeant. (Technical Sergeant, I hope). (MC/NB/4-6-41)

> Yesterday I was promoted to Technical Sergeant by the Colonel (the 46th Brigade commander). The colonel is going to be a Brigadier General. His nomination was sent to the Senate by the President yesterday. (MC/EC/4-13-41)

I was transferred to the 351st as supply sergeant for the 2nd Bn. as expected, and on April 12 was promoted from sergeant to technical sergeant, skipping the grade of staff sergeant. Thus, within a period of 27 days I had advanced four enlisted grades from private first class to technical sergeant.

Service Battery had a personnel strength of about 100 enlisted men, with about a dozen of them assigned to the battalion supply section. The battalion supply activities for both the 1st and 2nd Bns. of the 351st were conducted in the same building that housed the Regimental Supply Office, and were under the supervision of the regimental supply officer (a captain) and a regimental supply sergeant (a master sergeant). We (the battalion supply sergeants for the 1st and 2nd Bns.) discovered that the Regimental Supply Office was primarily concerned with policy and planning and was not concerned with day-to-day supply operations. Accordingly, after a few trial runs, we decided to consolidate the administrative and operational supply activities of our two battalions. I would be the "inside man," supervising all of the administrative "paperwork"—including acquisition of supplies and maintenance of records of their utilization and disposition—while my fellow supply sergeant would be the "outside man," supervising all of the receipt and distribution of the supplies. We eventually gained the reputation of having one of the outstanding supply operations in the IV Corps area.

At frequent intervals, outstanding entertainment, such as the Etta Moten Concert, was provided for the troops at Camp Livingston. Miss Moten's concert included spirituals, Negro lullabies and love songs, American art songs, and popular requests. The written program noted:

> Negro spirituals were originally sung unaccompanied. Miss Moten has chosen some of the simpler arrangements in which the traditional melody remains unaltered. Moreover, she insists that "Spirituals should be sung with the heart rather than the head;" they should be listened to in like manner.

Alexandria also provided a number of organized activities to occupy soldiers during their off-duty time, as indicated in the following examples pertaining first to the U.S.O. (United Service Organizations) and then to a social club.

> Dear Soldier:
> The USO Club, 815 Casson Street, Alexandria, is a place where you may visit and take part in the things you would like to do.
> You would help the Director of the USO Club, Mr. Thomas M. Bond, Miss Annabel Sawyer, Director of YWCA and in charge of work with women, and Mr. Ashton Kitchens, Program Director, a great deal if you will fill in this blank. Check the things that you would like to take part in. (Special Interest and Hobby Blank, Casson Street U.S.O. Club, Alexandria, Louisiana)

This was followed by about 50 items, which included dancing instruction, meeting nice families, visiting churches, appearing on radio programs, recording your voice, joining any of several clubs, and participating in card game contests.

Louisiana was a state of the deep South, where discrimination against blacks was a matter of public policy and "Jim Crow" laws required segregation of schools, transportation, and other public places. There, in June 1941, I joined with two other noncommissioned officers in a joint purchase of a 1937 Nash-Lafayette sedan. We used it primarily to visit cities other than Alexandria, which was much too crowded to suit us because it was the camp town for as many as 30,000 soldiers from Camps Polk, Beauregard, Claiborne, and Livingston, and from three airfields—Alexandria, Pollock, and Esler. Instead, we visited New Orleans, Lake Charles, Baton Rouge, and other cities some distance away from Camp Livingston.

In the summer of 1941, we accepted an invitation from a friend to visit his home near McComb, Mississippi. After an interesting weekend, we started our return trip to Camp Livingston and stopped at a country filling station for gas. As the proprietor started filling our tank, his wife came out of the office, looked at us in our uniforms and remarked: "I didn't know there were any niggers in the Army."

***

During my first year at Camp Livingston, my duties as battalion/regimental supply sergeant prevented me from having any "hands on" training experience in the tactics and technique pertaining to field artillery. However, there were certain circumstances peculiar to my situation that permitted me to keep informed:

1. The regimental supply sergeant, with almost 30 years of Army service, could obtain a copy of any Army publication that he ordered pertaining to the organization in which he was serving. Accordingly, his files contained an up-to-date copy of every Army Regulation, Training Circular, Field Manual, Technical Manual, and Technical Bulletin pertinent to the mission of the 46th Field Artillery Brigade, as GHQ Reserve Artillery.[4] Needless to say, I made good use of the publications in his files during both on-duty and off-duty time.

2. We had a club for noncommissioned officers of the first three grades—staff, technical, first and master sergeants—called The 1st Three Graders Club. Although most of the members tried to forget their on-duty problems during their off-duty time, I was one among the few who felt that we should take advantage of the opportunity and devote both on-duty and some off-duty time in an attempt to make the organization successful, since we had the largest black field artillery organization in history.

3. All of us contributed some information to our off-duty discussions. I discussed the supply problems peculiar to field artillery and, because of my direct access to the most up-to-date file in the brigade, I researched specific questions posed by the group on other pertinent matters, and kept them informed concerning new and revised publications. The other NCOs discussed the training problems and solutions they had encountered in the training of the firing batteries and the operations and intelligence sections

of the headquarters batteries. As a result, we were all better informed and were better prepared to do our individual jobs.

The *351st F.A. News*, dated September 15, 1941, included the following editorial comment from Lieutenant Colonel J. E. Jacobs, Executive Officer, 351st Field Artillery:

> The men of this regiment are making history, as this is the first time that Colored troops have been formed into Artillery units of the regular Army. For over sixty years the Colored regiments 9th and 10th Calry [*sic*] and the 24th an 25th Infantry have been among the crack troops of the army. On parades, reviews, and inspections they have made a continious [*sic*] record of excellence. Back in the Indian fighting days Colored troops were in constant service in the west and were more feared by the Indians than any other troops. No matter how greatly outnumbered by attacking Indians the Colored troops would form a rough circle and beat off all attacks just as the buffalo on the planes [*sic*] fought off attacking wolves and for this reason Indians called them Buffalo Soldiers. With the fine record of the Colored troops of the old army as an example, every soldier in this regiment should try his best to make this Artillery outfit take its place, in excellence beside the older Cavalry and Infantry Regulars.

The United States Declares War

As I indicated in a letter to my mother, some things began to change at Camp Livingston after the December 7, 1941 Japanese attack on Pearl Harbor and the declaration of war by the United States:

> Any minute we may leave here. We were in the show a few minutes ago when we got word to report back to our batteries.
>
> It could be practice just to see how fast we can get ready, or it could be the real thing. One never knows these days …
>
> … The war has changed some things down here, maybe for the better. For the first time I heard them say, "Regardless of race, creed or color." (MC/EC/12-15-41)

Little more than a month after the United States joined World War II, on Saturday, January 10, 1942, a disturbance occurred in Alexandria which reached riot proportions, "involving hundreds of soldiers and civilians, after the clubbing of a Negro soldier by a military policeman in front of a theater in the heart of the Negro district." (Lee, 1966, 356)

I remained at Camp Livingston during the riot, as indicated in the letter I wrote to my mother on the following Tuesday:

> I suppose you heard about our riot [in Alexandria] Saturday night … So far as I can find out, none of my friends were among the 50 or more individuals reported hurt and 3 or more reported dead.
>
> General [B. O.] Davis is here investigating the situation. He was in my office this morning and said that he would be here indefinitely … He couldn't have picked a better time. (MC/EC/1-13-42)

Officer Candidate School

In order to fulfill the junior officer requirements for the new black units, the Army decided to use existing officer candidate schools to commission additional black officers. In common with many other commanders of black units, unit commanders within the brigade were urged to advise mentally qualified enlisted personnel (categories I and II) to apply for officer candidate school.[5]

By that time, the enlisted strength of the brigade was almost 5,300 men, and of that number about 120—or a little more than 2.5 percent—were in the two upper mental categories. (Lee, 1966, 239–47) I did not find out how many of these applied for OCS, but on the basis of discussions with regimental personnel sergeants, I concluded that eligible privates, corporals, and sergeants were much more likely to apply than NCOs of the first three grades. Among these latter personnel, there was some reluctance to give up the certainties and privileges of their NCO rank for the uncertainties of a second lieutenancy.[6]

My battery commander, my regimental supply officer, and the regimental personnel sergeant major (who offered me his assistance by furnishing me a draft letter of application to use as a guide) all urged me to apply for OCS. But the regimental supply sergeant, a master sergeant who was a veteran of World War I and within a few months of retiring, urged me not to apply. He stated that he had personal knowledge of the unfair treatment received by Negro officers during World War I, and believed that they would be treated the same way during World War II. He stated that it was a foregone conclusion that if I stayed in the 46th Brigade, I would get his job when he retired, and as a senior NCO I would be respected throughout the Army. On the other hand, he said the bias against Negro officers was so widespread and intense that it would be especially destructive to the military careers of Negro officers with outstanding potential.

He stated that when the Army began to expand in 1940, there were only two Negro line officers on active duty, and that by the end of 1941 only two Negroes had been permitted to graduate from West Point in the past 50 years.[7] Furthermore, he warned that the outlook was particularly bleak for Negro artillery officers, since on the basis of World War I experience most would remain permanent second lieutenants throughout their careers as officers. Few would be promoted to first lieutenant and none to captain, since all jobs requiring captains and above, even in the Negro combat divisions, would be reserved for white officers.

Thus, the reality facing a black Army officer during World War II was a system based on institutional racism, justified by the assumption of the inherent inferiority of blacks. The most overt manifestation of bias against black officers, which was completely inconsistent with any claim of "separate but equal" or "separation without discrimination," was an outgrowth of the army staff practice of forbidding black officers to outrank or command white officers serving in the same unit. This "not only limited the employment and restricted the rank of black officers but also created invidious distinctions between white and black officers serving in the same unit." (MacGregor, 1981)

In the face of such an unpromising outlook, I decided to follow the advice of the regimental supply sergeant, and in spite of repeated urgings and reminders from the proponents, I had not applied for OCS by the middle of May 1942. It is likely that I would have continued to procrastinate indefinitely if the brigade commander had not intervened. He did so by directing me to report to his office on Tuesday, May 19.

When I reported to the brigade commander, Brigadier General W. H. Paine, he did not waste time asking questions. Instead, he stated that he knew the reasons for my reluctance to apply for OCS, but was confident that in spite of many unavoidable difficulties that had been faced by Negro officers during World War I, a Negro officer with outstanding potential would have a good chance to succeed during the current conflict. He was convinced by my service as an NCO in the brigade that I had outstanding potential. Furthermore, he stated, it was my patriotic duty and my duty to my race to become an officer so that Negro soldiers could have some officers of their own race to lead them in combat. He told me that he expected to see a copy of my application for OCS on his desk before the close of business on the following Friday, May 22.

Within the next 72 hours my application for FA OCS at Fort Sill, Oklahoma, had been submitted and forwarded to the Brigadier General Paine:

> In reference to Circular 126, War Department, dated April 28, 1942, I hereby make application for selection to attend the Field Artillery Officer Candidate School ... I agree to serve in the capacity of Second Lieutenant for one year or longer. (MC/OCS/5-22-42)

A few days later, I discovered that Camp Livingston included a camp for Japanese prisoners of war (Marshall, 1943, 246–48):

> May 30, 1942, Sat. Decoration Day
> Saw about a thousand Japanese prisoners of war being marched to PW Camp after being unloaded in front of property office. There were plenty of guards around ...
> ... Made corrections to OCS application which was submitted on 22 May.
> ... Will resume compiling history of my life in the Army. (MC/NB)

Within a few days, I appeared before the OCS Screening Board and discovered that, since the general had already decided that I would go to OCS, my appearance there was just a formality. It was extremely unlikely that they would have disapproved my application for any reason.

As I expected, I received orders transferring me to the Field Artillery Officer Candidate School at Fort Sill, to attend class No. 33 beginning on July 14, 1942.[8]

I reported to OCS on July 14, when for the first time in my life I was introduced to a desegregated environment, that included all training, eating, living quarters, etc., within the OCS area. However, this desegregated environment did not extend to the remainder of Fort Sill or to the nearby city of Lawton.

OCS Hall of Fame Induction for Lt. Col. Major Clark, Fort Sill, Oklahoma.

Class 33 included about 600 students, six of whom were black. I had no difficulty with the course, and on October 8, after the prescribed 12½ weeks, I was commissioned a second lieutenant along with 399 other survivors. The new second lieutenants included two other black officers—one who had started the class with me in July and another who had started out in an earlier class but had failed to keep up. All three of us new black officers were assigned initially to the 93rd Division. However, the order was corrected on the same day to assign us to the 92nd Division at Camp Atterbury, Indiana, and for us to report for duty on October 20.

During the period between graduation from OCS and the date I had to report to Camp Atterbury, I visited my home town for several days, and as indicated in a news item in a Muskogee newspaper, attended an American Legion meeting. The master of ceremonies was a county judge who "presented Lt. Major Clark, local youth who dropped in at the meeting while home on furlough, having graduated from Officers Training School, Fort Sill, earning his present official rank. Lt. Clark responded with fitting brief remarks—the crowd giving him a big hand." (*Oklahoma Independent*, October 16, 1942)

Part II

The Color Barrier—An Obstacle to Progress

CHAPTER THREE

Camp Atterbury, Indiana

At the beginning of World War II, the War Department estimated that four black divisions would be organized as part of the 200-division Army needed to carry out offensive operations during the war. However, only about 90 U.S. Army divisions were actually involved in combat during the war, and only two of these were black. (Matloff, 1973, 426; Lee, 1966, 127)

The 93rd Infantry Division, the first black division of World War II, was activated at Fort Huachuca, Arizona, on May 15, 1942. Five months later, in September 1942, the 93rd furnished a cadre of 128 white officers and 1,200 black enlisted men to prepare for the activation of the 92nd Infantry Division.

When the 92nd Division was activated on October 15, 1942, its major elements were at four widely separated locations. This was necessary because Fort Huachuca, then occupied by the 93rd Division, was the only location in the United States considered suitable to accommodate an entire black division. (Goodman, 1952, 1; Lee, 1966, 106)

On October 15, 1942, the 597th Field Artillery Battalion and the 365th Infantry were activated at Camp Atterbury, Indiana; the 598th FA Bn. and 370th Inf. at Camp Breckenridge, Kentucky; the 599th FA Bn. and 371st Inf. at Camp Robinson, Arkansas; and the 92nd Division Headquarters and all remaining elements of the division, including the 600th FA Bn., at Fort McClellan, Alabama. (Goodman, 1952, 1)

The activation was noted in the camp newspaper:

365th COMBAT TEAM REACTIVATED OCT. 15; PART OF 92nd DIVISION

On Oct. 15, 1942, the 365th Infantry and the 597th Field Artillery Battalion, composing the 3654th Combat Team of the 92nd Division here, was reactivated in stirring ceremonies.

The original 92nd Division saw service during World War I from October 24, 1917 until March 7, 1919. It was ordered overseas in June 1918, occupied the St. Die sector in Lorraine from Aug. 23 until Sept. 20, participated in the Meuse Argonne operation from Sept. 26 until Oct. 3, and from Oct. 9 until Nov. 11, 1918 it occupied the Marbache Sector (Lorraine). The

The 597th was armed with 12 105mm howitzers, classified as light artillery. (OHS)

183rd [Infantry] Brigade, of which the 365th Infantry was a part, was demobilized at Camp Upton, N.Y. March 7, 1919.

The 92nd was known as the "Buffalo" division, and the reactivated division carries on the nickname, wearing the insignia with the buffalo silhouette.

... Maj. Don K. [*sic*] Workizer commands the 597th Field Artillery Battalion.

... Three other parts of the division are located at Ft. McClellan, Ala., Camp Robinson, Ark., and Camp Breckenridge, Ky. (*The Atterbury Crier*, 12–31–42)

The difficulties caused by the wide dispersion of the battalions of division artillery as well as the inferior quality of the cadre received from the 93rd Division were noted in the 92nd Division Artillery Operation Report:

Such an arrangement made exercise of command by Brigadier General William H. Colbern, the 92nd Division Artillery Commander, a most difficult problem ...

... The cadre from the 93rd Infantry Division Artillery was notably poor, far inferior to the filler replacements received [later during] the first two weeks in December 1942.

The cadre from the 93rd Division Artillery (white officers and black enlisted men) reported to Camp Atterbury to prepare for activation of the 597th FA Bn. They were joined on September 25 by a group of white officers who had graduated on September 10 from FA OCS Class No. 29. (597 A Hist)

I reported for duty as ordered on October 20, five days after activation of the 597th, and discovered that all of the officers already there were white, including the battalion commander, Major Daniel T. Workizer.[1] I was technically the first black officer

Buffalo insignia, 92nd Division.

to report for duty with the battalion, but later that same day I was joined by my two black classmates from OCS Class No. 33. We were all given a cordial welcome by the white officers, perhaps because they were having a promotion party. Captain Elkins, Battalion Executive Officer, was celebrating his promotion to major, and although they had not yet completed a full month in their first assignment as officers, several of the white second lieutenants from OCS Class No. 29 were celebrating their promotions to first lieutenant.

We found that all key command and staff positions in the battalion—including those for battalion staff officers, battery commanders, and battery executive officers—had already been filled by the white cadre-officers from the 93rd Division or from OCS Class No. 29. This reminded me of the prediction made to me by the regimental supply sergeant back at Camp Livingston that certain positions in the unit would be reserved for white officers.

The 597th was organized with a Battalion Headquarters battery, three firing batteries, and a service battery, and had an authorized strength of 28 officers, two warrant officers, and 561 enlisted men. It was armed with 12 105mm howitzers, classified as light artillery, which were towed by 2½-ton trucks. The maximum range of the howitzers was about 12,000 yards. As a divisional light artillery battalion, the normal mission of the 597th would be direct support of the infantry.[2]

During the next month, several more black officers reported for duty with the battalion, each within about two weeks after his class had graduated from OCS. These officers were initially assigned as battery motor officers or as assistants to white officers in the primary firing battery positions.

My first assignment was to Service Battery as Battery Motor Officer:

> The following named officer having reported for duty with this Battalion is assigned as indicated; ... 2nd Lt. Major Clark, FA, AUS, 0–1171088, Service Battery, Motor Officer. (597SO#4/10–20–42)

The authorized strength of the Service Battery was about 100 enlisted men. My job as Battery Motor Officer was (before the fillers arrived) to prepare to supervise 17 men in the battery maintenance section. I knew from previous experience that the battery maintenance section included the men who fed and supplied the battery and maintained the battery motor vehicles.

However, I did not have much time to benefit from my previous experience, because on November 18 I was transferred from Service Battery to Battery B. There I was assigned as Battery Reconnaissance Officer, in which capacity I was the supervisor of the battery detail section. Major Harry W. Elkins, then the Battalion Executive Officer, would later write: "Lieutenant Clark was the best qualified lieutenant in the battalion. I believe he was in Battery B with a red-headed lieutenant as battery commander." (HWE/MC/10-10-75)

At that time the authorized strength of a firing battery was four officers and more than 100 enlisted men. About 25 of these men were in the battery detail. I knew from my previous experience that the battery detail performed the battery survey, established wire and radio communications, established battalion observation posts (when ordered), and assisted in the reconnaissance, selection, and occupation of position. As I held the position of battery reconnaissance officer for Battery B for 14 months, I finally had adequate time to learn from my previous experience.

During November, a basic school was established for the newly commissioned officers and noncommissioned officers of the combat team, to be conducted in several consecutive classes of one week's duration. I was a student in the first class, then was selected as an instructor for the subsequent classes. The officer in charge of the basic school was Captain Edward Rowny, who 30 years later as a retired lieutenant general would become President Reagan's special advisor on disarmament.

During the last week in November, I met Truman Gibson, Assistant Civilian Aide to the Secretary of War, when he visited Camp Atterbury and made a speech to the black officers of the 597th FA Bn. and the 365th Inf.[3]

At about the same time, I noted with interest the efforts on behalf of black Americans by Mrs. Clare Booth Luce, the Congresswoman-elect from Connecticut who was the wife of the noted publisher, Henry Robinson Luce. In the November 28, 1942 issue of the *Chicago Defender*, she was quoted as saying that the black people should be given assurance that they are not fighting for the white man's supremacy anywhere, but for freedom for all on the "noble proposition that all men are created free and equal ... We are still guilty of practicing some of the hard discriminations and perpetuating some of the same cruel oppressions against our own colored citizens while we condemn our Axis enemies."

During the last week of November and the first two weeks of December, the 597th received enough fillers from the reception centers at Fort Custer, Michigan; Fort Bragg, North Carolina; Fort Meade, Maryland; and Fort Still, Oklahoma, to bring the battalion up to full strength. (92A Hist) In a letter to the author written in 1975, the Battalion Executive, Maj. Harry W. Elkins, recounted some of his experiences during that period:

> Early one morning in the late fall, I went to meet a train bringing in new enlisted men. The temperature had dropped to near zero during the night. I had just completed a two-year tour of Panama a few months before and I felt like my face was going to freeze off before reaching the train.
>
> The battalion motor officer [who was white] hanged himself in an old barn near the barracks and I went over to identify him. His dead body, hanging by the neck, was a gruesome sight. He had come to my room just the previous evening to discuss what to do about his mother, who had just lost her husband. (HWE/MC/10-10-75)

The 597th's Individual Training Program began during the second week of December. As the majority of the fillers had not yet received their basic training, additional time was devoted to training in discipline and physical conditioning. (597A Hist)

According to the grapevine, the 597th battalion commander and members of his staff began an elimination process late in December 1942 to select two black officers to be promoted to first lieutenant along with the remaining white second lieutenants from OCS Class No. 29.

The selection process seemed somewhat devious to the black officers, especially as demonstrated in my own case. On the one hand, Battalion Training Memorandum No. 6, dated December 9, 1942, assigned me as an instructor for two field artillery gunnery classes. On the other hand, along with all of the other black officers, I was subjected to conditions which seemed to be designed to generate reactions that could be documented as grounds for reclassification.

The condition we encountered most frequently was the "two places at the same time" game, which two white senior officers appeared to be playing, either intentionally or because of the lack of staff coordination. My records include more than one example of this apparent game. For example, the Battalion Executive would direct me to be at locale "A" at 1300 hours. A few minutes before I was scheduled to report there, the battalion S-3 would direct me to be at location "B" at the same time I had previously been directed to be at location "A." I would therefore report to locale "B" at 1300 hours (complying with last order received). My absence from location "A" at 1300 hours would be documented and the Battalion Executive would send a letter through channels directing that "You will state by indorsement hereon [the] reason for your absence."

Fortunately, I had been forewarned about the things that could happen to "green" black second lieutenants, and I was prepared with the proper response in each case.

Early in January, the grapevine reported that some of the junior white officers in the battalion had heard about the possibility of and were opposed to the promotion of any black officer to be first lieutenant. This seemed to be confirmed when one of my fellow classmates, who was considered likely to be recommended for promotion, was deliberately provoked into a no-win confrontation with a white senior officer. Predictably, the black officer was eliminated from consideration for promotion at that time. When he left the battalion several months later, he was still a second lieutenant.

I was the other officer considered to be in the running, but I began to feel very uncertain about my chances after his experience.

***

The fillers participated in the firing of the howitzers for the first time on January 15, 1943, when the battalion furnished overhead artillery fire[4] for an infantry problem. One section each from A and C batteries and two sections from B Battery participated. Thereafter, beginning during the third week in January, the battalion conducted service practice at least once each week.

My conduct of fire during the first battalion service practice had a significant effect on my career, as I indicated in a letter to my mother:

> We had our first service practice last week—that is—we actually fired our guns …
>
> Each officer fired at a target and was graded on how well he did. I made the highest grade—100%—a perfect problem. (MC/EC/1-24-43)

The day of the practice was cold and windy and it was extremely unpleasant on the hill that was used as an observation post. If a wind chill index had been computed, it would have been far below zero.

When my turn came to fire, the instructor (Captain Hughes, battalion S-3) identified the target as a small bush in a flat area about 2,000 yards away. As soon as I took my position in front of the class, I realized that I was more exposed to the chilling effects of the wind than I had ever been in my life.

After transmitting the firing data to the guns for the first shot, I began "double timing in place" to keep from freezing. After about two minutes of fighting a losing battle against the cold, I estimated that I would have about five more minutes before the deterioration of my body functions would reduce me to a state of helplessness.

I knew that I could not finish my problem in five more minutes if I followed the artillery school procedures, which would require a minimum of five rounds to ensure the proper effect on the target. Since the firing battery was in a very early stage of training and required relatively long delays for safety checks before each round could be fired, it would take 10 more minutes to fire the five rounds. Accordingly, since I felt that I could retain my normal mental and physical capacity for only half that time during which I could only fire two more rounds, I had to make the first major decision of my career as an officer.

I decided on a course of action which would complete the problem with two more rounds and stay within the critical five-minute period of time remaining. To do so, I would disregard standard procedures and take some short-cuts, in an "all or nothing" gamble that would result in a grade of zero if I did not succeed. And the chances for success were not good, because in order to succeed I would need a target hit or an impact so close to the target with the third round that there could be no doubt that it had a significant effect on the target.

I knew that even with the most accurate artillery pieces, it was difficult to obtain a target hit by indirect fire[5] without following the prescribed step-by-step procedure. And because of the dispersion characteristics of light artillery such as the 105mm howitzer, it was difficult to obtain a target hit using precision fire even under ideal circumstances, and any attempt to do so without following procedures was almost certainly doomed to failure.

I had to take the risk. I followed standard procedure for the first two rounds in order to establish the location of the target within a 400-yard bracket. Then, with my time running out and knowing that my entire future in the field artillery might be determined by what happened in the next two minutes, I abandoned the prescribed procedures, changed to my own emergency procedures, and prayed for a miracle.

After I observed the point of impact of the second round, I mentally computed the elevation and deflection change necessary for the howitzer to move the point of impact of the third round to the target. I then announced the necessary data to the telephone operator for him to transmit to the firing battery.

Before the telephone operator could start transmitting, the instructor held up his hand as a signal to stop the problem. He then advised me to reconsider the data I had just sent in the light of what was required by procedures that I had been taught only a few weeks before at Fort Sill. Since my self-allotted time had run out, I did not reconsider my decision, but informed the instructor I was completely aware of the implications of my action and assumed full responsibility for the results.

After replying "It's your funeral," the instructor signaled the operator to transmit my data to the firing battery.

The next two minutes seemed like two hours as I waited for the impact of the third round. I was becoming numb all over and it was difficult to see the target any more. But my vision improved quickly when the shell finally hit the ground and I saw clearly that it had exploded directly beneath the target bush, causing the bush—complete with roots—to be tossed several feet into the air. The instructor suspended service practice for the remainder of the day and drove into the target area to observe, at close range, the effect of my third round.

The following week, I was promoted to first lieutenant along with four remaining white officers from Class No. 29. It was more than a year later, after all white officers had been transferred out of the battalion and replaced by black officers, before another black officer in the battalion was promoted.

Although War Department policy dictated that no black officer was to outrank a white officer in the same unit (Lee, 1966, 211; Macgregor, 1981, 37), a new white second lieutenant was transferred into the battalion and assigned to my battery for a short period of time after I was promoted to first lieutenant. However, I was required only infrequently to exercise the prerogatives of my rank during that period, and when that did occur, there was no hint of resentment or insubordination by the white officer.

The men of the 597th spent the last week in January and the first week in February qualifying on the M1 rifle (they had not yet been issued carbines):

> Army Regulations on eyes—If a man's eyes do not test better than 20/50 he is not required to fire.
> Tonight at sick call assemble all the men and find out whether they have bad eyes. Send them over to the Battalion Surgeon at Sick Call for a preliminary examination but do not put their names in the Sick Book.
> Any man with bad eyes report to Battery Commander. Get Glasses in Martinsville—$8.80. Furnish Optician with list by Battery. (MC/NB)

We were gratified that, when we finished, a larger percentage of our men had qualified than had qualified in the infantry element of our combat team:

> Training [which began] during the latter part of December 1942 [and continued during January and February 1943] consisted of individual and section training, rifle marksmanship, forced marches and school of the soldier. Realizing the necessity of establishing an esprit de corps, the artillery commanders placed great stress on rifle marksmanship and, as a result, the artillery battalions in qualification firing with the M1 rifle, did far better than the division average. (92A Hist)

***

During the short time I was stationed in Indiana, I remained so busy carrying out my military duties that I had no direct experience with anything that indicated the state's public policy toward blacks. However, I was told that the Ku Klux Klan had been active in certain sections of the state since World War I.

Nevertheless, the following excerpts from the camp newspaper indicate some examples of the provisions made for the off-duty activities of the men:

PERMANENT WEEKEND TRAIN SCHEDULE ANNOUNCED; FITS IN WITH PASS RULING

> A permanent train schedule has been set and will be used this weekend and all future weekends according to ... Post Transportation Officer.

The Atterbury Special train will make two trips to Indianapolis each Saturday—the first at 1330 (1:30 p.m.) and the second at 1800 (6:00 p.m.) arriving there at 14:30 (2:30 p.m.) and 1900 (7:00 p.m.)

Coming back to camp from Indianapolis, the train will leave the Union Station at 2330 (11:30 p.m.) Sunday night. The return schedule fits in with the new ruling affecting most of the camp whereby weekend passes end at 0100 (1:00 a.m.) Monday morning. Since the train will arrive at camp at 0030 (12:30 a.m.) all passengers will be able to reach their barracks by 0100 (1:00 a.m.)

… The fare is $1 for a round trip. The ticket is good for 90 days, and the two parts of the ticket can be used for fare on the train going either way." (*The Atterbury Crier*, 12-31-42)

Negro Troops Using Temporary U.S.O.

Negro troops have been taking welcome advantage of the facilities offered them at the Franklin U.S.O. according to Tom Johnson, director, located at Madison and Main Streets. The spot is near the center of town and easily accessible to any troops visiting Franklin. Social and recreational programs are being presented every day of the week. (*The Atterbury Crier*, 12-31-42)

SERVICE CLUB No. 3

North End of Gatling Street

… Sunday, Feb. 7—TEA DANCE—1500. 75 Girls from Indianapolis, 75 girls from Cincinnati. (*The Atterbury Crier*, 2-5-43)

***

Early in March, the 92nd Division Artillery commander received approval from Second Army to consolidate the division artillery at Camp Robinson, Arkansas:

During the time the (artillery) battalions were attached to the infantry regiments the training deviated a great deal from that prescribed for newly activated artillery units. Artillery ranges at each station were very poor …

Interruptions in training caused by command inspections, reviews, forced group songfests and demonstrations interfered a great deal with the training program and left little time for actual artillery training …

Realizing that his problem could be solved only by consolidating his battalions on one post … the Artillery Commander immediately started working toward this goal. By the first week of March, approval of Second Army was obtained, and the staff began work on the task of moving three battalions and Headquarters Battery with inexperienced drivers and only one half of their authorized transportation from their respective stations to Camp Joseph T. Robinson, Arkansas, a move of over 500 miles for each unit. (92A Hist)

The 365th Infantry was to remain at Camp Atterbury.

CHAPTER FOUR

Camp Robinson, Arkansas

In March 1943, the 92nd Division Artillery gathered at Camp Robinson, Arkansas for about six weeks of unit training. During that period, Major Crockett relieved Major Workizer as battalion commander; President Roosevelt visited Camp Robinson; and the 93rd moved from Fort Huachuca to the Louisiana Maneuvers area for the continuation of its training.

On March 9, the 597th published the order for movement of the battalion from Camp Atterbury, Indiana to Camp Robinson, Arkansas the following day.

On March 10, the 597th left Camp Atterbury for a four-day motor march to Camp Robinson, near Little Rock, where all of the 92nd Division Artillery was being assembled for unit training. During the first day, the 597th traveled through southern Indiana, across the Ohio River into Kentucky, and stopped at Camp Breckenridge, Kentucky. There, the 598th was preparing to join the 597th on the morning of the 11th for the remainder of the journey to Camp Robinson.

The 597th bivouacked for the night at Camp Breckenridge, and on the next morning continued the journey in a convoy with the 598th. The convoy crossed Kentucky, a small bit of Illinois, crossed the Mississippi River into Missouri, and spent the night in a pasture near Charleston, Missouri. On the 12th, the convoy moved through Missouri into Arkansas and spent the night at Newport Air Force Base, Arkansas. On March 13, the 597th completed the last leg of the journey and reached Camp Robinson in the middle of the afternoon. The 597th had traveled a total distance of 598 miles. (597A Hist)

Immediately upon their arrival at Camp Robinson, an intensive training program was initiated for the 92nd Division Artillery:

> With his command consolidated for the first time, General Colbern began an intensive program to improve the technical artillery training. Unit training began on 15 March.
>
> But the time was short and the week of 15–21 March brought the III Corps Inspection Team to give the "13th Week Battery Firing Tests." Tests were run on the artillery Range at Camp Robinson, and the neglected artillery training was obvious; no battalion was rated satisfactory. (92A Hist)

After failing the firing tests, the battalions immediately began practice for the retest, which was to take place about a month later.

On April 3, Major Clement W. Crockett relieved Maj. Daniel T. Workizer as the battalion commander of the 597th.

Some of the provisions for off-duty activities of the soldiers in Camp Robinson are indicated by items in the division newspaper, *The Buffalo*, and the Camp Robinson newspaper, *The Military News*:

New Library Opens at Camp Robinson

The Library of the 371st Infantry was recently opened to the enlisted Personnel and the Civilian employees of the camp.
    The Library is located in the left wing of Service Club No. 3. (*The Buffalo*, March 27, 1943)

371st INFANTRY REGIMENT

(Chapel on North Dakota and 6th Street)

Chaplain: Sideboard
Protestant: Sunday 9 a.m.; 10 a.m.
Wednesday 7 p.m. Prayer Meeting
Friday 7 p.m. Choir Rehearsal

599th FIELD ARTILLERY [BATTALION]

Chaplain: Bowden
Protestant: Sunday 10 a.m. (*The Military News*, April 9, 1943)

Major Clark

In Little Rock, the U.S.O. for black soldiers was located on 9th Street. Soldiers stationed at Camp Robinson told me that this U.S.O. was the only one in Little Rock they could attend. They were also told not to go west of Pulaski Street; mostly white people lived west of there.

Occasionally, Philander Smith College would invite soldiers to a coed dance. Soldiers desiring to go to the dance were selected. Girls would forward their names on a tag, and a soldier would pin the tag of a girl on the lapel of his coat. Invited soldiers were carried by truck to the dance to meet their blind date. No stragglers were invited. (Tanner/MC/4-17-87)

Meanwhile, Second Lieutenant Roscoe C. Cartwright—a future brigadier general—who had been assigned to the 599th Field Artillery Battalion at Camp Robinson, Arkansas since November 1942, was married to Miss Gloria Lacefield of Little Rock on April 13, 1943.[1]

On Palm Sunday, April 18, a significant event took place at Camp Robinson that, because of wartime censorship, was not reported in the Little Rock newspaper until the next Wednesday. The following are excerpts from the *Arkansas Gazette* for Wednesday, April 21, 1943:

PRESS NOW CAN TELL OF VISIT BY ROOSEVELT
President at Camp Robinson Sunday

Elaborately guarded, carefully avoiding the limelight and with a censorship clamped down on newspapers, President Roosevelt visited Camp Robinson last Sunday ...

Mr. Roosevelt attended Palm Sunday services with 3,400 officers and enlisted men, on his second wartime inspection tour of the country ...

Governor Adkins ... greeted the president at his special train, toured the post with him in an open car, and sat beside him at the church services ...

The three-day rain prevented holding the Palm Sunday service in the large outdoor arena at Camp Robinson. Instead, it was moved into the Field House, with seats for several thousand persons ...

The president met Chaplain Crawford W. Brown, told him he would always remember the services, and remarked: "I've never heard anything in my life as wonderful as those boys singing 'Onward Christian Soldiers'."

That was the processional hymn, accompanied by a band, and it was sung as a white-robed soldier bearing a cross marched slowly down the center aisle and up a flight of green-carpeted stairs to the altar. He was followed by soldiers, Negro and white, carrying American flags and regimental colors, and by the chaplain and an assistant. (Copyright 1943, *The Arkansas Gazette*. Reprinted by permission)

The 597th was part of the honor guard for the president, and one officer and 10 enlisted men from the battalion participated in the services in the Camp Robinson Field House. As the participating officer from the 597th, I saw the president "at close quarters," and found out for the first time that he had a physical handicap, when he entered the Field House.

The retest of the batteries took place during the week of April 21–25, 1943, with encouraging results; all units were rated satisfactory with ratings in the low 80s.

Second Lieutenant Charles M. Brown, who had joined the 597th the previous November following graduation from OCS Class No. 35, left the 597th to take basic flight training at the Army Air Force Training Detachment in Pittsburgh, Kansas, followed by advanced flight training at Fort Sill, Oklahoma. Upon completion of the latter, Brown became the first black army aviator. He did not return to the 92nd Division Artillery but was assigned to another field artillery unit elsewhere.

Near the end of April, we were informed that the 93rd Division had left Fort Huachuca on a permanent change of station to participate in the April–June Louisiana Maneuvers. This made it possible for the entire 92nd Division to assemble at Fort Huachuca.

Members of the 92nd Division Staff made a reconnaissance to Fort Huachuca and reported the results in a staff memorandum dated April 15, 1943:

TROOPS:
a. Present Garrison:
   (1) Post Service and 9th Service Commands

(includes 2 WAAC companies and 780th MP Bn) ...	203-O;	4-WO;	2180-EM[2]
(2) Third Army Service Units ...	36-O;	2-WO;	2175-EM
b. 92nd Inf Div (when concentrated) ...	917-O;	14-WO;	15211-EM
TOTAL	1156-O;	20-WO;	19556-EM

LOCATION, CLIMATE, AREA:
... The fort Huachuca Military Reservation is located in Cochise County, Arizona, in the southern part of the State, and situated: 98 mi W of Douglas; 65 mi E of Nogales ...
... The climate is warm and dry; rainfall scanty. Rainy season starts in July. Short rains until September ...
... Elevation: Approx. 5000 ft; prevailing SW wind.
... Area: 73,000 acres; Approx. 120 Sq. Mi. (92D S Mem/4–15–43)

On April 23, 1943, 92nd Division Artillery published the order for movement from Camp Robinson to Fort Huachuca, Arizona: "92d Inf Div Arty, moving by rail, concentrates at Fort Huachuca, Ariz, for per sta..." (92A F04/4–23–43)

During the last week in April, the 597th packed and crated organizational equipment for rail movement and, on April 29, the first of three trains left Camp Robinson carrying the 597th to Fort Huachuca.

CHAPTER FIVE

Fort Huachuca, Arizona

The 597th completed the movement from Camp Robinson to Fort Huachuca during the first week of May 1943. From then until December, the battalion would conduct unit training and combined infantry–artillery training in and around the Fort Huachuca Military Reservation.

During the rail movement from Camp Robinson to Fort Huachuca, Maj. Harry W. Elkins, 597th Battalion Executive, was the train commander. In a 1975 letter to the author referred to previously, he recounted some of his experiences in connection with the move:

> I was a train commander on the rail move from Camp Robinson to Fort Huachuca. It was a mixed train with passenger cars, baggage cars, and flat cars carrying vehicles. As the train was stopped at some station along the way about 2:00 A.M., I was awakened by the conductor calling to the station master "Where's the train commander? Some of those trucks back here have busted loose." I had visions of wrecked trucks scattered alongside the tracks. However, it turned out that the only trouble was that some of the strands of cable securing the trucks to the flat cars had broken. This was taken care of without much difficulty.
>
> One day on the rail move, while the train was stopped in open country between towns, a couple of lieutenants and I walked back to the flat cars to check on the vehicles. Before we got back to the passenger cars, the conductor gave the engineer the go-ahead signal. The train began to move so that the three of us had to hop aboard the flat cars and ride in the cabs of trucks until the next stop about a half hour later.
>
> Fort Huachuca was hot and dry. One of our lieutenants caught rattlesnakes by hand (he may have used a stick to hold them down while he grasped them by the head).
>
> Gasoline rationing kept us close to the post while off duty. Several of us did get down to Nogales, Mexico, for a bull fight. There were a good many US soldiers there. The Mexicans cheered for the matador and the US soldiers cheered for the bull. (HWE/MC/10–10–75)

I commanded Car No. 2514, which had a capacity of 29 men, on the train carrying the 597th from Camp Robinson to Fort Huachuca. By May 2, the entire battalion had de-trained at Fort Huachuca. We discovered several problems there that had not been encountered at Camp Atterbury or Camp Robinson. Fort Huachuca was surrounded by a desert, had no camp town—except the dirty, squalid, and unsatisfactory town of Fry just outside of the gates—and it was located in a part of the country with practically no black population.

Officers of 597th FA Bn. at Fort Huachuca, Arizona, 1944. Col. Wendell T. Derricks is on the front row, sixth from left and Lt. Col. Major Clark is on the front row, last on the right. (OHS)

In order to ameliorate some of the morale problems resulting from Fort Huachuca's isolated location, the Fort Huachuca and 92nd Division Special Services Officers initiated an ambitious athletic and recreation program. This was extended down to the infantry regiments, and through the division artillery headquarters to the field artillery battalions. Since the more than 15,000 black men of the 92nd Division constituted 80 percent of Fort Huachuca's population, segregation on post was of minor significance to the enlisted men.

An example of some of the special provisions being made for the entertainment of the troops was included in the 92nd Division Artillery Special Service Bulletin dated May 17:

> … 4. Various dances are now being scheduled. All dances held at the Service Clubs will be open to all enlisted Personnel [sic]. A Division "Merit Dance" will be scheduled twice each month. Tickets for this dance will be prorated to units for distribution as a reward for outstanding exemplary conduct and attention to duty. The cooperation of all is requested to maintain the distribution of these tickets on a reward basis. Closed unit dances may be held by any organization by prior arrangement for the use of an RBI [Recreation] Building. Advance notice is requested …
> … 7. Each battery or similar unit will appoint a qualified man to set as "Battery Reporter," who will turn in a weekly report by each Tuesday on the activities of the unit, or personal items that are of general interest, for publication in the "Buffalo."

I became involved when, on May 31, while retaining all of the duties in my primary assignment as Reconnaissance Officer for Battery B, I was assigned additional duties as the 597th Field Artillery Battalion Special Services Officer and Athletic and Recreation Officer.

The new duties required me to coordinate all athletic and recreation programs for the battalion and to supervise the battery reporters for *The Buffalo*, the 92nd Division weekly newspaper. One result of this assignment was that, because of the 597th's preeminence in athletic and entertainment talent, I was mentioned in *The Buffalo* more frequently perhaps than any other black officer in the division.

The baseball team received a trophy for being second in the division artillery competition, and it placed 10 men on the unbeaten division artillery team. In the 11 final events in the division artillery track competition, the 597th won seven first places, four second places, and one third place for a total of 49 points, as compared to 25 points for the nearest competitor. (597A Hist)

In the following account, published in *The Buffalo* on June 26, 1943, Corporal R. M. Cain (a battery reporter) "brags" about the outstanding entertainment talent in the 597th. The last paragraph is a sample of one of the subjects considered humorous at that time:

> Men of the 92nd Division, you don't know what you missed if you didn't see the show given by the 597th Field Artillery Bn. last Friday at the Service Club No. 1 Carnival Area.
>
> It was presented under the direction of the Division Special Service Officer, and Lt. Clark, Battalion Special Service Officer; and was produced by Cpl. Charles Harmon, former drummer and singing star of Blanche Calloway's Band. Judging by the applause, the show went over in a big way …
>
> The entire show was great and was much enjoyed. We will let you know when the next one will be. You are all invited to attend.

During this period, I remained so busy carrying out my assigned duties as Reconnaissance Officer for Battery B and as Battalion Special Services and Athletic/Recreation Officer, that one visit to Tucson, one to Tombstone, and one to a Mexican border town was the extent of my off-post visits to the surrounding area. My visits to the town of Fry (just outside the gates) took place only when I was assigned there as a patrol officer.

The officers' clubs at Fort Huachuca were segregated: Mountainview for black officers and Lakeside for white officers. The following is an example of one activity at the Mountainview Club.

> EXHIBITION
> Of the work of 37
> NEGRO ARTISTS
> Officers Mountainview Club
> Fort Huachuca, Arizona
> May 16 to 22, 1943

> … Our efforts have resulted in one of the largest collections of works by Negro artists ever assembled in this country …
>
> … Mr. Lew Davis has kindly consented to arrange the works of arts in the Mountainview Club, Fort Huachuca, Arizona, where they will find their permanent home. (Program for Exhibition, printed at Fort Huachuca, Arizona, May, 1943)

One of my few visits to the officers' Mountainview Club took place in May, to view the exhibition, and another was in August, when the popular black entertainers Lena

Horne and Pearl Bailey visited there after they had performed (for the first time on the same program) at the dedication of a new Fort Huachuca theater.

***

With the entire division assembled at Fort Huachuca, it was possible for a much greater number of the black officers in the combat elements of the division to meet each other and compare notes. After doing so, they agreed that one common problem affected all officers in these units: the disincentives barrier. This was the barrier that separated two groups of officers (white and black) based solely on the color of their skin and rewarded their performance according to the group they belonged to.

On the one hand, no matter how mediocre the performance of a white officer, he could expect his minimum award to be greater than the maximum award received by the most outstanding black officer. Conversely, no matter how outstanding the performance of a black officer, he could expect his maximum award to be less than that of the most mediocre white officer. The black officers believed that the disincentives barrier, if it remained in place during combat, would have a significant adverse effect on the division's performance.

The outline of the disincentives barrier was contained in the draft of a letter given to me by an officer in the 365th Infantry shortly after we were reunited at Fort Huachuca. The letter was written to call attention to certain conditions existing in the organization which were detrimental to the morale and fighting efficiency of its black officers and troops. It pointed out that, laboring under such adverse and obviously prejudicial conditions, it was extremely difficult most of the time, and nearly impossible some of the time, for them to go about their work with diligence and self-confidence, instilling in the men the will to train and fight. Among other things, the letter stated that:

> Incompetent white officers, who openly admitted that they did not understand the functions of and had no experience in certain positions, were assigned to those positions rather than retain black officers who had been performing satisfactorily. Upon assignment to the positions, the white officers admitted openly that they were relying wholly and completely on the knowledge and experience of the black officers until they became proficient in their duties.
>
> White officers received the rank commensurate with the positions they held, while black officers serving in the same capacities were not promoted to commensurate rank. Additionally, certain white officers were recommended for promotions falsely, in that they were not holding and had never held the positions shown on the letters of recommendation for the promotion.[1]

Shortly thereafter, Gen. B. O. Davis arrived at Fort Huachuca to visit the 92nd Division for the first time since it had been assembled at one location.[2] A reliable source reported that the information in the 365th letter had been made available to him. However, in the public accounts of General Davis's report of his visit to the division, there was no specific discussion of any findings relating to that information.

Early in June, an incident occurred which prevented me from even temporarily serving in an assignment reserved for white officers.

Usually, in a field artillery battery, when the assigned commander was absent for a few days, the Executive Officer (who was the senior officer present) would temporarily assume command, and the Reconnaissance Officer (who was the next most senior officer) would temporarily serve as Executive Officer. Accordingly, when Battery B's commander, First Lieutenant Witenhafer, was scheduled to be absent from the battery for a few days beginning on June 10, we expected that First Lieutenant Enderson, the Battery Executive, would assume temporary command, and I would serve as Executive Officer in his place. However, the battalion commander decided to handle the situation differently, transferring a Captain David C. Shapard from another battery into Battery B to take over as battery commander in Witenhafer's absence. When Witenhafer returned, Shapard returned to his previous assignment, leaving unanswered the question of why it had been necessary to make the unusual changes in assignments.

There was general agreement among the black officers that my presence in Battery B had caused the problem. Enderson was technically the next most senior officer because he had been commissioned as a second lieutenant one month before I had. But both he and I had been promoted to first lieutenant on the same date, and as the Battalion Executive later admitted, I was considered the best-qualified lieutenant in the battalion.

It was agreed that the battalion commander must have considered it necessary to transfer a captain to Battery B during Witenhafer's absence to avoid letting me serve as Executive Officer, avoiding any possible chance that I might command the battery even temporarily.

During the summer of 1943, a number of black officers left the battalion to attend liaison pilot's school. I was urged to do so, but I was the senior black officer in 92nd Division Artillery and did not see any advantage in leaving at that time. However, by the middle of the summer, only five black officers remained in the 597th.

Meanwhile, a number of the enlisted men were transferred to the infantry as cadres for the newly formed 2nd Cavalry Division at Fort Clark, Texas.

***

On July 2, I gained a practical lesson in range safety practices. The regulations provided that, while only certain specific individuals were authorized to give the command to "fire" the howitzers, any individual could call "cease fire."

We were practicing for battery firing tests and, to provide some variety in the exercises, North Mountain and Needle Peak—the highest points on that end of the range—were being used alternately to observe from one day and as the target area the next day. For example, the favorite OP (observation post) on North Mountain one day became the favorite base point the next, and vice versa for Needle Peak.

On the day of the occurrence, North Mountain had been designated as the area to observe from, and Needle Peak the target area. However, Battery C did not get the word.

I was acting as the forward observer for Battery B and, shortly after I established my OP behind a large rock on the side of North Mountain, Battery C began to register on the same large rock, which was a favorite base point. When the first round impacted about 200 yards beyond me, I realized that a serious mistake had been made and immediately broadcast a "cease fire" over my radio.

Unfortunately, the battalion commander disregarded the intent of the "cease fire" command and, instead of ensuring that it was executed immediately, first wanted to know why I was calling for a cease fire. While I was explaining the situation to him, the battery fired a second round, which impacted about 200 yards short. Luckily, before Battery C could split the bracket,[3] they realized they were making a serious mistake and changed the direction of fire to the correct target area on Needle Peak.

The lack of obstructions to observation on the portion of Fort Huachuca used for artillery problems made survey operations almost too easy because it was possible to see the target area and several distant aiming points from the battalion position area. On many problems, it was possible to do a connecting area survey with an absolute minimum of measuring and other field work.[4]

Battery tests were given by 92nd Division Artillery from June 29 to July 14. One battery in each battalion was rated unsatisfactory, but Battery B of the 597th and Battery C of the 600th made the two highest test scores: "We had our battery test last week and were considered the best battery in the whole division artillery." (MC/EC/7-4-44) As a result of our achievement, we were awarded a streamer for our guidon[5] and, with Battery C of the 600th, were later selected to participate in the Armistice Day parade in Tucson.

With battery tests out of the way, the AGF (Army Ground Forces) firing tests were the next goal. It was decided that the best method to train for the tests was to take the tests.

An inspection team was formed from the Division Artillery Staff, and from mid-July until August, each of the four battalions was run through the three battalion tests at least once each week. If results were below the expected standards, the offending battalion was retested that same week on the particular test in which it had failed.

The actual tests were given by a team from VIII Corps during the week of August 16–20. Two of the four battalions (the 597th and 600th) failed the first battalion test so badly that the grades made on the other two tests were not sufficient to raise their average to the 70 percent required for a satisfactory rating. (92A Hist)

***

As Battalion Special Services Officer, I continued to carry out activities designed to maintain the morale of the battalion personnel: "Highlights of the Battalion Dance last Saturday night was a jitterbug contest for a prize of $10.00. Competition was so keen that Lt. Clark had to award two $10.00 prizes." (by Sgt. Wells, *The Buffalo*, August 1, 1943)

On August 21 and 22, a new theater in the division area was dedicated with the showing of *Stormy Weather* and special entertainment by some of its stars, including Lena Horne and the Nicholas Brothers. Lena was the niece of John Horne, sports editor of *The Buffalo*. Also present at Fort Huachuca during this period and participating in the theater dedication was USO Troupe No. 65, featuring the singer Pearl Bailey. A notice of the forthcoming events was published in the 92nd Division Daily Bulletin for August 21:

> Theater #5, Fort Huachuca's newest theater, located at 3rd Avenue and E Streets, in the contonment [*sic*] area, will be opened and dedicated Saturday, 21 August 1943. Lena Horne and the Nicholas Brothers will be present to entertain. Following the program, the moving picture "Stormy Weather" starring Lena Horne and the Nicholas Brothers will be shown. Lena Horne and the Nicholas Brothers will appear at the Outdoor Arena outside Service Club #1 at 20:00 with an SCU 1922 Variety Show on Saturday, 21 August 1943. Lena Horne and the Nicholas Brothers will appear Sunday, 22 August at the matinee and evening performances at Theaters #3 and #5, and also at the Outdoor Arena outside Service Club #1 at 20:00 with the Variety Show at which time Lena Horne will be crowned "The Queen of the 92nd Division." (92 Div DB)

I was a part of the large audience that witnessed a milestone event in entertainment history on August 21 when Lena Horne and Pearl Bailey appeared on the same show for the first time. Lena's performance was delayed because of the unexpected reaction to Pearl, whose appearance was intended to warm up the audience for Lena. According to the account documented by Pearl on pages 26 and 27 of her book *The Raw Pearl*, the Army newspaper had reported that she would sing one song. But when she started singing, "the fellows screamed and carried on ridiculously. My one song became four." Lena was permitted to start her performance only after Pearl had responded to several encores.

On August 22, Lena made matinee and evening show appearances at two theaters. She also made an evening appearance at a Division Variety Show held in the Outdoor Arena outside Service Club No. 1, where she was crowned as the Queen of the 92nd Division.

Whether or not by happenstance or design, the Hook area of Fry[6] was placed off limits, effective from noon on August 22. Consequently, during the afternoon and evening of August 22, thousands of soldiers were in the stands at baseball games or lined up outside theaters. (Lee, 1966, 284–85)

***

Beginning in mid-August and continuing until December 1, the 597th Field Artillery Battalion and the 365th Infantry participated in a combined training program in infantry–artillery coordination, based upon newly perfected tactics that had contributed to the success of the Tunisian campaign in North Africa. Artillery officers accompanied infantry companies as forward observers, and adjusted fire as close as 300 yards to troops (we expected that distance to be reduced to 100 yards in combat). During one of these problems, an incident occurred that provided a type of experience many World War II field artillery officers had at some time during their careers.

I was acting as Safety Officer for Battery B and Lieutenant Enderson was acting in his normal capacity as the Executive Officer. It was my responsibility to check the guns before any firing command was given by the Executive Officer, to ensure that the rounds would impact within safety limits; and it was the Executive Officer's responsibility to wait until I signaled "safe to fire" before he gave the firing command.

The problem was complicated by the fact that the primary coordination with the infantry was accomplished by the designation of three successive phase lines, with different safety limits for each phase. The infantry was to advance to each phase line in accordance with a specified time schedule.

At the time of the incident, there had been a 10-minute lull in the firing since the last mission, which had been fired as the infantry approached Phase Line II. According to the schedule, the infantry was approaching Phase Line III and it was time to prepare to fire the mission which had been planned for this phase. However, instead of transmitting the data for Phase Line III, the fire direction center inadvertently transmitted the same data that had been transmitted for the previous mission at Phase Line II.

When the Executive Officer received the data, he noted that there were no changes from the previous mission in the elevation and deflection settings for the howitzers. Therefore, he believed it was merely a repetition of the previous mission and viewed the situation as an opportunity to see how quickly the battery could respond. Since he did not believe a safety check was necessary under those circumstances, he gave the command to fire without waiting for me to make the specified safety check to determine if the data met the requirements of Phase Line III.

When the mission was fired, the infantry had almost reached Phase Line III, and although there were no casualties, the rounds fell much closer to the troops than was permitted by the safety regulations.

An investigation confirmed that the fire direction center personnel had made the basic error by inadvertently transmitting the wrong data and that the Executive Officer had erroneously fired without waiting for me to make the safety check and signal that it was safe to fire.

The battalion commander decided that the battery Executive Officer and I should share equally in the blame for the violation of safety regulations and pay for the eight "short" rounds that were fired. Accordingly, he directed that we should each purchase enough U.S. Savings Bonds to cover the cost of four rounds of 105mm howitzer ammunition.

Lt. Clark—   6 Sept 43
Information coming to me over the weekend indicates that the proper price of a round of HE Fz M54 is $19.24—not what I was previously told.
   Therefore, amend what I directed before to be: purchase of two—$50.00 bonds and $2.00 worth of War Stamps.

C. W. Crockett[7]—
   The total cost to the government of four rounds at the price of $19.24 each was $76.96. I bought two $50.00 U.S. Savings Bonds at $37.50 each for $75.00, and $2.00 worth of War Stamps to cover the remaining $1.96.

About mid-October, my request for 10 days' leave was approved, as noted by our battery reporter in *The Buffalo*: "We wave Lt. Clark on his way to enjoy a well-earned leave, hoping that every moment of his time will be well spent." (*The Buffalo*, October 23, 1943) I also recorded the event in my notebook:

Left Fort Huschuca, Sunday 17 Oct at 0950. Left Hereford (by rail) at 1230, arrived Kansas City, 1930, Monday, 18 Oct; left Kansas City 1030, Tuesday 19 Oct; arrived Muskogee, 0530 Wednesday, 20 Oct; arrived Haskell 0630 same day. Left Haskell, 1430 Sunday 24 Oct; arrived Muskogee, 1530; left Muskogee 2230 and arrived in Kansas City at 0630, Monday 25 Oct. Left Kansas City 0930, Tuesday 26 Oct; arrived Hereford, 1645, Wednesday 27 Oct; arrived Fort Huachuca, 1830 same day. (MC/NB)

I was the junior member (recorder) and the only black member on a board of officers appointed to examine applicants for second lieutenant commissions in the U.S. Army. In November 1943, we examined Staff Sergeant James S. Christian, Headquarters Battery, 597th, who was a rated liaison pilot, and approved his application for a commission as a second lieutenant. After receiving his commission, Christian remained with the 597th as a liaison pilot and was promoted to first lieutenant on January 27, 1945. During combat he earned the Air Medal with one Oak Leaf Cluster. In 1977, Christian was elected to the Virginia House of Delegates and had a distinguished career as a legislator until his death on December 29, 1982.

On November 9, 1943, 92nd Division Artillery published the order for movement of Battery B, 597th, and Battery C, 600th, to participate in the Armistice Day Parade. Accordingly, on Armistice Day, Battery B received the reward for its outstanding battery test performance during the previous June.

Our battery reporter noted the event in an item published in *The Buffalo*:

We congratulate our battery commander, Capt. Witenhafer on his recent promotion from 1st Lt. and on his first anniversary as Commander of Btry. B.
   We also congratulate Lt. Enderson and Lt. Clark on their first anniversary as Executive and Reconnaissance Officers, respectively.

> We are sure everybody enjoyed the trip to Tucson and the parade that followed, and the little affair at the Blue Moon afterwards. We have never seen a greater percentage of wolves in one battery before. (*The Buffalo*, November 20, 1943)

From December 3–23, the 597th participated in division (D-series) exercises during which all combat and combat support elements of the division moved out into the "field," which included the Fort Huachuca Military Reservation and some adjacent land:

> We have been out 9 days and will be out 11 more. It is cold at night but we have plenty of clothing to keep us warm. (MC/FDP/12–12–43)

We returned to Fort Huachuca on Christmas Eve:

> Today is Christmas Eve. I have just returned from 20 days spent in the mountains and desert around Fort Huachuca, Fairbanks, Tombstone and Gleason. The weather has been cold at night, early morning, and late afternoon, but warm during midday. Each morning, except one, there has been a frost and it rained one night.
>
> My bed feels strange. After the nice soft rocks I've been sleeping on, I cannot seem to sleep on a mattress and pillow anymore. I really slept better out there than I did at home. I couldn't even contract a cold out there.
>
> My biggest complaint concerns the stickers and thorns … In this part of Arizona every living thing is either poisonous, in the case of snakes, etc., or has thorns on it, in the case of vegetation. So anything you touch will cause you to painfully remember it.
>
> … In the report that was made concerning our field exercises, a list was included of those officers and men who did an excellent job. The one officer listed from my battery was "M. Clark, 1st Lt."
>
> My conviction that we will leave here soon has been almost certainly confirmed. Before the end of January, we will probably go to Louisiana for maneuvers. (MC/FDP/12-24-43)

Major Clark

Immediately after the division returned to Fort Huachuca for the Christmas holidays, First Lieutenant (Chaplain) Alfred G. Dunston, the new 92nd Division Artillery Chaplain, arranged a meeting between the black artillery officers and Brigadier General Colbern, the Division Artillery Commander. Chaplain Dunston had replaced Chaplain Bowden during the division exercises. The purpose of the meeting, which had been requested by the black officers, was to discuss the assignment and promotion policies within 92nd Division Artillery.

At the meeting, a spokesman pointed out to the general that, although several infantry officers in the division had already been assigned as company commanders and promoted to captain, not even one black artillery officer in the 12 firing batteries of division artillery had been assigned to command a battery or promoted to captain. Furthermore, less than half a dozen black officers had even been promoted to first lieutenant despite the fact that some of the second lieutenants had been in the division artillery since shortly after it was activated more than a year before.

The Division Artillery Commander made no attempt to explain the real policies concerning the assignment and promotion of black field artillery officers. Instead, he stated that he followed the recommendations of the artillery battalion commanders in the assignment of both black and white officers and that, so far, he had not received any recommendation for assignment of any black officer to command a battery or for the promotion of any additional black officers to first lieutenant. Nevertheless, he stated that he would look into the matter.

I wrote to my fiancée that the return address on my most recent letter from my brother, William, a staff sergeant in Headquarters, 332nd Fighter Group, included an APO number:

> William (my brother) now has an APO number, which means that the 332nd (Fighter Group) will probably be pulling out for overseas soon.
>
> I will also have an APO number in about three weeks ... APO 92, c/o Postmaster, Shreveport, LA ...
>
> We will go near Camp Livingston, where I spent 18 months in 1941 and 1942; also Alexandria, Bunkie, Marksville, Shreveport, Monroe, Lake Charles, Baton Rouge (Southern University), New Orleans and a few other places.
>
> I am enclosing the 92nd Division insignia[8] ... The living counterpart of this (a buffalo) has a pen behind Service Club No. 2 here at Fort Huachuca. He is very ugly. He is also from Oklahoma (the 101 Ranch). (MC/FDP/12-30-43)

During January 1944, the 597th prepared for participation in the Louisiana Maneuvers, which were scheduled for February and March.

A few days before we left for Louisiana, I obtained a three-day pass to visit my fiancée in San Francisco effective on or about January 20. When I returned to Fort Huachuca, I received a copy of 597th Battalion Special Order No. 12, which indicated that I had been transferred from Battery B to Battalion Headquarters to be Assistant S-2 (Battalion Reconnaissance and Survey Officer). I regretted leaving Battery B, where I had been assigned since November 1942, but as I explained in a letter to my fiancée: "this is a promotion [in that I am] ... the only colored officer in the 92nd Division on an artillery battalion staff ... My fellow officers of both races seem prouder of this than I am." (MC/FDP/1-27-44)

CHAPTER SIX

Maneuvers in Louisiana

According to War Department policy announced in October 1940, black units were to be provided in all the areas and services of the U.S. Army, and blacks would be assigned to the combat arms in the same ratio as whites. (Lee, 1966, 111) However, at a press conference with black newsmen in November 1942, Secretary of War Henry L. Stimson indicated that he would not follow the policy as it pertained to the combat arms. (*Defender*, November 28, 1942) As a result, although the Army activated a total of seven black field artillery regiments,[1] plus the separate field artillery battalions necessary to support two black infantry divisions and one black cavalry division (Sawicki, 1977/1978, 1,279–80), the promised ratio of black artillery units was never reached. For example, although the Army eventually reached a total of almost 700 field artillery battalions during World War II, the highest total number of black battalions was never greater than 30, and this high point occurred in 1943 after each of the field artillery regiments had been reorganized into two separate battalions. (Clark, 1985) Thereafter, many of those battalions were periodically stripped of most of their personnel to provide fillers for Army service units or were inactivated and directly converted to service units. (Lee, 1966, 425) In 1944, the entire 2nd Cavalry Division, including its field artillery battalions, was inactivated for this purpose. (Nalty, 1986, 167) These actions resulted in the reduction to only 17 black field artillery battalions that were eventually committed in combat by the Army. (*FA Journal*, 1946)

The 184th Field Artillery had been inducted into Federal service on January 6, 1941. Early in 1943, the 1st and 2nd battalions of the 184th Field Artillery had been reorganized into the separate 930th and 931st Field Artillery battalions. (Lee, 1966, 474–78) A few months later, the two battalions were stripped of 80 percent of their personnel to provide fillers for Army service units. (Lee, 1966, 425) Then, early in 1944, both battalions were converted to engineer combat battalions[2] and their field artillery officers were left without assignment. This removed all black field grade officers in the U.S. Army from assignment to field artillery units. (*Pittsburgh Courier*, March 4 and 11, 1944)

Late in January 1944, the 597th traveled to Louisiana as part of the 92nd Division to participate in maneuvers in February and March. A few weeks before the end of the maneuvers, most of the former officers of 930th and 931st Field Artillery battalions were transferred to the 92nd Division. (Lee, 1966, 474–78) The officers from the 930th joined the division in the Louisiana Maneuvers area and were attached to the 597th Field Artillery Battalion as observers. (597A Hist) The officers from the 931st traveled to Fort Huachuca to await the return of the 92nd Division from maneuvers.

The battalion entrained at Fort Huachuca on January 28 for movement to the Louisiana Maneuvers area, and detrained at Merryville, Louisiana, on February 3.

When the maneuvers began on February 6, I was the Battalion Survey and Reconnaissance Officer for the 597th and was responsible for supervising the battalion Instrument and Survey Section. Although there were less than a dozen men in the section, they were all highly qualified and had been selected because of their proficiency in mathematics.

I also coordinated, when necessary, the activities of the Instrument and Survey Sections of the firing batteries of the 597th. We were responsible for performing all of the necessary surveys for the battalion, for operating the battalion observation post(s), and when needed, to participate in the Division Artillery survey effort.

Unlike Fort Huachuca, where the lack of obstructions to observation made survey almost too easy, Louisiana's tall trees and other obstructions to observation made survey operations very difficult and time consuming, especially at the outset. It took me several days to realize that I needed to plan my complete survey before starting—instead of planning it as I went along. I found that with adequate advance planning, I could accomplish the survey with much less field work, thereby saving a great deal of time.

In letters to my fiancée, I noted that we had also participated in certain non-tactical activities:

Feb. 12, 1944—… We are having what we call a "break" … Every 4 or 5 days we get to rest a day, but after the first two weeks of maneuvers, things will begin to get tougher …

Feb. 20, 44—… Last night, I took some of our men to Alexandria on pass. Somehow it was like revisiting the scenes of my childhood. Although it has been 20 months since I was there, nothing seemed changed; and the USO, Lee Street, Third Street—everything was almost the same.

Driving down the familiar streets in my jeep, I instinctively drove around bad places in the road which were still there. On Lee Street, there was the usual fight every few minutes and the police station was full of intoxicated people. There are more liquor stores in Alexandria than there used to be filling stations before gas rationing.

I met several old friends. Some, who had bid me goodbye when I left there on 10 July 1942, were still in the same intoxicated condition when I saw them last night. (MNC/FDP)

On February 26, during the fourth week of the Louisiana Maneuvers, I was transferred from the battalion staff back to Battery B. There I was assigned as the Battery Executive Officer, a position previously reserved for white officers. Perhaps, in making the assignment, consideration was given to my status as a senior first lieutenant and the ranking black officer in the 597th Field Artillery battalion and the 92nd Division Artillery.

As Executive Officer, I was responsible for training and supervising a total of more than 50 men in the four howitzer sections and the ammunition section, and I was also in charge of the local security of the battery position.

In one of the highlights of the maneuvers for the 597th, the battalion participated in a defense against an armored attack in which it successfully turned back an assault aimed at the division command post (CP). (597A Hist)

In the meantime, events were taking place in Washington, D.C., which would have a significant impact on the future of the 597th. The Secretary of War, Stimson, had caused a political storm when he approved the plan to convert to engineers the all-black 930th and 931st Field Artillery battalions, which contained all of the black field grade officers in the Army assigned to field artillery units at that time. After the 930th and 931st were converted to engineers, the field grade officers as well as all of the other field artillery officers in the units were left without assignments.

Although I had no reason to believe I was going to be affected by the storm, I did have an interest in the outcome of the matter because of my brief contact with the senior officers of the affected units more than three years before. It had taken place back in December 1940, soon after the 8th Illinois Infantry had been converted to the 184th Field Artillery. Ten of the converted artillery officers—including the future regimental commander, battalion commanders, and senior staff officers—had been attached to the 349th Field Artillery at Fort Sill for their preliminary artillery training (see Chapter 1). I had been an enlisted man in Battery A, 349th Field Artillery, assigned as the instrument operator at the observation post used by the new artillery officers when they participated in their first artillery service practice. I had no further contact with any of the officers after that time.

During the fifth week of the maneuvers, I had received a copy of *The Pittsburgh Courier* for March 4, 1944, which began to document the details of the controversial action taken by the Secretary of War. The political storm had increased in intensity when it became known that Stimson's excuse for the conversion of the two battalions to engineers was that "they had been unsatisfactory as artillery."

The situation was brought to the attention of the general public as a result of a speech made in Congress on February 23 by Hamilton Fish of New York. In a letter dated February 9, he had requested certain information from Stimson concerning the conversion of the 930th and 931st. (Congressional Record, 1944, A659 and A660)

In his letter responding to Congressman Fish's inquiry, the Secretary of War had stated that "many of the Negro units ... have been unable to master efficiently the techniques of modern weapons" and that the 930th and 931st Field Artillery battalions were not being retained as artillery owing to the unsatisfactory records of both units. (Congressional Record—House, February 19, 1944, 2007–08)

In his speech, Congressman Fish stated:

> I do not agree at all with the official policy of the War Department in using colored soldiers as service troops, particularly with the policy of breaking up such a well-known and gallant Negro regiment as the former Eighth Illinois National Guard, which served with distinction and heroism in both the Spanish-American War and the World War ...
>
> I cannot speak for the people of Chicago, but I think they will be shocked when they learn that the old Eighth Illinois National Guard Regiment, of which they rightly have been so proud because of its service in the last war, is now turned into an engineer regiment after more than two years of training in preparation for front line service as a field artillery unit.
>
> ... I cannot agree with the Secretary of War's inference that colored solders' efficiency ratings are so low that "many of the Negro units have been unable to master efficiently the techniques of modern weapons."

Congressman Fish's speech caused a strong adverse reaction to the Army's policies by some of the other congressmen and by black newspapers and opinion leaders; policies which, until then, had prevented the use of black ground combat troops in their primary role. (Nalty, 1986, 167) Although about 20 white US Army divisions had seen some combat action during the two years in which the United States had been involved in the war (Combat Divisions, 1946), no black field artillery or infantry unit had been committed to combat.

To counter adverse reaction, the War Department accelerated plans to commit black combat units, such as the 93rd Division, the 24th Infantry, and eventually the 92nd Division. The most immediate effect was to ensure that a place was found for the black artillery officers deprived of their units by the conversion of the 930th and 931st FA Bns.

Accordingly, in an action that was amazingly inconsistent with a statement he had made just 10 days before, the Secretary of War announced new assignments for the officers who had commanded the two field artillery units being converted to engineers. Although he had stigmatized them by indicating that they had been unsatisfactory as commanders in their former field artillery battalions, he announced that they would be reassigned to the 92nd Infantry Division, scheduled for early deployment to a combat zone, to replace white officers in command of two of the field artillery battalions in that division. (597A Hist)

During the following two months, my frequent letters kept my fiancée informed of the developing situation:[3]

> Mar. 15, 1944—... It seems that we may go back to Fort Huachuca for a few days, weeks or months ...

> The division is somewhat upset over the assignment of the high-ranking colored officers from the 930th and 931st Field Artillery Battalions to join us at Fort Huachuca, and we don't know whether or not it will delay us from going overseas. (MC/FDP)

On March 16, I discovered that the 597th was one of the two battalions affected by the change, when I met Lieutenant Colonel Derricks in front of the 597th Battalion Headquarters tent, sitting on a stump and writing in a notebook. Derricks had commanded the 930th before it was converted to combat engineers, and he and several of his similarly displaced officers were assigned to the 597th as observers.

Since Derricks was alone at the time, I introduced myself and informed him that I had been present at the observation post at Fort Sill, Oklahoma, in December 1940, when he had participated in his first artillery service practice. He replied that he remembered the incident clearly and, as a matter of fact, specifically remembered me. I was flattered but somewhat skeptical that he could remember an enlisted man as the result of a single meeting more than three years before.

> Mar. 20, 1944—... Our battalion is going to be taken over completely by the officers from the old 184th Field Artillery (Chicago National Guard). All the white officers are to be transferred out, I don't yet know how we (the original colored officers) will be placed. We will find out when we get back to Fort Huachuca.
>
> Mar. 25, 1944—... Maneuvers are nearly over. I think this is our last problem. We will leave here early in April to go back to Fort Huachuca where will then be congregated 90% of all colored combat arms officers not yet overseas. In the 597th, we will have Colonel Derricks and his whole group of officers from the 930th (their enlisted men were converted to engineers and sent overseas, according to the *Defender* and *Courier*) ...
>
> Colonel Derricks and his officers are presently attached to the 597th as observers, but after we return to Fort Huachuca, they will take over. It is interesting to note how it is affecting the white officers, who will be transferred out of the battalion when we get back to Fort Huachuca.
>
> Mar. 28, 1944—... The first time I saw Colonel Derricks was in December of 1940 at Fort Sill on top of a hill on a very cold and windy day. His regiment (the Old 8th Illinois Infantry) had just been changed to the 184th Field Artillery. We both recalled the incident, and he claimed that he remembered me but I found that hard to believe. (MC/FDP)

When Derricks and his officers first arrived, the black officers and enlisted men of the battalion were proud, at long last, that the 597th had black officers equal in rank and numbers with the white officers of the battalion. But afterwards, as they began to consider the practical effects of the takeover, they began to wonder about their chances for retention in their individual assignments.

The NCOs were concerned about the possibility that they might not be able to retain the status for which they had worked so hard for so long, and fearful that they would have to start all over again and prove themselves to the new officers.

The outlook for the original black officers was especially gloomy because it was easy to predict what would happen to most of them. After being reduced to a total of five the preceding summer, the number of black officers had increased to thirteen by the time the new officers arrived. During maneuvers, five of these officers had been assigned to primary battery positions, with two of those positions being first lieutenant slots. At that time, I was not certain of the effect of the change on those black officers already assigned to the battalion.

Mar. 28, 1944—Less than two weeks of Louisiana Maneuvers left, then returning to Fort Huachuca. After that???

You may remember reading the accounts in the *Courier* and *Defender* concerning the conversion of the men in the 930th and 931st FA Bns into engineer units. The former commanders were field artillery officers and were left without assignments. The 930th and 931st were both descendants of the old 184th Field Artillery regiment from Chicago. All of the high-ranking officers are powerful

Lieutenant Colonel Wendell T. Derricks, Commanding Officer, 597th Field Artillery Battalion, 92nd Infantry Division, 1944–45.

politically (their detractors say that's how they got to be high ranking). Therefore, it created a political storm when they were pushed around that way. So now the plan is to give them the artillery battalions in the 92nd Division.

We have been told that all of the white officers will be transferred out and we will stay. But what about our assignments? There are about 75 of us in all of Division Artillery, with thirteen of us in the 597th. Only a few hold what is known as a Table of Organization position (a position in which you have a definite assignment), because almost all of those positions previously were reserved for white officers. We are wondering what will happen to those few of us colored officers who do hold such positions.

I am now the colored officer in the 92nd Division with the longest service in an artillery unit, or to put it another way, the colored artillery officer with the longest service with the 92nd Division. And I am the senior, colored artillery officer serving continuously with the 92nd Division. For these reasons, my friends believe that I will not be adversely affected by the change. I am not banking on that though … (MC/FDP)

I received your [Mar. 28] letter this morning, and somehow, I have a feeling that the results of the changes and developments in your division will be in your favor (whatever that is) …

In your particular case, I know how you must feel not knowing what to expect and, in a way, "out on a limb." I am pulling for you with all my might. If anyone deserves something great from these changes, you certainly do. (FDP/MC/4-10-44)

Maneuvers over, the 597th made another movement by rail, the first elements leaving Merryville, Louisiana, on April 3 and the last elements arriving in Fort Huachuca on April 8. I was a part of the last element to leave:

Apr. 4, 1944—Yesterday was the last day of maneuvers. When you read this, I will either be on my way to – or in – Fort Huachuca. We have been told that some parts of the division will be going overseas soon; not all, however …

Apr. 8, 1944—I am back in Fort Huachuca. We left Louisiana on the 6th and arrived here this morning. Everything seems the same, although we have been away 2 months …

Apr. 9, 1944—Today is Easter, a snowy Easter. At the time set for the sunrise services, a small blizzard was raging. Now, two hours later, the sun is peeping out every few minutes then wrapping itself up again in the clouds.

I arrived back in Fort Huachuca yesterday after a fifty-hour ride through Louisiana, Texas, New Mexico and Arizona.

… When we arrived, the battalion commander announced that there would be no passes or leaves until certain things were done incident to transferring the command of the battalion to Colonel Derricks and his officers. As a result, we are not even giving proper observance to Easter …

Apr. 11, 1944—… We seem to be sitting on a powder keg waiting to see what is going to happen when Colonel Derricks takes over day after tomorrow. General B. O. Davis and Truman Gibson will be here next week.

Most of the colored artillery officers in the Army who are not overseas are here-wondering who will get the "table of organization" jobs available. There are about three times as many officers here as there are such jobs available.

Well, we will know on Thursday. (MC/FDP)

CHAPTER SEVEN

Programmed for Failure

At the end of maneuvers, General Almond announced to the assembled officers and enlisted men of the division that, according to a recent War Department decision, the 92nd Division would be sent to an active theater for combat duty in the near future. (Lee, 1966, 495; Goodman, 1952, 10–11) The 370th Regimental Combat Team, to be formed of specially selected personnel from the other division units, was scheduled to go first.

Following maneuvers, the division began the return to Fort Huachuca to conduct an intensive training program in preparation for overseas movement. The program included lessons learned during maneuvers, correction of individual and unit training deficiencies, and the latest published lessons from the battle fronts. (Goodman, 1952, 11)

Preparation for overseas movement was conducted in two phases. In the first phase, top priority was given to preparing for the earliest possible deployment of the 370th Regimental Combat Team, consisting of the 370th Infantry, 598th Field Artillery Battalion, and detachments from special units of the division. Thereafter, priority was given to preparing the remainder of the division for deployment. (Goodman, 1952, 11–12)

The 597th and 600th Field Artillery battalions were reorganized by the block assignments of black officers to replace the white officers who had previously occupied all of the key command and staff positions in the battalion. This was the first and perhaps the only time in history that black combat arms units had been reorganized in that manner.

The black officer composition of the division was changed significantly when the two groups of officers were transferred from the 930th and 931st, since in addition to several captains, each group included three field grade officers. Thus, for the first time in history, black field grade combat arms officers were assigned to the 92nd Division.

The change was even more significant for the 92nd Division Artillery where, before the arrival of the new officers, there had not been a black officer above the grade of first lieutenant in any of the field artillery battalions.

Both groups of new officers had served in 155mm medium howitzer battalions, similar to the 600th, with a general support or reinforcing mission; but none had served in a 105mm light howitzer battalion, similar to the 597th, with a direct support mission. Accordingly, the new officers assigned to the 600th were already familiar with the "hardware" and mission of their new unit, but the new officers allocated to the 597th were not.

Nevertheless, in spite of the difficulties that would be encountered, an opening had been made in the color barrier by the assignment of Colonel Derricks to the 597th. This provided an opportunity for black officers to cross over the barrier and prepare for future progress by establishing a bridgehead on the other side. However, since the new black officers assigned to the 597th were in an extremely vulnerable position, the division expected and planned for the bridgehead to be held for only a short time. Thus, a maximum effort was required by all personnel assigned to the 597th to prevent a return to the status quo.

Less than a week after the 92nd Division returned to Fort Huachuca, all of the officers were transferred out of the 597th and 600th Field Artillery battalions. At the same time, Lieutenant Colonels Derricks and Ray assumed command of the 597th and 600th respectively. In the 597th, Colonel Derricks filled all of the key and staff positions, previously held by white officers, with the two majors, five captains, 10 first lieutenants, and five second lieutenants he had brought with him from the 930th.

In his reorganization of the 597th, Colonel Derricks changed every officer's assignment except mine: I remained assigned as Executive Officer, Battery B. However, the other original black officers—including those assigned to first lieutenant slots during maneuvers—were relieved of their assignments and attached unassigned as assistants to the officers who replaced them, or were transferred out of the battalion. The change-over occurred on April 13. "I am the only officer in the battalion who kept the same job." (MC/FDP)

When the first rumors began to circulate early in March concerning the impending takeover of the 597th and 600th by black officers, 92nd Division officers at all levels expressed their dread of the probable results. White officers were shocked at the possibility that black field-grade combat arms officers were to be assigned to the division for the first time. In particular, white officers in the 597th and 600th dreaded having to leave an institutional environment in which they had been protected from their most-qualified potential competitors in their opportunities for choice assignments.

The original black officers—those who had been assigned to the 92nd Division Artillery before maneuvers—were ambivalent concerning the change. On the one hand, they were relieved that the institutional policies and practices based on race, and manifested most openly by officer promotion and assignment policies, would be discontinued in the 597th and 600th, and perhaps tempered in the 598th and 599th.

But the original black officers in the 597th and 600th dreaded the almost certain prospect that they would be replaced in their jobs, because both Colonels Derricks and Ray had brought enough officers with them to fill all the key assignments in the two battalions.

I sympathized with the plight of the original black officers:

> Apr.–May, 1944—… It seems to be somewhat unfair to some of my fellow original officers. For example, Lieutenant Smith, who has a Master's Degree from Tuskegee, and who has been in the battalion only two weeks less than I have, has been placed in a position as an assistant to one of the new officers from Chicago …
>
> … The original group of colored officers got a pretty raw deal in this change. Most of them have been in the battalion for several months, and some of them since late 1942 or early 1943. They had been enduring all the hardships taking eight months of Huachuca, and two months of maneuvers. And, since the head men were all white, they have been held back, not because of the inability to do their jobs but because of their race.
>
> By maneuver time many colored officers in the infantry were in command of companies and several had been promoted to captain. But in the 92nd Division Artillery, not even one colored officer had been assigned to command a battery and, in all of the battalions of division artillery, only five officers had been promoted to first lieutenant. Furthermore, in the 600th no colored officer had been promoted even to first lieutenant.
>
> When I consider my own situation in comparison with that of some of the other original colored officers, I really have nothing to "beef" about; I have been promoted once and do have a primary assignment. But more of the others do have reason to be unhappy. When it seemed that they were about to get a break because some of the white officers were being transferred out, the War Department sent in two whole battalions of colored officers to fill all the high ranking positions. Now most of the original officers are in worse positions than before. (MC/FDP)

The new officers encountered major differences between the hardware and mission of the 597th and that of their previous battalion. Although the overall method of decision-making and planning by the battalion commander and staff of a 155mm battalion was not significantly different from that of the battalion commander and staff of a 105mm battalion, a detailed knowledge of the operation of the firing batteries was essential to the effectiveness of the decisions and plans. Furthermore, there were significant differences between the firing batteries of a 155mm battalion and those of a 105mm battalion.

- The howitzers. The 155mm howitzer weighed almost 6½ tons; the 105 less than 2½ tons.
- The ammunition. The 155 fired separate loading ammunition with a projectile that weighed over 90lb; the 105 fired semifixed ammunition with projectiles that weighed from 29–35lb.
- The rate of fire. The rate of fire of a 155 varied from two rounds per minute for the first four minutes to 40 rounds per hour for prolonged firing; the rate of fire for the 105 varied from four rounds per minute for the first four minutes to 100 rounds per hour for prolonged firing.

- The maximum range. The maximum range of the 155 was more than 16,000 yards; the maximum range of the 105 was a little more than 12,000 yards.
- The prime mover. The 156 was towed by a 4-ton, 6×6, cargo truck or an 18-ton, high-speed tractor, M5; the 105 was towed by a 2½-ton, 6×6 cargo truck.
- Time to get ready to fire. 155—5 minutes; 105—3 minutes.

Apr.–Jun., 1944—… When the new group took over they started doing their jobs as they had done in their old outfit, which had a mission which was of a type different from that of our battalion. Although we [the original officers] cautioned them that the division had different operating procedures, they didn't take our word at first. (MC/FDP)

***

In the *Courier* for the week of April 23, I noticed that Brigadier General Davis was to visit Fort Huachuca, specifically the 92nd Division. I supposed he was anxious to see the results of the recent changes and developments. (FDP/MC)

My Most Unpleasant Task

Shortly after we returned to Fort Huachuca, a Special Court Martial was appointed for the 597th and I was assigned as the Trial Judge Advocate (prosecutor), a role I was to undertake in addition to my other duties.

One of my first cases involved a soldier "who, on or about 23 April 1944, did wrongfully take and use, without proper authority, a quarter (1/4) ton truck of the value of about nine hundred and ninety-seven dollars ($997.00), property of the United States and intended for the Military Service thereof."

The soldier was found guilty and sentenced to have $14 of his pay detained for six months. The sentence was modified by the Division Artillery Commander to change the six months' detention of pay to three months. (92A SCM Order #46, 5029044)

***

During this period, I kept my fiancée informed of other activities at Fort Huachuca:

Apr.–May, 1944—… I attended chapel service today [April 16], the first time since returning to Fort Huachuca. Only two line officers were present: Lieutenant Colonel Wendell Derricks and myself …

Lieutenant Richardson's wife, who is teaching in Wynnewood, Oklahoma, is coming out here the last part of May; also, Sergeant Scott's wife.

A portion of our division is going over [to Europe] pretty soon and they have asked for volunteers. Shall I go? …

...Today, Sunday (May 7) the whole division went to the Stadium to hear Reverend Richardson, the Chaplain and Vice President of Tuskegee Institute ...

... Today (May 21) is Sunday. I spent the morning with the battery in a phase of training which had to be completed today. None of us liked to give up our "day of rest," but it is one of those things that will happen more and more often now.

Yesterday we had a division display of weapons and vehicles common to each unit. I had to explain and demonstrate the display for my battalion.

Last week I caught up with the various vaccinations and inoculations that are required for us: smallpox vaccination, typhoid and tetanus toxoid shots, all in one day, all in the same arm.

Despite all the signs to the contrary, I believe we will be here for three or four more months. I don't believe Uncle Sam is going to send an all-colored artillery outfit over yet. (MC/FDP)

Within a few days of the reorganization of the 597th, I began to feel that all was not well in the battalion. I compared notes with some of the other original officers and key noncommissioned officers and found that the morale of the battalion was going downhill in a hurry. We discussed some of the facts applicable to our situation and reached a startling conclusion: the new officers were being programmed to fail. The most significant factors considered were:

1. Black officers had been programmed to fail previously when the Army wanted to get rid of them or remove them from certain specific assignments.
2. Even if all other factors were favorable, the block assignment practice used in the change-over was, in and of itself, extremely detrimental to a unit.
3. The new officers lacked training and experience in the hardware and mission of a direct support battalion.
4. The 597th was already the least satisfactory battalion in 92nd Division Artillery.
5. No black officer had ever before commanded a direct support field artillery battalion.
6. Success or failure of the 597th was to be determined by white officers who previously commanded the 597th but who had been involuntarily displaced from their jobs.

This was not the first time that Army officers had programmed black officers to fail when they wanted to get rid of them. During World War I, black officers were commissioned after graduating from the black Officers Infantry Training Camp at Des Moines, Iowa. The Army programmed a number of these officers to fail by assigning them directly to field artillery units without any previous field artillery training (see Introduction). During World War II, in addition to the rumors we had heard of many similar examples, we knew that the Secretary of War had already tried to get rid of Derricks and his fellow officers. He had done so by removing them from their previous assignments and converting their battalions to engineers on the grounds that they had failed to produce successful artillery battalions.

The block assignment practice used in the 597th would have been detrimental even to a service unit, and was certainly detrimental to a combat arms unit making final preparation for deployment overseas. It was confirmed years later (Lee, 1966, 216–17) that when a unit was reorganized by block assignments, a serious leadership crisis was produced. The results of simultaneous removal of all white officers from the unit and the substitution of black officers, wrote Lee,

> ... not only suddenly destroyed on a unit-wide basis the leadership relations between the officers and men, but often interrupted training, setting the unit back several weeks in extreme cases; destroyed whatever esprit had been built up among the officers and men of the unit; and forced each element of the organization to alter its mode of operation. The resulting letdown in operating efficiency, discipline and morale was often attributed to the new Negro officers when actually the method of substituting new—and in these cases quite different—officers for the old, familiar troop leaders, schooled in their knowledge of the men of the unit, and the peculiarities of life for the unit under its particular headquarters and on its particular post, was often at fault.

In order to understand the implications of this particular block assignment, it is important to realize that Army policy had prevented any of the original black officers in the 597th, the 92nd Division Artillery, or anywhere in the Army from gaining the training and experience necessary to qualify them for key command and staff positions in a direct support field artillery battalion. Thus, since the only qualified officers were white, the block assignment removed all of the qualified officers from the 597th, assigned officers who were not considered qualified (see below), and because of the policy of "blacks shall not command whites," deprived the battalion commander of any access to qualified officers other than those who could be provided by on-the-job training.

According to reports, Colonel Derricks was an outstanding troop commander and was proficient in the tactics and techniques pertaining to field artillery in general. Although he did not seem well versed in certain special field artillery techniques pertaining to fire direction, survey, etc., many of the officers he had brought with him, especially those who had been commissioned through Field Artillery OCS, displayed an excellent knowledge of those techniques.

Colonel Derricks, formerly an infantry officer, had been a field artillery battalion commander for more than three years. During that period, he had commanded three battalions—all medium artillery—training in tactics and techniques applicable to general support or reinforcing missions.

In programming them for failure, the Army took advantage of the fact that neither Derricks nor his officers from the 930th had any previous training and experience in a 105mm howitzer battalion with a direct support mission. Under normal circumstances, the officers would not have been considered fully qualified to hold key command and staff positions in a battalion scheduled for early deployment to a combat zone, without first gaining additional on-the-job training and experience with the type of unit to which they were assigned. However, the Army assigned them to such positions in the 597th in the expectation that they would fail.

To the best of my knowledge, no other combat arms unit in the history of the U.S. Army was ever faced with a similar situation as it began final preparations for deployment overseas.

Although Battery B (the battery to which I was assigned) was one of the two best batteries in all of 92nd Division Artillery, the 597th as a unit—on the basis of its scores made during the previous year in battalion firing tests—was considered to be the least satisfactory field artillery battalion in the division. It seemed highly unlikely that, having known this, the Army really expected the new officers to produce a successful unit in view of the following considerations:

(a) The new officers were unfamiliar with the hardware and mission of the 597th and, although they had been completely familiar with the hardware and mission of their previous unit, they had allegedly been unsuccessful in producing a satisfactory battalion.

(b) In like manner, the white officers who had commanded the 597th had been completely familiar with the hardware and mission of the 597th but had been only marginally successful in producing a satisfactory unit.

(c) In view of (a) and (b), we were certain that the new officers were facing a much more difficult task than they had faced in their previous unit. Thus, we did not consider it logical that the Army expected the new officers to do as well with the 597th as they had with their previous unit. In other words, the Army expected them to fail.

Colonel Derricks was faced with a situation and a task without precedent. In addition to the other disturbing factors, he knew that no black officer had ever before been assigned to command a direct support field artillery battalion. As a matter of fact, no black officer had ever been assigned to command any type of field artillery battalion in combat, and no artillery battalion had ever been committed to combat with black officers in key command and staff positions.

Furthermore, the success or failure of the 597th would be determined by the white officers who had formerly been assigned to the battalion but had been involuntarily displaced from their jobs. Within a few days after Derricks assumed command of the 597th, these officers had returned to the 597th to begin their new task of inspecting the training of the battalion. Subsequently, they had reported a seemingly unending list of discrepancies targeted on the new officers with the apparent intent of discrediting them.

While commanding the 597th, the white officers had been about as fair as the racist system permitted them to be, but they had all been an essential part of the institutionalized barrier to advancement based on color. Because of that barrier, I had been stuck in the grade of first lieutenant for more than 14 months. This situation affected my motivation since I was confident that, without the impediment of the color barrier, I could compete successfully for a key command and staff position within the battalion. Accordingly, when the white officers were finally transferred out of the battalion, I felt relieved to be "free at last." However, my relief was soon tempered by the fact that the officers returned to the battalion in a new capacity:

> Apr.–Jun., 1944—... It is a relief to get all of the white officers out. Last summer when there were only five of us (colored officers) left and they seemed to want to get rid of me, I said that I would see them go before I went; and so it has come to pass at last ...
>
> ... Some of the white officers transferred out of the 597th have been given temporary jobs on the division artillery staff with the duty of inspecting the training of our battalion. Naturally, they are looking for things they can use to discredit the 597th—and they found plenty. However, the reports are targeted on the new officers and the original officers are spared.
>
> Now the new officers are finally beginning to listen to the few original officers that are left. (MC/FDP)

In their first reports, the white training inspectors limited or entirely omitted any criticism of the original black officers and NCOs. It was clear that the new officers were the targets for their reports and, although the reports reflected some dissatisfaction at being involuntarily displaced from their jobs, they did reflect many valid deficiencies. Most of these flaws related to the tendency of the new officers to react in tactical situations as they had been trained, and which was correct, in their former battalion, but which was not correct in the 597th.

As a result of that special situation, the inspectors documented many deficiencies against Battery A and Battery C, but few against Battery B and none against me as Executive Officer of Battery B. Actually, they commended me for having an efficient firing battery, which thereafter was used as the firing element in most of the battalion demonstrations.

Accordingly, Battery B was the busiest firing battery in the battalion and I was the busiest battery Executive Officer:

> Apr.–Jun,. 1944—... The past week was a very busy one for me. I have been executive officer of Battery B since 26 February, the only one of the original colored officers in the division in such a position ... I am the person in the battery directly responsible for firing the four guns.
>
> Battery B was chosen as the first battery to fire since the return of the division to Fort Huachuca. So the first shot fired under the new command was fired at 1005 hours on 28 April 1944.
>
> ... Friday after (5–07–44) we went out again to fire with the 758th Tank battalion. We stayed out Friday night and fired Saturday morning. We made a direct hit on an old abandoned ranch house causing it to burn for four hours.
>
> ... Last Saturday we fired a demonstration. This Saturday we will fire another demonstration. This Sunday I am battalion duty officer ...
>
> Today my battery fired for service practice and was commended by the General. It is definitely the best firing battery in the battalion. Perhaps that is why we fire for so many demonstrations.

... Friday night we stayed out in the field. Saturday morning at 0600 we began shooting for the demonstration. In less than one hour we had expended $2,500 worth of ammunition. This week my battery has expended about $7,500 worth in all, more than twice as much as the other two batteries combined. (MC/FDP)

Eventually, the delay in the adjustment of some of the new officers to the changed tactical requirements began to impact significantly on the performance of my battery during training exercises. In one case I considered it necessary to document the facts in a letter to Colonel Derricks describing the adverse impact on the performance of my battery because of the inconsistent actions of one of the new captains assigned to my battery as Safety Officer.

About two weeks after Derricks assumed command of the 597th, my battery was firing in support of the 758th Tank Battalion and the problem required the utmost speed consistent with safety. Since both the target and the supported tanks could be seen from the position, it was relatively simple to assure a safe elevation and deflection. However, the Safety Officer repeatedly delayed the firing by unnecessarily repeating accuracy checks that were insignificant from a safety standpoint.

Although I expressed my dissatisfaction at the firing delays caused by the Safety Officer, I recognized that some of his caution could have been caused by an experience similar to that I had as Safety Officer several months before. In that case, an impatient Executive Officer had fired rounds which landed outside safety limits, and although he did so before I could check the data and announce my decision concerning whether or not it was safe to fire, I had to share the blame and cost of the mistake.

My battery was used as a showcase for the battalion. During the first two months of post-maneuver training, Under Secretary of War Robert Patterson, some members of Congress, and many of the top generals in the U.S. Army not yet assigned to overseas commands visited the 92nd Division. When they visited the 597th, the division commander would bring them around to my position and ask numerous questions:

Apr.–Jun., 1944—... General Almond comes around my position every time we go into the field, which is every day. He seems very interested in our activities and he comes to me to ask about anything and everything. Now that the 597th has a Negro battalion commander, some members of the general's staff, who accompany him on his visits, wonder out loud why I have not been assigned to command a battery. (Why didn't they show this concern when the 597th had a white battalion commander?)

I am writing about my own activities more than I intended but I assure you I am not attempting to brag. I hope it will help you to understand why all of my time is devoted to doing my part to make this a successful unit.

Few seem to realize that this battalion is on trial now and I will stand or fall with it. Although I dislike some of the things that are being done, I realize that this trial holds the fate of the Negro field artillery officer in the balance and I have a critical interest in our success ...

... We seem to have more inspections than anybody. Even General George C. Marshall, Chief of Staff of the Army, was here last week. About ten generals have inspected us this week. Keeps us busy straightening up ...

In the last month, it seems that every high Army official in the U.S. … has visited us. Last week it was Lieutenant General Leslie J. McNair, Chief of Army Ground Forces. He was the general who was wounded in North Africa last year. There is a rumor that the second lieutenant nurse who attended him on the plane that returned him to the U.S. was promoted to lieutenant colonel …

… The division commander brought General McNair to the area where I was instructing a class and I had to "report" to him. He asked me about maneuvers, etc. General Almond advised me to speak a little louder than normal because General McNair was hard of hearing. (MC/FDP)

Major Clark

Shortly afterwards, General McNair was transferred to Europe to take over command of an army group. However, a few days later, while observing a saturation bombing attack by the Eighth and Ninth Air Forces in support of the U.S. First Army break-out of the Normandy beachhead, he was one of those killed when some of the bombs fell short of the target. (Blair, 1983, 280)

I recognized at this time the historic significance of our effort and the difficulties associated with ensuring that it would be documented from reliable sources:

> Apr.–Jun., 1944—… Some day—after the war—various accounts will be written about the Negro in the war. A lot will be written about the Negro officer, especially in the 92nd Division, since there are more Negro officers in the 92nd Division than in any other organization.
>
> If I am still alive, I will probably write a history … The other histories will be based on reports from many sources—some not very reliable. Mine will be taken from personal experience because I am in a position to know what actually happened and why.
>
> The 597th Field Artillery Battalion will take up a lot of space in my history because it is the first all-Negro unit in a combat division and, together with the 600th Field Artillery Battalion, constitutes the only all-Negro units in any combat division. (MC/FDP)

Part III

Bridging the Obstacle

CHAPTER EIGHT

The Tide Turns

With such unprecedented problems facing him, there were times when Colonel Derricks concluded he was being programmed for failure; but he did not allow that to adversely affect his response to the situation. Instead, he responded by putting into practice all of the skills he had gained during his previous three years as a battalion commander, using racial pride to motivate the personnel to "do their very best." Accordingly, he was successful in implementing an on-the-job training program for all of his key officer personnel and, at the same time, preparing the entire battalion for movement overseas according to schedule.

The outstanding manner in which Derricks performed his task was recognized later by the commanding general of the 92nd Division, who awarded him the Army Commendation Medal for superior performance of duty in preparing the 597th for overseas service.

The combined effect of many repetitive inspection visits and reports, which increased the insecurity of Colonel Derricks and his new officers, was noticed by the men and adversely affected their morale. However, we believed that there was one significant advantage gained by the change that could be used in an attempt to overcome the overwhelming short-range disadvantages and improve morale. That advantage was the motivation potential inherent in racial pride. Accordingly, each member began a maximum effort in his sphere of influence to use racial pride to improve morale and as a motivation for excellence as a path to success. There was an attitude of rallying around the new officers to protect them as much as possible until they could overcome the cause of their vulnerability.

Within a few weeks of Colonel Derricks assuming command, the performance of the newly assigned officers and the battalion as a whole began to improve, but not soon enough to satisfy Derricks. By the first week in June, he was "fed up" with the embarrassment caused by the unending list of deficiencies turned in by the 92nd Division Artillery training inspectors. Consequently, he decided to get tough. In a letter to all officers of the 597th dated June 1, 1944, he outlined his standards of performance. Afterwards, he began tough remedial action in cases where performance did not meet his standards.

> TO: All officers, 597th FA Bn.
>
> … insufficient and improper supervision of Training activities … by battery officers and Staff officers has caused embarrassment to this command. This reflects either a lack of knowledge of duties and responsibilities required of officers or a failure to accept them and honestly attempt to efficiently discharge them. This condition must be corrected immediately. (WTD/D/6–01–44)

A major test of his new "get tough" policy came after he evaluated the results of the battery tests that had been conducted by division artillery. Battery B and Battery C passed the tests on their first try, but Battery A failed on the first try and did so again on the retest. Upon being informed of Battery A's second failure, Colonel Derricks decided that the battery needed a new commander.

He selected me for the job on June 5, and I became the first of the original black officers in the 92nd Division Artillery to be assigned to command a firing battery. However, he did not confirm my assignment in writing until after I had demonstrated that I was capable of overcoming the problem that the previous command had not been able to solve, by earning a passing score for Battery A on the next retest four days later.

> I am now Battery Commander of "A" Battery, 597th Field Artillery Battalion … the first of the Original colored officers of the 92nd Division to receive such an assignment. (MC/FDP/6-09-44)[1]
>
> Jun. 15, 1944—Congratulations and the very best of wishes for your success. I know you will always do your job well. This assignment should have been given to you a long time ago, you certainly deserve it and more. (FDP/MC)

The requirements of my new assignment could be stated in very simple terms. It was my duty to command the battery and be responsible for everything the four other officers and more than a hundred enlisted men did or failed to do. The main components of my battery, in addition to the battery headquarters, included the battery detail, the firing battery, and the maintenance section. I was fortunate that I had some practical experience in the activities associated with each component.

Some of the areas of my concern included:

> Check laundry roster; Check furlough roster; Check training roster; Check organization roster; Check stencil roster; Check number of broken window glasses; Check names of men who went through the gas chamber; Check the names of men who fired the carbine on Saturday; Check quota for motor school; Check names of radio operators; Check door-jam in kitchen; Have Bn Surgeon check Private Taylor's physical qualifications. (MC/NB)

Although the battery had a large number of men who were fast learners, it also had its share of slow learners who contributed to a multitude of daily frustrations endured by me as a battery commander. It may have happened more than 40 years ago, but there is one ego-deflating incident that I still remember. It concerned a young man who was an outstanding truck driver and mechanic but a slow learner in other areas. I had been a battery commander for only a short time when it happened. In preparation for a visit by a team from the Inspector General's Office (IG0), we set aside some time each day to instruct the men and check their knowledge concerning the names of the officers in the chain of command from their own unit commander, First Lieutenant Clark, to the commander-in-chief, Franklin D. Roosevelt, the President of the United States. Since we had been informed that this was a subject on the team's checklist, I personally spot-checked the progress of the men at each battery formation.

The IG team arrived as scheduled and, as expected, checked the men for their knowledge of the officers in their chain of command. Some of the men responded without error, while many responded with minor errors; I was feeling quite satisfied until the inspector, with me beside him, asked the driver/mechanic, "Who is your unit commander?" Looking directly at me, the man responded, "I don't know."

During June, several men were transferred out of the battalion to replace the physically unqualified men in the 598th FA Bn., which left Fort Huachuca for overseas deployment on June 28.

We were extremely busy during the summer of 1944.

> Jun. 15, 1944—... I haven't been asleep before 2 a.m. for over a week now. There is a forest fire in the Huachuca Mountains that we go out and fight in our spare time.... I have really been busy since I took over "A" Battery. All the other officers in the battery are married and they spend some of their time trying to figure a way to get their wives out here. ... Today was the first break we have had in a long time. We celebrated Infantry Day with a division parade. Lots of visitors from Mexico and other places.

> Jun. 24, 1944—Several of my old friends in the battalion left us today for other units. Now, only Lieutenant Jacobs and I (of the original group) remain.

> Jun. 27, 1944—On Sunday, for the first time, I was able to relax for a little while ... I went to chapel at 0900 and stayed for an Open Forum discussion of something about "Our Pre-war Ambitions in the Post-war World." It seems to be a little premature to me to be doing that ... My relaxation did not last long, however. There were many things to do in preparation for Monday, so my Sunday afternoon was all taken up. I didn't even get to see the baseball game between the 365th Infantry and Division Artillery.
>
> Tonight, Tuesday, I am the duty officer, which means that I have to stay here all night. I will be duty officer every second night from now until the last part of July, maybe longer. The other nights we have school until late at night. A little confining but you get used to it.
>
> Lots of things are happening here that I cannot discuss. However, I can report that the officer's club still has its big Saturday night affair which, I am told, gets very undignified near the last.
>
> More and more wives are trying to get into this already overflowing place, although husbands are kept so busy they very seldom see one another after they get here.

I have lasted three weeks as a battery commander and am not quite ready for the booby hatch, although, if things continue at the present pace, I may be soon.

Captain White, our Assistant 5-3 (from Chicago) had an appendectomy Sunday night. He is doing ok now.

Major Campbell, a real Chicago politician, announced this afternoon that he is a grandpa.

I have several Oklahoma men in my battery, including one or two from Muskogee [Corporal Bowen].

Lieutenant Cartwright of Tulsa just returned from leave and reported that Tulsa is doing all right.

Jul. 9, 1944—Colonel Derricks' wife came from Chicago to visit him.

Jul. 23, 1944 … Having some nice cool rainy weather. A little electrical storm every day. You can see lightning strike something 50 miles away … It's a strange feeling you have—out in the desert—20 miles from anything and lightning striking all around. (MC/FDP)

During the week of July 24–29, Battalion firing tests were given by XXIII Corps. The 597th and 600th were graded unsatisfactory on the first try, but managed to come through with a satisfactory score on the retest. (92A Hist)

Next came the task of getting the units qualified in POM (Preparation for Overseas Movement). Inspections, required movies, required training, and medical examinations were the order of the day. (92A Hist)

Those battalion personnel who had not been authorized any leave during the preceding six months were permitted to go on leave. All remaining bachelor officers in the battalion, including me, changed their status to married. Each already-married officer who could find accommodation within a reasonable distance from Fort Huachuca tried to arrange for a visit from his wife. Mrs. Derricks thus made her first visit to Fort Huachuca.

During the last week in July, my request for a two-week leave to get married was approved. I left Fort Huachuca on July 26, was married in my hometown on July 31, and returned to Fort Huachuca on August 9.

First Lieutenant Major and Mrs Frances Clark, wedding photo, July 1944.

While I was away, Colonel and Mrs. Derricks visited California. After I returned to Fort Huachuca, I wrote to my wife (whose initials had now changed from FDP to FDC):

> Aug. 13, 1944—Colonel Derricks got his leave after I left Fort Huachuca and he came back two days after I did ... I understand that he spent his leave in California ...

> Aug. 18, 1944—Louis Armstrong was here tonight. He made his "Spotlight Band" broadcast from our field house. (MC/FDC)

During July and August, eight of the newly assigned officers were promoted: four first lieutenants to captain and four second lieutenants to first lieutenant.[2]

As I had been in command of Battery A since the first week in June, I looked forward to the first week in September when I would complete my first three months in that job, and would then be eligible for promotion to captain:

> Aug. 25, 1944—My promotion is held up until I have been in command three months (that is according to regulations). That will be in September. One of the officers I told you about received his promotion when he came back from leave. The last bachelor battery commander married last Tuesday. The battery had a group picture made yesterday. If I get one in time, I'll send you a copy.

> Aug. 29, 1944—I am going to send you two pictures as soon as I get some stamps. The other afternoon, we were told, quite unexpectedly, that the photographer was going to take our pictures. So, we gathered the men who were left in the area and had our picture taken. We also had a group picture taken of the officers in the battalion. (MC/FDC)

I did not get promoted as I had expected. I was later informed by one personnel officer that, although the recommendation for my promotion was submitted on time, there was some confusion concerning the date of my eligibility for promotion—because of the four-day delay (June 5–9) in confirming my command assignment in writing. Accordingly, the recommendation was returned for administrative corrections. Then, on September 5, before the processing of the corrected recommendation was completed, the 597th left Fort Huachuca en route to an overseas assignment. Apparently, when we left Fort Huachuca, we also left the jurisdiction of the command to which my recommendation had been submitted, and there was no carryover of my eligibility from one command to another. Therefore, the recommendation was returned without further action.[3]

With the men about to be posted overseas, censorship was an important issue:

> All personnel will be familiar with censorship ... regulations prior to departure ... unit censors ... one for each 100 men or fraction thereof will be designated ... Censors will receive [censorship] stamps at the staging area. All mail and telegrams written subsequent to departure will be collected by the train commander, censored at the staging area and held until after departure of writer from POE ... [Lieutenants Johnson and Mundy were designated as unit censors for Battery A.]
> ... Personnel will not be permitted to communicate with, see or visit friends or relatives enroute to staging area. Censored telegrams and letters may be written and monitored phone

calls made at the staging area. Families and friends are not permitted to know routes, times and location of staging. No officer nor man will inform relatives as to the port he is to go to. (92Div DM #1)

During the first week in September, we accomplished the final inspection of records and equipment and completed the loading of all unit equipment on trains for shipment to the port of embarkation.

Much later, General Almond awarded Colonel Derricks the Army Commendation Medal for his outstanding achievement in preparing the 597th for overseas service:

As Commanding Officer, 597th Field Artillery Battalion, 92nd Infantry Division, you were required to surmount all normal problems inherent to the training of a unit which was being prepared for overseas movement. By your physical endurance, and hard work during this period of training, you were responsible for your unit's outstanding achievements. Your enthusiasm, energy and devotion to duty were reflected in the completeness of your unit when it was ordered to a staging area for overseas movement.[4]

CHAPTER NINE

Going Over

On the morning of September 5, 1944, after seeing a motion picture film on safeguarding military information, the 597th Field Artillery Bn. left Fort Huachuca by rail for Camp Patrick Henry, Virginia, the staging area for Hampton Roads Port of Embarkation (H.R.P.E.), arriving there on September 8. The battalion remained there until September 19, then boarded the USAT (U.S. Army Transport ship) SS *Colombie* at H.R.P.E. for voyage to Italy.

The 597th debarked at Leghorn, Italy, on October 6 and moved to the Peninsular Base Section (PBS) Forward Staging Area near Pisa, where it began to receive and process organizational equipment. Key personnel were attached to units already in combat for brief periods of battle indoctrination.

On November 10, the 597th moved up to assembly area south of Viareggio for final checks of personnel and equipment before moving to the battalion's first combat position.

Lieutenant Colonel Derricks was detailed as the train commander as the 597th had entrained for Camp Patrick Henry and the Hampton Roads Port of Embarkation.[1]

The train carrying the 597th, identified as Main No. 37871, had a personnel load of 34 officers, three warrant officers, and 524 enlisted men. They traveled over the tracks of the Southern Pacific; Chicago, Rock Island and Pacific; New York Central; and Chesapeake and Ohio Railroads, and were routed through El Paso, Texas; Chicago, Illinois; and Richmond, Virginia.

> 0700 hours, Sept. 5, 1944—Left Ft. Huachuca, Arizona for HRPE. Traveled by rail over S.P., C.R.I. & Pac., N.Y.C, and C.O.R.Rs. Arrived Staging Area HRPE (Cp Patrick Henry, VA) 2200 hours 8 Sept 1944. Remained there receiving equipment and staging training until 19 Sept 1944. (WTD/D)

The importance of keeping their movements secret continued to be hammered home to the men of the 597th:

> All classes of mail originating with personnel of staged units are subject to censorship ... Personal mail ... Enlisted men: censored by unit censor or officer designated by him. Sealed. Stamped by unit censor or signed with name and rank of no censorship stamp is available.

... Officers: Officer will sign his name in the lower left-hand corner of the envelope in addition to the return address in the upper left-hand corner. (Camp Patrick Henry security regulations, Aug. 1, 1944)

The 597th arrived at Camp Patrick Henry at 0800 on September 8 and, during the following 10 days, prepared for final staging, which included individual equipment inspections, prescribed shots and physicals:

There will necessarily be a long wait until you begin again to receive letters steadily from me. Don't be alarmed. You will receive them in time. (MC/FDC/9-11-44)

On the night of September 19, the 597th—consisting then of 46 officers, three warrant officers, and 518 enlisted men—entrained for the short trip to Hampton Roads Port of Embarkation and boarded the U.S. Army Transport SS *Colombie* the same night:[2]

Sep. 19, 1944—Entrained at CPH, VA about 2030 hours for HRPE. Arrived HRPE about 2130 hours and embarked immediately on U.S.A.T.–S.S. *Colombie*. Sailed at 0800, 20 Sept 1944. Trip pleasant and uneventful. Many civilian passengers were aboard (Red Cross workers, Camp Shows people and specialists). (WTD/D)

The next morning, September 20, the *Colombie* sailed out of port and joined a convoy for the voyage across the Atlantic. Also sailing on the *Colombie* were the 599th Field Artillery Battalion, the 317th Engineer Combat Battalion, 92nd Division Headquarters, 92nd Division Artillery Headquarters, troops from other 92nd Division units, and officers from the Brazilian Expeditionary Force.[3] Military personnel continued to implement a training program on-board ship that included orientation, physical training, and "abandon ship" drill.

On October 1, after 10 days at sea, the convoy entered the Strait of Gibraltar, left the Atlantic and entered the Mediterranean. It then proceeded close to the North African coast, passing within view of Algiers and Tunis. On the night of October 3, it left the coast of Africa, passed north of Sicily and, during the morning of October 4, anchored in Naples harbor.

In his diary, Capt. Hondon B. Hargrove, then commanding Battery C, described what he saw at Naples:

Oct. 4, 1944—Entered Naples Harbor, saw for the first time the destruction visited on the Italian cities by Allied and German planes. The harbor is littered with sunken ships; buildings are gutted and even from out in the harbor, it can be seen that the former beautiful city of Napoli is only an empty shell. Almost every building on the waterfront has been blasted by bombs or shells. Saw Mt. Vesuvius for the first time this morning. A P038 is flying around it and at one time seemed to dive right down into the crater and the ship deck was lined with men watching it. (HBH/D)

Colonel Derricks also noted his battalion's arrival in Italy:

Allied Gains in Italy, 6 October–15 November 1943

> Arrived at Naples, Italy, at 1200, 4 Oct. 1944. Stayed in harbor there until morning 5 Oct. Sailed for Leghorn, Italy, arriving there on 6 Oct. Disembarked about 1500 same day. Traveled by truck from port to staging area. (WTD/D)

Early on the morning of October 5, the *Colombie* and one escort vessel sailed north along the Italian coast and arrived in Leghorn's harbor on the next day. The *Colombie* was reported to be the first Allied troop transport to enter Leghorn harbor subsequent to the capture of the city from the Germans, who, before they had been driven out, had managed to destroy the city's port facilities and partially block the harbor with sunken ships.

In the middle of the afternoon on October 6, the 597th disembarked in pouring rain.[4] I recorded the event in my notebook that night:

> Oct. 6, 1944—"Fall out with your raincoats on!" I passed the word to my first sergeant as I removed my field gear so that I could put on my raincoat. That done, I replaced my gear, spot checked to see that the order was being carried out and that my battery was lined up in the passenger list order. Then I placed myself at the head of my battery in the proper passenger list order and began to disembark in the rain. (MC/NB)

After debarking, the 597th moved by truck convoy to the Peninsular Base Section (PBS) Forward Staging Area just south of the Arno River, 4 miles southwest of Pisa:

> Oct. 8, 1944—I had a wonderful crossing—saw everything that geographies and histories tell about—plus a lot they haven't gotten around to. Had a lot of surprises, both pleasant and unpleasant, concerning people and places.
> Nothing you read tells half the story. Hope our country never suffers similar experiences. (MC/FDC)

***

The campaign on the mainland of Italy had started the year before, in September 1943, when British units under General Bernard Montgomery landed on the toe of the Italian boot and U.S. Army units under Lieutenant General Mark W. Clark landed at Salerno, 25 miles southeast of Naples. The Germans had seriously considered abandoning southern Italy to pull back to the Northern Apennines, but Field Marshall Kesselring, the German commander, insisted that he could hold for a considerable time on successive lines south of Rome. This proved to be an accurate assessment. (Matloff, 1973, 481–82)

The Germans successfully delayed the Allies by holding first at the line of the Volturno River; then at the so-called Winter Line, anchored on the towering peaks around the town of Cassino; then by containing for several months the beachhead established by the Allies at Anzio in January 1944. It was not until June 4, 1944, two days before the D-Day landing in France, that the Allies took Rome and the

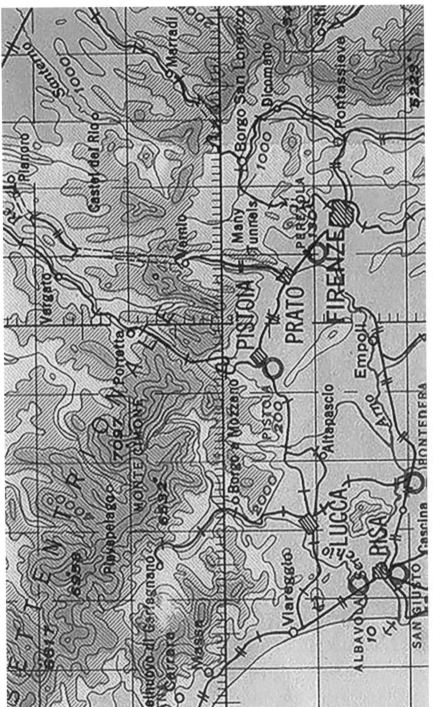

Staging area just south of Arnor River, 4 miles southeast of Pisa

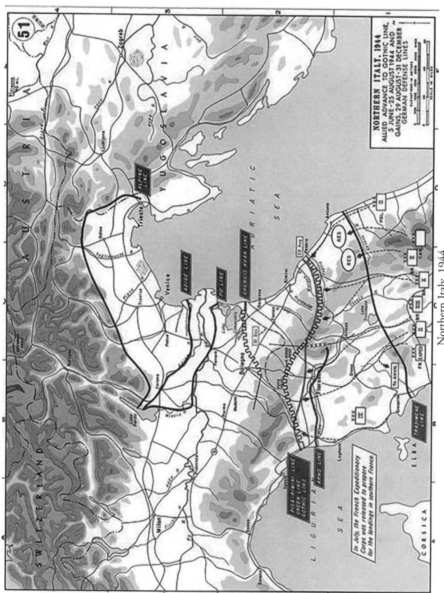

Northern Italy, 1944

Germans finally decided to pull back to the Gothic Line, their prepared position in the Northern Apennines.

The Gothic Line was an elaborate defense system extending through the Apennines from the Mediterranean to the Adriatic. It had been started while the Allied armies were still 200 miles south, breaking through the Winter Line. Under the direction of the German Todt Organization, which had built German's West Wall and Eastern defense lines, approximately 15,000 Italian farmers and laborers were herded into labor camps and forced to do the manual labor of digging anti-tank ditches, gun emplacements, and machine-gun and rifle pits. The Gothic Line was sited to take advantage of the rugged mountains and the limited number of roads across them.

In general, it followed the south side of the water divide rather than the crest line. Starting from the west coast near the town of Massa, it swung along the heights overlooking the coast, then followed an irregular course through the mountains north of Lucca, Pescia, and Pistoia, across Highway 65 near the Futa Pass, then along the main Apennine ridge to reach the Adriatic near Pescara. Its total length was about 170 miles. (Carleton, 1947, 3; Goodman, 1952, 20)

The Allies continued to pursue the Germans beyond Rome and, by August, the U.S. Fifth Army was on the south bank of the Arno, where the troops rested, trained, regrouped, and prepared to cross the river and reach the plain beyond. There they would attempt to crack the Gothic Line before winter caught the Allied forces in another mountain campaign. (Lee, 1966, 536–537) The planned attack was the beginning of a three-month campaign that achieved penetrations of the gothic line but did not break out of the mountains. (Matloff, 1973, 482)

When the 597th arrived, the 370th Combat Team was already in Italy, participating in an attack by IV Army Corps with the immediate objective of capturing Massa and then proceeding on to La Spezia. (Goodman, 1952, 41) However, that objective was not reached until more than six months later.

During the first week after arrival in the staging area, key officers and noncommissioned officers of the 597th were selected for battle indoctrination.[5] Colonel Derricks and two of his staff officers, Major Percy Turnley and First Lieutenant Briggs, traveled to the 91st Division in the II Corps zone, which was about 100 road miles east by northeast of the staging area. There, they were attached to the 347th Field Artillery Battalion for battle indoctrination:

> Oct. 12—Major Turnley, Lt Briggs and I went to 91st Div Arty for battle indoctrination. Were attached to 347th FA Bn comd. by Lt Col Linn, for 3 days. Our first experience with being shelled came a few minutes after we arrived at the C.P. of 347th (88[mm] shell frag. Fell near us.) Col. Ketchum, a [Fort] Sill classmate of mine, was Exec of 91st Div Arty.[6] Remained there until Sat 14 Oct. (WTD/D)

Also on October 12, I traveled with another group of officers from the 597th to a position about 20 miles north of the staging area and was attached to the 598th Field Artillery Bn. for battle indoctrination; I was the only battery commander in the group, which included Captain Pickett, Lieutenant Connor, and Lieutenant Conquest.

I recorded my first impression of the area in my notebook:

> Throughout most of its length, Highway #1 is forced to follow a route out into the side of precipitous mountains along the western Italian seacoast. However, between the great ports of Livorno and La Spezia, the highway is routed on level ground. Proceeding north of Livorno on Highway #1, a traveler soon comes within view of the Pisa (of the leaning tower). Just before entering Pisa, the highway crosses the Arno River, whose importance as a barrier during World War II was in sharp contrast to its mere 75 miles in length. The highway skirts the northwest edge of Pisa, comes within 500 yards of the Leaning Tower, then turns northward once more.
>
> After about five miles, the highway crosses the Serchio River, then continues through Migliarino and the King's Hunting Preserve until close to Torre del Lage (of Puccini). From there to Via Reggio the farmland is well tilled.
>
> Highway #1 skirts the east edge of Via Reggio and Lido di Camalore, then turns slightly northeastward toward Pietrasanta at the bottom of the mountains. At Pietrasanta, the highway turns northward again and, keeping the mountains close to its right, with the sea 3 to 5 miles to its left, it goes through Querceta and on to Massa, La Spezia and eventually to Genova. (MC/NB)

On the way to the 598th, we stopped at 92nd Division Headquarters in Viareggio just in time to hear that Colonel Barber, the Division Chief of Staff, had been killed by an enemy artillery shell. He had arrived with us on the *Colombie* on October 6, and after we landed had gone immediately to the II Corps front. The fact that he was killed the day after his arrival at the front was a reminder to us that we finally were "playing for keeps."

The 598th had preceded us overseas as part of the 370th Combat Team and had been in combat since August 28, primarily in the area north of Lucca in the Serchio Valley. The 370th CT had moved from the Serchio Valley to the coastal sector on October 4, and within two days had become involved in an operation with the objective of pushing the Germans beyond Massa. When we arrived at the 598th, they were still furnishing artillery support for that operation.

I was attached for battle indoctrination to one of the firing batteries of the 598th, located in Pietrasanta, about 3 miles inland from the Ligurian Sea. I knew many of the men and officers in the battery and was relieved to hear that they had not suffered a large number of casualties. However, the battery commander and first sergeant had been wounded to the extent that they would not return to the unit but would be sent back to the United States.

I was surprised to see civilians still living in their homes in the area.[7] Those in Pietrasanta were very cooperative in taking care of the soldiers' laundry and permitting them to stay in their homes. As a result, some of the artillerymen at the front were better dressed and better housed than some soldiers in the rear areas.

During the three days that I remained with the 598th, Pietrasanta was shelled frequently by enemy artillery. I learned very quickly to recognize, by its sound, whether or not a shell was coming close to me or going somewhere else. However, during the first day or two I did not take any chances—I hit the dirt immediately upon hearing the sound of any incoming shell.

The 598th was firing hundreds of rounds of ammunition, day and night, in support of the unsuccessful attacks on Mount Cauala that were being made by the 370th Infantry. On my last day with the battalion, I was informed that Captain Gandy had been killed in action.

Captain Gandy had received considerable publicity about six weeks before when he was promoted "on the spot," soon after his company entered the combat area, by the Fifth Army commander, Lt. Gen. Mark Clark.

During my stay with the 598th, I was warned that the Germans were very ingenious in their use of mines and booby traps. The beaches along the Ligurian coast, just a few miles to the west and northwest, had become one of the most extensively mined areas in the combat theater, the Germans having expected the Allies to make a seaborne landing there. There were also booby traps throughout the area which were intended by the Germans to exploit the tendency of many U.S. Army soldiers to hunt for souvenirs and pick up anything they found. Soldiers were warned to assume that everything that could be booby trapped was booby trapped, and that there was a high probability that they would be blown to bits when they picked up mementoes or opened doors of abandoned houses.

I heard stories from civilians concerning atrocities committed by the Germans before they left the area. There was one story about the mass killing of some men in a nearby village. Although many of the tales were hard to believe and I was able to verify only a very few, I was convinced that the Germans had treated the local civilians badly because they seemed genuinely happy to have us there instead of their former allies.

While our first group was away from the battalion, a special issue of *The Buffalo* was published to explain the Division Post Exchange (PX) system and include other information of interest to division personnel:

THE "PX" SYSTEM EXPLAINED ...

Every two weeks the Division PX Officer fills a requisition for supplies at the PBS depot in Livorno. At the PBS "PX" office, he is shown a list of articles that are available for distribution based on unit strength. (Items are rationed.) When the supplies are stored in our warehouse, they are broken down by units based on strength (some items are so few that they are distributed so that each unit gets some in spite of strength).

In the future, each "S.S.O." [Special Service Officer] or "PX" Officer will be given a list of items allowed his unit and the price of each item. He will post this on a bulletin board in a Company or Battery street. Orders will be taken in cash in advance collected by the unit Special Service Officer or the unit "PX" Officer before he comes to the warehouse.

He will pay cash on the spot for what he takes out. This should avoid losses in money and items and insure tighter control all the way around …

… Should you want a book to read, see your unit Special Service Officer or his representative. Each Company of battery has available fifty-one different books given it by the Division Special Service Section. These books are on a lending library basis to insure that each man gets his turn at a favorite story.

… 597th is first in with the "PX" cash; nice work Lt. Harris …

… BTRY "C" 597th FA BN … The personnel of this battery are proud of their ability as sportsmen and Captain Hondon B. Hargrove, our C.O. … challenges any battery in the battalion to a game of any kind including Whist and Dirty Hearts … Many men in the battery are very much interested in learning to speak Italian and so far most of them have learned to say, "Good Morning," and "Have you any wine?" We are all very grateful for the arrival of the PX and are really enjoying the necessities that they afford us …

… Bobby Young, accompanist for that fine singer Sgt. Warren, will give a boogie woogie recital in the officers' lounge at 2300 hours. Bobby has played at the Village Vanguard in New York. (Special edition of *The Buffalo*, Oct. 14, 1944)

On October 15, our first two groups of "battle-indoctrinated personnel" returned to the battalion, and another group, including Lieutenant Mundy, went up to the 598th for their battle indoctrination.

From then until November 10, we continued to check personnel and equipment for combat readiness. My mail to my wife noted some recent impressions:

Oct. 15, 1944—Sherman was right to a certain extent. After my baptism of fire, I agree with him. However, my experiences have made me realize that some things are even worse.

The people who live around here are hard to understand. Some leave to seek safer places but others remain to take what fate has to offer. Those that leave return as soon as they think the worst is over. Some return to a pile of rocks or dust; others to an untouched home. Those that remain still cling to the hope that destruction will pass them by but when death comes, it surprises them.

The roads are avenues of both escape and return for the people and one cannot tell which is being done because there is civilian traffic in both directions. (MC/FDC)

During this period, Colonel Derricks accompanied General Colbern on a visit to the 598th Field Artillery Bn.:

On 24th October at 1620 hours General Colbern with Lt Colonel Derrick[s], Battalion Commander, 597th FA Bn, visited the Battalion Command Post and discussed fire plans and possibilities with the Battalion Commander. (598A Hist)

I wrote to my wife inquiring about how the Army Postal Service was handling my mail, also noting the lack of overt racial prejudice by the Italian civilians in the area, and describing the establishment of a "cable radio" system in my battery:

Oct. 26, 1944—I have been sending letters on V-MAIL forms with air mail stamps affixed. How are you receiving them, in the original or processed?

The M. Clark you see on the outside of my letter is me. Officers are required to sign their names on the outside of each of their letters to certify that it has been personally censored. However, it is still subject to other censorship.

Oct. 29, 1944—The people here in places where recent hostilities have occurred are in no condition to display any racial prejudice. However, I have heard that it is different in areas where they have had an opportunity to recover.

Most of the men in my battery like this area, all things considered. They are learning enough of the language to make some friends.

Oct. 30, 1944—One of my battery officers had a radio which had quit operating and, since he could not repair it himself, he turned it over to me. I succeeded in restoring it to operation, using methods based on long experience.

Since it covers only the commercial broadcast band, reception is limited primarily to the foreign language stations. However, it can receive three of the London (BBC) stations and the stations that the Army operated (Armed Forces Radio).

It is [the] only radio working around here, so I had to devise a way to permit as many as possible of battery personnel to listen when they are off duty. I did this by having a number of field telephones installed around the area connected to a "relay station" in the battery headquarters tent. (MC/FDC)

Within a few days of us arriving in the staging area, I became aware of a situation that surprised me. The two enlisted men of the battery who were considered the least proficient in English grammar had become the most proficient in talking with the local civilians in a special version of the Italian language. Later observations, involving a large sample of similar personnel, indicated that this seeming paradox was the rule and not the exception.

On November 10, the 597th moved from the staging area to an assembly area about 5 miles from Viareggio. All of the officers and some enlisted men "celebrated" Armistice Day in a castle owned by an Italian princess:

Moved up to an assembly area 5 miles south of Viareggio. Hq and all officers and some EM housed in a castle owned by an Italian princess (Barbona). (WTD/D/11–10–44)

Nov 11, 1944—I was wondering today how you were recognizing this Armistice anniversary at home. I was made very much aware that there was no armistice here as I saw and heard the evidence of war all around me.

When you think of war, you think of mud and trenches and rain and tents. Well, there is all that here. But there are also some very sharp contrasts here. I have been in the rain and mud and tents, but I have also stayed in some of the finest houses that I have ever seen. And the owners (if they haven't moved out) seemed only too glad to let us stay for however long we needed to stay. (MC/FDC)

After we moved into the assembly area, we began the final checks of personnel and equipment in preparation for moving into our first combat position. Four days later, I accompanied Colonel Derricks, some members of his staff, and the other firing battery commanders on reconnaissance to select our first firing

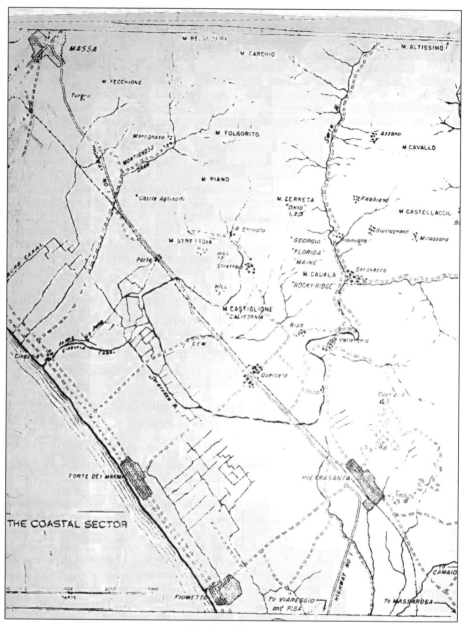

The Coastal Sector

battery positions in combat. We found that we had been assigned positions in the vicinity of Forte dei Marmi, which had been a seashore resort during peacetime, with beautiful beaches and a splendid seashore drive.

Since the Germans could observe most of the Forte dei Marmi area from their positions in the hills 3 miles to the northeast, we took advantage of all available cover and concealment in order to attract as little enemy attention as possible to our activity.

The position assigned to Battery A was on the east side of Forte dei Marmi, away from the sea, near the road which ran between there and Querceta, a village about 2 miles east of Forte dei Marmi located on Highway 1, 3 miles northwest of Pietrasanta.

After all firing battery positions had been selected, we returned to the assembly area to make final plans for occupying the position the next day. I announced the instructions to the officers and section chiefs in Battery A:

> Each section will work in shifts ... Italians will dig and help unload ammunition ... Install four phones to firing battery (one each section) and one to Exec's night post ... Each truck (prime mover) to carry forty rounds of ammunition ... Each fifth section truck to carry 200 rounds ... After firing, brass (cartridge cases) will be taken back to Service Battery ... Trucks will reload at Battalion Ammo Dump ... FO [Forward Observation] parties will consist of the FO, a radio operator, a wireman-telephone operator and a driver. (MC/NB)

The plan for the preparation and occupation of the position included three phases. In the first phase, Lieutenant Jacobs, my Executive Officer, would accompany me to houses in the vicinity of the battery position to find suitable places for a battery CP and adequate accommodation for the men. In the second phase, the key non-commissioned officers and their teams would go to the assigned battery positions to prepare pits for the guns and install communications. In the third phase, I would return to the staging area and lead the battery into position just as it became too dark for the observing Germans to distinguish our movements.

On November 15, our plan was carried out without a major hitch. We had no difficulty in finding a place for our battery CP and accommodation for the men. The only difficulty encountered was in the preparation of gun pits where an overabundance of Italian civilians volunteered to help both in their design and construction. Some of the civilians professed to be civil engineers, a claim difficult to dispute after observing the results of their work.

When I went back to the staging area to prepare to lead my battery into position, I found that the order of march for the batteries had been confirmed as A, B, C, Headquarters, and Service. Accordingly, riding in a jeep as the first vehicle in the order of march, I had the honor of leading the 597th into its first combat firing position—the first, last, and only all-black-officered direct support field artillery battalion to be committed to combat in the history of the United States Army.

When the 597th entered combat, it had a personnel strength of 44 officers, three warrant officers, and 518 enlisted men.

Part IV

Gaining a Foothold

CHAPTER TEN

By the Sea

During this period, the 597th was introduced to combat operations and began to provide artillery fire support for our front-line troops.

The eastern (right) flank of the front line occupied by the Allied armies in Italy was on the Adriatic coast near Rimini, and the western (left) flank was just north of Forte dei Marmi, along the Ligurian coast south of Massa. The British Eighth Army was disposed on the eastern portion of the front and the U.S. Fifth Army on the western part. In the Fifth Army sector, the U.S. II Corps was on the right and U.S. IV Corps on the left.

The 92nd Division assumed responsibility for the left portion of the IV Corps zone next to the Ligurian Sea. It held an approximately 20-mile-wide line from the sea to the town of Barga, east of the Serchio River. (Goodman, 1952, 56–57) The mission of the 92nd Division, now under Fifth Army control, was to command the coastal sector, prepare its remaining elements for action, and protect the left flank of the Fifth Army. It was to hold the maximum enemy force in the coastal sector by continuing to exert pressure and occupying any areas the securing of which was considered to be within its capabilities.

The mission of the 597th was direct support of the 365th Infantry, the left regiment of the 92nd Division, which occupied a sector extending from the Ligurian Sea in the west to Highway 1 in the east. The front lines began at the mouth of the Cinquale in the west and passed just north of Querceta in the east.

Near the end of November, the 366th Infantry was attached to the 92nd Division because additional troops were needed by the division to ensure an adequate defense of its area of responsibility. Then, for reasons not adequately documented in available records, the division reduced its strength by an even greater amount by releasing the 365th Combat Team for movement to the Bologna front for attachment to the 88th Division.

On November 15, the occupation of its first combat position by the 597th was carried out without any major difficulties. Then, early on the morning of the 16th, Battery B—commanded by Captain Buchanan—made the initial registration firing on the base point.[1]

The officer in charge at the firing position was Lieutenant Leonard L. Jackson, battery Executive Officer; the observer at the observation post was Lieutenant James R. Mundy, the Reconnaissance Officer. Later on that same day, Battery A and Battery C also registered on the base point. Colonel Derricks was pleased with the performance of the battalion:

> Nov. 15, 1944—Bn moved to position in vicinity of Forte dei Marmi.
> CP in Forte dei Marmi proper.
> First rounds in combat fired (Fired 16 No. 1944) by Btry B, with Capt Buchanan, commanding, and 1st Lts L.L. Jackson, Exec, and James R. Mundy, RO, adjusting on the base point. Base point a castle on hill (Castle AGHINOLFI) about 5700 yds from GP. All batteries made good adjustments and reacted to combat conditions excellently. (WTD/D)

The battalion was divided generally into a forward and a rear echelon. The forward echelon (which was primarily tactical) consisted of the three firing batteries—A, B, and C—and the elements of Headquarters Battery required to operate the 597th Battalion CP. The rear echelon (which was primarily administrative) consisted of the Service Battery and elements of the firing batteries and Headquarters Battery not needed in the forward area. In the first and all subsequent moves made during combat, the 597th rear echelon was generally located approximately midway between the battalion forward echelon and the division service area to facilitate its activities as the conduit of support from the division technical service agencies to the battalion.

The division technical service agencies—Medical, Quartermaster, Ordnance, Engineer, and Signal (the latter two classed as both technical service and combat)—had supply and service functions and carried out most of these in the division service area, located to the rear of the division headquarters, and generally out of enemy artillery range. However, some of their service functions required them to operate in the forward area of the combat zone.

Most of the battalion personnel in the forward area had frequent direct contact with only one of the technical services—the Quartermaster Corps—which provided baths. The third group could man the guns until the men in the first group could take their showers and return to the battery to relieve them.

The Quartermaster Corps also supplied the rations to feed the troops. The type of rations depended on whether or not there was adequate refrigeration and organized cooking facilities in the unit to preserve perishable items and prepare the food. Where both types of facilities were available at fixed posts in the United States, Field Ration "A" was supplied, which included fresh meats, fresh fruits and vegetables, and other items which were highly perishable.

In the combat area, where organized cooking facilities were available but adequate refrigeration was not, Field Ration "B" was supplied. This was similar to ration "A" except that processed, canned, or other non-perishable products replaced the perishable components.

The "Grasshopper" Artillery Air OP. (OHS)

In the front lines, where neither refrigeration nor organized cooking facilities were available, individual combat rations "C", "D", or "K", or small group "10-in-1" combat rations were supplied (see Glossary: C-ration).

The 597th was authorized two liaison-type (grasshopper) airplanes and two pilots.[2] However, there was an excess of black pilots in the Mediterranean theater of operations, so additional pilots were attached to the 597th. Air observers were assigned, on a rotating basis, from among the officers and qualified enlisted men in the battalion.

With very few exceptions, calls for fire were routed through the Battalion Fire Direction Center. There, the requests were converted into data which could be transmitted as instructions to the firing batteries. However, in exceptional cases, each firing battery was prepared to respond directly to requests from its own forward observers.

The targets attacked most frequently by artillery fire were enemy personnel, guns, trucks, tanks and other armored vehicles, buildings, bridges, and supply installations. When a target could be seen by a ground or air observer, fire was adjusted on the target by the observer, who reported a "sensing" for each round (over or short, right or left, etc.) to the fire direction center. The fire direction center made the necessary corrections to subsequent rounds to place effective fire on the target.

When the target could not be observed, the fire direction center computed data based on the coordinates of the target specified in the fire request and made necessary corrections based on weather conditions and data obtained by registration on check points.

There were several methods for attacking targets. The method selected for each target was influenced by the results desired from the fire, for example destruction, neutralization, harassing, and interdiction (see Glossary), Generally, the requests for harassing and interdiction fire came from the supported unit or from Division Artillery.

Since only the key officers and noncommissioned officers had participated in the October battle indoctrination program, most of the enlisted men of the 597th received their initial battle indoctrination immediately after the first occupation of position by the battalion. For the next few days, in common with most soldiers entering combat for the first time, they were jittery during hours of darkness, and as noted below in Colonel Derricks' diary and in the battalion journal, responded by reporting anything they saw or heard that they could not identify as friendly:

> Night of Nov. 16, 1944—Men of A & C jittery and fired quite a few rounds of S/A ammo at imaginary hostile patrols. BP Castle AGHINOLFI. 1800 hrs 16 Nov—Bn in direct support of 365th Inf. 1700. (WTD/D)

> Nov. 16, 1944—
> 2300—Able Battery Reports flares near area
> 2355—Able Battery Reports tampering with aiming stakes
> 2357—All Batteries alerted

> Nov. 17, 1944—
> 0230—"C" Btry reports intruders
> 0400—"A" Btry reports tampering with aiming stakes
> 0400—"B" Btry reports flare left front; small arms fire right front
> 1930—One soldier did not know the password ... carried to 365 CP for questioning and identification (597A Jnl)

Each infantry regiment in the 92nd Division included a cannon company.[3] The 92nd Division Artillery had adopted the policy of attaching the cannon companies of each infantry regiment to its corresponding direct support artillery battalion. Accordingly, on November 17, the 365th Infantry Cannon Company was attached to the 597th and designated as Battery "D."

Early in November, the 371st Infantry relieved the 370th in the coastal sector and the 370th returned to the Serchio Valley sector. On November 18, the 597th joined with other units of the 92nd Division Artillery in supporting the 371st Infantry in their first unsuccessful masking of the troops from enemy observation by firing smoke shells on a hill with the code name "California," one of the numerous hills occupied by enemy troops in front of the 371st Infantry.

During the following two weeks, the 597th was credited with receiving important intelligence information from an Italian prisoner; with causing many enemy casualties with artillery fire; with destroying a great deal of enemy equipment, ammunition, and other supplies; and with discovering an important Germany communication cable buried near Battery A's position.

> Nov. 18, 1944—
> 1900—German cable found in the ground by Lt Clark near Able Battery Position. (597A Jnl)
> Nov. 1944—The 597th reported locating a German communication cable near one of their battery positions which an Italian civilian reported Germans had buried in June and which extended from Forte dei Marmi to Viareggio, to Camalore to Pietrasanta. (92A Hist)

A few days after the 597th moved into its first combat position, I heard that the all-black-officered 366th Infantry was on the way to the Leghorn area for attachment to the 92nd Division. Like many other officers in the 597th, I had friends in the 366th. In my case it was Hubert Locust, the son of my high school English teacher.

Colonel Derricks' friends in the 366th included two officers who had served with him in the 184th Field Artillery: Lieutenant Colonel Oscar Randall, Commanding Officer, 3rd Battalion, 366th; and Captain Errington Johnson. Another officer in the 366th had an indirect connection to Colonel Derricks. He was Lieutenant Colonel James Robinson, Commanding Officer, 2nd Battalion, 366th, whose sister, Vicky, was a close friend of Colonel Derricks' wife.

On November 19, our first Sunday in combat, Colonel Derricks accompanied two visitors around the firing battery positions:

> Nov. 19, 1944—Sunday (The first in actual combat). Not much activity last night. Had dinner with the Meconis.[4] They are nice people and are anxious to make me comfortable. Accompanied the Chaplain (Diggs) to Btry positions where we chatted with the men and he (Chaplain) offered prayer in each gun position. Later same morning, accompanied Gen'l Colbern around positions. He was pleased with what he saw and said so. Inspected Service Btry at 1400 and had red beans and rice for dinner with them. Heard that the 366th Inf was near so will see Randall and Errington Johnson soon.[5] Doing very little firing now.
>
> Nov. 20, 1944—No unusual occurrences. Attended meeting w/CG Div Arty at 1100 and conference w/CO 365 at 1400. Have head cold and slight one in chest. (WTD/D)
>
> Nov. 20, 1944—The people here amaze us with tales of what the Germans did to them before we came. It is hard to believe that some of things actually happened. But when you see how glad the people are to have us here, you realize that some of those tales must be true. (MC/FDC)

Enemy artillery was very active over the entire area. Even Service Battery, several thousand yards to the rear of the firing batteries, was shelled periodically. Among the three firing batteries, Battery A's position was nearest to the front lines and was shelled first. However, Batteries B and C received the bulk of the shelling thereafter. Battalion observation posts were also subject to a considerable amount of enemy harassing fire—because they were usually in a relatively exposed position and could be easily identified by the enemy:

> Nov. 20, 1944—1355. Lt. Dix's OP shelled heavily. Building next to OP demolished. One man hurt. (597A Jnl)

Most enemy shelling in the 597th area came from the 152mm coastal guns on Punta Bianca, 10 miles northwest along the Ligurian coast. These guns were beyond the range of counterbattery fire from artillery available to the 92nd Division. Later, they were attacked repeatedly by light bombers, but without any apparent effect.

As noted by Colonel Derricks in his diary, Headquarters Battery and the battalion CP received considerable shelling intended for the British heavy antiaircraft artillery (HAA) battery located nearby:[6]

> Nov. 21, 1944—Pickett came in early this a.m. All of his talk was about heavy shelling. While at supper tonight, a large shell-burst occurred just outside the northwest window of our dining room. I didn't feel very comfortable—so suggested to Page, Chaplain Diggs and the doctor that we go downstairs until Tedesche [slang for Jerry, i.e. the Germans] completed his firing in that area for the evening.
>
> I believe that the British 3.5s have made him a bit angry for he has plastered my C.P. area for two nights in succession. The remarkable part of it being that he has not followed a regular schedule of shelling. He is usually very methodical—so much so that the hour when one of his shells will come can be easily predicted. One of my cooks had an unusual experience that did not add much towards his mental comfort today. A shell fragment from an undetermined artillery piece (said to be an Italian 165) cut one of his leggings without scratching his leg. He was too surprised to be frightened.
>
> The tempo of shelling has been stepped up considerably. They are evidently disturbed over the activity on our side. From all indications this war will last for some time to come. Germany will not stop.
>
> One of my batteries got a lucky hit on an enemy ammunition dump. Very pleasing to us all. Morale high and the men are settling down and losing their jitters. Performance of the battalion as a whole is satisfactory and is improving daily. (WTD/D)

Colonel Derricks noted that the 597th was at this time the first battalion of its kind to enter combat:

> I failed to mention earlier that we have made history in that we were the first all-Negro battalion of field artillery to enter combat as a complete battalion. Batteries A & C of the 600th (Ray's battalion) were in before us—but the battalion as a whole did not get into position until we had registered all batteries of our battalion. And too, we were the first all-Negro field artillery unit to land on the European continent, on 6 October 1944, at Livorno (Leghorn), Italy.
>
> Many of the flyers of the Brazilian Air Force, who were passengers on the same transport with us are now flying combat missions in this area. They were fine shipmates and I wish them much success. (WTD/D)

During the Italian campaign, several types of 105mm ammunition were furnished to the 597th to perform its tactical mission. These included high explosive (HE) shells with impact or mechanical time fuses—and later with VT (proximity) fuses—to inflict casualties on enemy personnel, facilities and equipment; white phosphorous (WP) shells for incendiary purposes and to produce smoke for obstruction of enemy observation; and propaganda shells—containing leaflets instead of high explosives—with information designed to reduce the enemy's combat efficiency by lowering the morale of their soldiers.

Although the participation of the artillery in psychological warfare operations had not been stressed in training, it soon became apparent in combat that, as a divisional 105mm howitzer battalion, the 597th was going to be an important medium for distribution of combat leaflets. There were other distribution media—such as fighter aircraft with leaflet bombs, liaison aircraft dropping leaflets free-fall, and patrols and special agents distributing leaflets by hand—but only the artillery could place the leaflet shells anywhere within range, at a moment's notice, in any kind of weather.

There were several types of leaflets, but most fell into one of the following categories (597A Hist):

1. General tactical leaflets with appeals to enemy troops dealing with the war in its largest strategic sense, with the surrender theme, treatment of prisoners, and the individual soldier's prospects for battles yet to come.
2. Local tactical leaflets written for a temporary situation against units of low morale, stressing unpopular unit officers and losses suffered by the unit.
3. News leaflets combining accurate and current military news from all available sources, and international news and that of the enemy's homeland gotten from enemy media or from secret intelligence sources.
4. Surrender leaflets which could be used even where the enemy's situation was favorable. Experience showed that enemy troops would frequently pick up and hide such leaflets for insurance against the future; their possession served to keep the surrender idea constantly in the soldier's mind.

The front-line soldiers, the intended recipients of the leaflets, were reluctant to expose themselves at the front to pick them up. However, if the leaflets were shot into the rear areas near supply installations and along main supply routes, they somehow got into the hands of front-line troops without too much delay. (597A Hist)

My 92nd Division records do not indicate how many prisoners were taken as a result of the 5,561 leaflet shells fired by the three light battalions, or the 40,000 leaflets distributed by partisans or dropped by liaison planes. The division did receive and process over 11,000 prisoners of war during the period October 6, 1944–April 30, 1945, with over 12,000 additional prisoners processed after the end of hostilities. (92A Hist) The overwhelming majority of prisoners taken before the end of April 1945 were captured as a result of attacks carried out by our troops. However, some prisoners surrendered during so-called "quiet" periods.

Leaflet shells were specially made so that the base plug could be easily removed and rolled leaflets inserted into the empty casting. Before firing, a mechanical time fuse was set to detonate a small charge and blow out the rear plug and the leaflets when the shell reached 100ft above the target area. Up to several hundred small leaflets could be packed into one shell, with lesser numbers of other printed documents commensurate with their size.

A copy of each type of propaganda leaflet, with the English translation, was available to operations and intelligence sections of the field artillery battalions involved in their distribution. (597A Hist)

Although 105mm howitzer HE ammunition was rationed at the rate of 10 rounds per howitzer per day during that period, Battery A was kept relatively busy firing. According to some of the personnel at the Battalion Fire Direction Center, many of the battalion observers preferred to use Battery A for their fire missions because of its speed and accuracy.

On November 22, Major Oscar J. Magee, Intelligence Division, Army Service Forces, visited the 597th and 600th Battalions:[7]

> Nov. 22, 1944
> 1000—ASF (Army Service Forces) Intelligence Representative, Major McGhee visited CP. Taken on tour of Bn installations by Bn Commander. (600A Jnl)
> 1045–1230—Col Ray visited CP. Major Oscar J. McGhee, representative of Mr. Truman Gibson, came with him. (597A Jnl)

Also on November 22, Colonel Marston, the Division Artillery Executive, was hospitalized:

> Wednesday, Nov. 22, 1944—
> 1515A—Colonel Marston left Div Arty CP for 33rd General Hospital and was entered into same. (92A Hist)

After Colonel Marston was hospitalized,[8] only General Colbern outranked Colonel Derricks in 92nd Division Artillery, and only six officers outranked Derricks in the entire 92nd Division.[9]

The 597th continued having to deal with the effects of shelling from German positions:

> Nov. 22, 1944—This day has been more or less routine with the exception that Jerry gave my CP its worst plastering of the time we have been here. A concentration of 15 or more rounds was fired in the area. No casualties but it came much too close for our mental comfort. At least three shell[s] scattered fragments on the CP proper. Now the British are firing—so we can expect a shelling from Tedesche shortly.
> Quis [Captain Quisenberry] went down to the staging area today where he looked for Randall and Erring. They had not arrived but were expected later in the evening.
> *Niente Bono! La bombe* is on again.

> Sgt Clarence Coleman (Med Detach) was shot by a man in Service Battery this evening—not seriously wounded.
>
> Yep—Jerry is answering the British guns. To date, he has not been able to find my guns; hence no counterbattery—for which I am glad. All of the shelling we have received in the CP area has been directed at the British guns that are located in our vicinity. (WTD/D)

I stayed in the home of a sculptor/painter in the little village just east of my battery, and he presented me with samples of his work: two marble peaches that seemed so real that my mouth watered each time I looked at them. Unfortunately, several weeks after we moved from that position to the Bologna front, the marble peaches were lost, together with several other items of my personal effects (see Chapter 13).

The Italian civilians in the village treated me as "headman." One house, situated between my battery and my "residence," belonged to a family with three cute little girls, aged 3, 5, and 7. No matter how many times I passed their house each day, the little girls would line up in stair-step order to greet me. Everybody in the village appeared to be cousins. All the children seemed limited to one of about eight names, meaning there were a lot of youngsters with the same name. (MC/FDC)

Our first Thanksgiving Day in combat was quiet:

> Nov. 23, 1944—Today is Thanksgiving Day and we had many things to be thankful for. We all had a turkey dinner and the enemy did not send over any shells to spoil our appetites.
>
> We had several civilian guests (from the village) and it was interesting to see people dressed in their best clothing and sitting down to a dinner which could have been interrupted at any time by enemy shells. (MC/FDC)

Some of the key officers of the 366th preceded the main body of the regiment, arriving in Leghorn on Thanksgiving Day, November 23. When Colonel Derricks visited the staging area that afternoon, he found Colonels Randall and Robinson already here:

> Nov. 23, 1944—Thanksgiving Day and a nice one. Not much firing by the enemy during day. We did very little because of lack of observation. Had dinner with Quis' battery after a trip to Via Reggio & points south on which I saw Randall and met Lt. Col. Robinson (Vicky's brother).[10] (WTD/D)

Colonel Derricks was asked to investigate the shooting of Sergeant Coleman by the man from the Service Battery. From this day, the commander was also involved in drawing up fire plans for operations in which the 365th Combat Team was expected to participate. One plan involved the "big push" or "show," a final offensive to include both the US Fifth Army and British Eighth Army in an effort to break into the Po Valley before winter set in. The next attempt was set for December, but it was postponed until later in the month and finally put off until April 1945.

Other typical items of interest during the 597th's second week of combat are indicated below:

Nov. 24, 1944—1237—Able Battery Commander has an old man ... [who] came from Massa last week ... [He] knows the exact home where the 2nd in command of operations of Massa lives. He claims two 92nd [Div.] prisoners are working there ... They are paid 70 cents per day and food. (597A Jnl)

Nov. 24, 1944—Nothing of moment to note. Heavy shelling by the Enemy on his schedule. Men are becoming accustomed to it and are beginning to joke about misses. Thank God we have no casualties to date.

Nov. 25, 1944—Saturday nite. Have written Vi [Mrs. Derricks] and mailed the *Stars and Stripes* to her.[11] This day has been the same as yesterday—routine duty inspections. Had dinner with General Colbern. He had C rations, so can't say that I enjoyed the food, although I did enjoy the company. Hope to get home by midnite tonight and hope to get some sleep. Mario [Meconi, Derricks' Italian "host"] brought me a bottle of whiskey and one of cognac. Good stuff—will save it for a state occasion. His family are very considerate and interested in my comfort. (WTD/D)

Nov. 25, 1944—2200—Lt Clark reported two soldiers, A Co. (365), molesting civilians 1000 yds east of A Btry position. Lt Jacobs apprehended them ... 365 requested 597 to pick them up. Colonel Derricks approved and men were brought to CP to await provost marshal. (597A Jnl)

Nov. 25, 1944—1300—Two war correspondents, Mr. Carter of the *Afro American* and Mr. Jordan of the *Norfolk Journal and Guide*, visited CP. They were taken on a tour of the Bn installations. (600A Jnl)

To carry out its direct support mission, the 597th provided one liaison officer to the 365th Infantry regimental headquarters and one to each of the front-line infantry battalions. In addition, it provided a forward observer to each front-line infantry company. Battalion OPs were established as necessary to provide additional depth to the observation and ensure that the entire zone of the supported unit was covered.

Both frequency-modulated (FM) radios and wire (telephone) lines were used for communication with liaison officers and forward observers. Each liaison officer party consisted of the liaison officer and three enlisted men, qualified in radio and wire laying and splicing. Each forward observer party was similarly manned and qualified.

All captains and senior first lieutenants were eventually carried on the liaison officer roster, and all lieutenants were carried on the forward observer roster.[12] In addition, the senior enlisted men of the forward observer and liaison officer parties were qualified as artillery observers. Any battalion officer was considered as qualified and available to man a battalion OP if needed.

On November 25, Colonel Derricks relieved the first group of forward observers and liaison officers after they had been up front with the infantry for about 10 days, initiating a practice in the 597th of frequently rotating such personnel:

Nov. 25, 1944—Relieved first group of FO's [forward observers] and LnO's [liaison officers] today. They did well and are entitled to a rest. That is about all for this day. *Hasta manana* [until tomorrow].

Nov. 26, 1944—Nothing of interest today. Routine duty and a trip to Div CP. While there I saw Chaplain Beasley and Major Watkins. Got to bed about 1230 [0030] and was awakened by the shells of the enemy's big guns. Everyone in the house, except Sandra, went down in the basement for safety. When awakened, she nodded and turned her head and nonchalantly went back to sleep. She is either tired of living or believes that Tedesche can't shoot. I personally believe the he is alright in his gunnery for he certainly has layed [sic] them in here. While in the basement, I gave Maria (Mama), Mario and Lina a lesson in Inglese. They are doing fine. Wish that I could learn as fast as they do. (WTD/D)

Meanwhile, there was plenty of action in the gun positions:

Nov. 26, 1944—1658—A (Btry) G.P. [gun position] reports at 1050–1100 enemy shelled Querceta 1000 yds to the right and that shells fell in GP, one—10 yds from No. 4 piece and one near switch board building [that] did not explode. It was turned over to CBO. (92A Counterbattery Officer)

Nov. 27, 1944—2100—Lt Jacobs turned in his report of apprehension of 2 Co "A" 365 ... soldiers. (597A Jnl)

In addition to the plans for the Fifth Army offensive, a 92nd Division plan was being formulated that would involve a crossing of the Cinquale Canal near its mouth at the sea in the sector of the 365th Infantry. However, that operation did not take place until February 8, 1945, at a time when neither the 597th nor the 365th were in the coastal sector (see Chapter 15):

Nov. 26 [27], 1944—Another busy day. Attended a conference and a sand table description of a "show" that we are to participate in soon. From today's G-2 Report, it seems that we are causing the enemy some concern with our fires. We are credited with 45 known wounded from one fire mission. Pretty good. (WTD/D)

On November 27, four men of the 597th were sent on rest leave beginning a program for each combat unit periodically to send a small number of personnel on leave to Rome and other selected cities:[13]

Nov. 27, 1944—I am sending four EM (enlisted men] for leave in Rome. Know they will enjoy that. Have one battery that is not doing so well because the officers have given way too much to fear of injury. Have made a temporary change that I hope will correct the deficiencies. Things are becoming more and more routine. (WTD/D)

On November 28, after enduring three days of intense enemy artillery fire, the personnel of one of the 597th's forward observer parties were ordered to abandon their OP:

Nov. 28, 1944—
0930—Lt Richardson, FO with I Co was ordered to abandon his OP.
1300—(Forward Observation Party) ... maintained observation for 3 days and nights while OP was under shell fire. There were 12 direct hits on OP while this party was there ... The names of the people in this party were Lt Richardson, Sv Btry, Pvt Allen Pugh, Btry C, Pvt Virgil Holder, SV Btry.

Nov. 30, 1944—
0930—It is reported that the 597th knocked out several artillery pieces this a.m. with 178 rounds. Bn stopped fire to permit ambulance service then continued fire to accomplish the mission. Observation was by plane.

1045—Lt Clark reports lines out between A and C Btry. He noticed that shelling was 5 min every 15 min. (597A Jnl)

The 366th is Attached to 92nd Division

IV Corps and Fifth Army were concerned about maintaining the 92nd Division's strength so that it could continue to hold its western end of the Fifth Army lines. For further bolstering of the numerical strength of the division, Fifth Army and the theater considered the use of Negro troops in other units. (Lee, 1966, 557)

The 366th was the only all-black-officered infantry regiment in the combat zone. Its officer complement consisted primarily of ROTC (Reserve Officers' Training Corps) graduates from Howard and Wilberforce Universities. Since its arrival in Italy a few months before, it had been assigned the mission of guarding the widely dispersed ground installations of the Fifteenth Air Force. On October 28, the Fifth Army had relieved it from its Fifteenth Air Force commitments and alerted it for movement to Leghorn for attachment to the 92nd Division.

On November 28, two days after the regiment arrived in Leghorn, the 366th was attached to the 92nd Division. This created a potential condition I had hoped for since arriving overseas. Never before in history had there been a more favorable condition for a demonstration of the ground combat arms capability of an all-black-officered combat team; a team of 3,700 officers and men that could be formed from the 366th Infantry and 597th Field Artillery Battalion; a team with an educational level well above that which the Army had previously claimed as the basic cause of unsatisfactory performance by black combat units.

I believed that, if the Army intended to carry out its stated policy of giving blacks an opportunity to prove themselves in combat, it could not afford to miss the unique opportunity afforded by this situation. For two days, November 28 and 29, a window of opportunity was open to carry out this policy, because all units were then under the control of the 92nd Division. During that period there was, in the Pisa staging area, about 20 miles south of 92nd Division Headquarters in Viareggio, the all-black-officered 366th Infantry, with a personnel strength of 157 officers, five warrant officers, and 3,000 enlisted men. At the same time, in the Forte di Marmi area, about 10 miles north of division headquarters, was the 597th Field Artillery Battalion, the only all-black direct support battalion committed to combat in the history of the United States Army, with a strength of 44 officers, three warrant officers, and 518 enlisted men.

I confidently expected that the division would organize the 366th Regimental Combat Team, which would include the 366th Infantry and 597th Field Artillery Battalion. But on November 30, my hopes were shattered and my worst fears were confirmed concerning the hypocrisy in the Army's statement of intentions to provide an opportunity for blacks to prove themselves in combat.

Actions taken by the division during those two days led to the conclusion that, instead of ever intending to combine the two all-black-officered units, the primary objective was to disperse the elements of the 366th and move the 597th as far away as possible before the potential inherent in their proximity was recognized by the black press.

The first step was to break up the 366th. For example, when Colonel Queen, the regimental commander of the 366th, reported to General Almond, he requested a period of 30 days to reassemble the units of his regiment for a concentrated period of retraining. During this time, he hoped to overcome the adverse effects of the long period of time his regiment had been involved in non-tactical operations and to properly prepare his organization for operations as an infantry combat unit.

According to a statement made to me by Colonel Queen in my last conversation with him in 1974, General Almond stated that he could not give him 30 days but that he would give him 15. On November 30, however, in spite of General Almond's promise, the integrity of the 366th as a combat regiment was destroyed by the piecemeal attachment of some of its units to front-line 92nd Division infantry units.

The second step was to move the 597th out of the area as soon as possible as part of the 365th Combat Team. For example, the statement that the "IV Corps and Fifth Army were concerned about maintaining the division's strength so that it could continue to hold its western end of the Fifth Army lines" was forgotten after the attachment of the 366th Infantry. The new statement to explain the movement of the 365th Combat Team out of the division was that with the arrival of the 366th Infantry, the 92nd Division was able to free some of its Army line.[14]

By the time the 597th returned to 92nd Division control in January 1945, the 366th had been overtaken by a disaster of such magnitude that the adverse effects plagued the regiment and the division for the remainder of the war, and, as a matter of fact, continued to do so for more than a generation after the war.

On December 1, General Colbern visited the Battalion Headquarters at about 0940 and stayed until 1025. A little while later, General Almond arrived at Battalion Headquarters, stayed about five minutes, then accompanied by Colonel Derricks, visited Battery C (597A Hist):

> Nov. 30 [Dec. 1] 1944—Gen'l Almond and his aid[e] visited Btry C and my CP. He evidently had no fault to find—for he made no comment. (WTD/D)

> Dec. 1, 1944—1140—Capt. Hargrove reported 40 rds 88's ... on C Btry. One truck damaged. CP hit 8 times. (597A Jnl)

Later that same afternoon, Colonel Derricks received notice that the battalion was going to move to a new area:

> Dec. 1, 1944—Received notice that we were to move to a new zone and that I would report to CP 88th Div by 1200—2 Dec for recon & instructions.
>
> Making preparation for moving battalion and my recon. Had a pleasant evening with the [Meconi] family. (WTD/D)

Colonel Derricks notified the battery commanders that each should organize a small reconnaissance party and report to Torre del Lago at 1600 the next afternoon to join up with a party of battalion and company commanders from the 365th Infantry. They would travel together to the new area as the advance party for the 365th Combat Team.

CHAPTER ELEVEN

In the Mountains

During this period, the 597th, as part of the 365th Combat Team, moved to the Bologna front, where it was attached to the 88th Division. The 365th Infantry, "in addition to receiving further indoctrination from more experienced units, … could ease the relief and rest problems for veteran white units in the line." (Lee, 1966, 559)

Specifically, the 365th Infantry was used to rest the battalions of the 349th Infantry of the 88th Division, whose sector it later controlled.

In the Bologna sector, the 597th was subjected to the most intense enemy artillery concentrations of the war. However, because of strict adherence to lessons learned in training, the battalion escaped with relatively small numbers of casualties.

The 88th Division, the first all-selective service division to enter combat on any front during World War II, had been heavily involved in combat ever since its first action at Cassino in March 1944. It had helped to smash the Gustav Line, liberate Rome, and was the first division in the Fifth Army to reach the Gothic Line. During the period September 10–October 26, it had engaged in actions so fierce that it had sustained over 5,000 casualties (Clark, 1950, 401), and although the division was back to full strength when the 365th Combat Team was attached, the combat troops were exhausted.

Like the 91st Division, the 88th Division was a part of the U.S. II Corps, occupying the right portion of the corps' front on the north slope of the Apennines south of Bologna. The U.S. 34th Division was on its left and the British 1st Division on its right.

The mission of the 88th Division was to participate in the active defense of the Bologna sector and prepare to participate in an Allied offensive before the real winter set it.

On December 1, the 597th was relieved of providing direct support for the 365th Infantry in the coastal sector of the 92nd Division and released from 92nd Division Artillery control to prepare for movement to the Bologna front for attachment to the 88th Infantry Division.

The following day, Colonel Derricks, accompanied by two battalion staff officers, traveled to the new area:

> Dec. 2, 1944—Off early for trip to 88th Div. Passed through Lucca, Padula (Pistola), Firenze and then on to 88th Div. Long, cold ride—use[d] ¾ ton truck and had Briggs and Gayles with me. They slept most of the way as usual. Met Brig. Gen. Kurtz (Arty Comm) at CP 88th Div. He directed me to his executive, Col Dunford, at Div Arty CP. (WTD/D)

The 597th was attached to the 88th Division Artillery to provide general support of the division, reinforcing the 337th Field Artillery Battalion in support of the 349th Infantry. The 597th was to be prepared to revert to its direct support mission when, later in the month, the 365th assumed responsibility for the front-line positions controlled by the 349th.

Unlike the 92nd Division, the 88th Division was "color blind" in its treatment of Colonel Derricks and his staff officers:

> Dec. 2, 1944 (continued)—Our reception at all installations of this Div has been very pleasant. Everyone seems disappointed if we cannot think of something for them to do for us. So different from Div. 92. We spent the night at Div Arty. Recon tomorrow. (WTD/D)

After Colonel Derricks spent the night of December 2 at 88th Division Artillery Headquarters, on the next day he selected the positions for the firing batteries, the battalion CP, and the Service Battery. Then he waited for the battery commanders to arrive; a longer wait than he expected:

> Sunday, Dec. 3, 1944—Went on recon and selected my GP and CP and rear for the Bn. Had to wait unduly long for my BV's [Battle Vehicles] because the 365th took them to the Inf CP instead of directing them to Div Arty. We finally got them oriented and began our wait for the battalion. My officers saw their first on-the-spot battle casualties. About eight Italian mule drivers and 15 mules were hit by shelling on the road near the RJ [road junction] at Molinetto on Hwy 6531 in what I call Death Valley. (WTD/D)

The battery commanders had an acceptable, though unusual, explanation for the delay, having been taken up front to the 349th Infantry Headquarters (instead of being directed to stop at the 88th Division Artillery Headquarters) and being further delayed by the shelling at Molinetto.

It had started the previous day when the 597th firing battery commanders, including me, had reported to Torre del Lago at 1600, as directed, and found the battalion and company commanders from the 365th Infantry already there. Major Johnson, 1st Battalion commander, 365th Infantry, was in charge. In his diary, Captain Hargrove described the trip from Torre del Lago to the 88th Division front lines, which began late in the afternoon of December 2:

> Dec. 2–3, 1944—I have with me two vehicles: mine with Vappie driving and Lt. Lee with a jeep. We left before dark. None of us have maps, except perhaps Major Johnson.
>
> It's raining like hell, and driving is pretty rough for everyone. Blackouts, and hard to keep up—but we dare not slow down. If we have motor trouble or anything like that, I'm just going

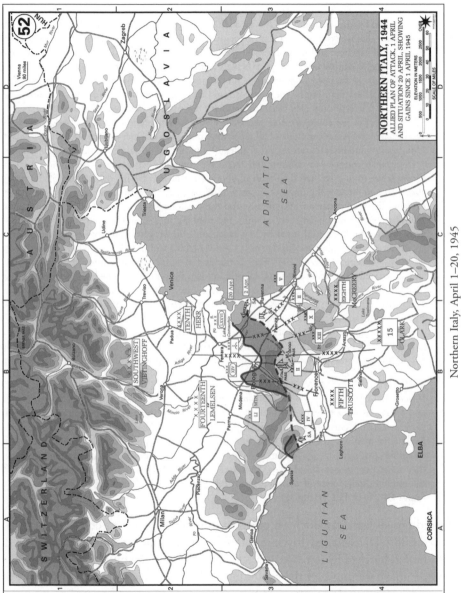

Northern Italy, April 1–20, 1945

to have to sit down and wait till daybreak and try to get some information from somebody. This seems about the dumbest damn thing I've ever seen. No battery commander knows where he is going, what's happening to his battery, or any inkling of the plan.

Rode all night long. About 10 p.m. we seemed to leave the flatlands and started going into the mountains. We passed near Florence, went northeast over icy mountain roads. We were passed often by huge ammunition trucks, all driven by Negroes. Vappie and I finally came to the conclusion that we were on Highway 5, where the German planes were known to swoop down from out of nowhere and strike everything in sight. Farther up, our units and the enemy were still fighting for control of it, and it was being shelled heavily, intermittently. About 2:30 a.m. we turned off of the highway high up in the mountains, and began to go down into a great valley. The road had been cut out by the Engineers and its [sic] rutted and muddy and slippery—and dangerous. It's terrifically cold as contrasted with the warmer climate of the west coast.

At daybreak we could see that we were in the colder section of Italy. There was snow everywhere, and American units of all types were dug in on all sides of the valley and in draws. Hundreds of antiaircraft guns on either side; 90 mm, lots of 40 mm's and multiple 50 calibers.

I began to notice our column and feel a bit apprehensive; nobody seemed to be going forward but us and we had a column of about 40 vehicles. We hit the bottom of the valley about 10 a.m. and, still going north, we wound our way through towering walls over Bailey bridges. The road is narrow and muddy, and the farther we go, the more units we see dug in. No infantry, just supply and service units and they dig in despite the mud and ice and snow. Then we see the 155 [mm] medium howitzers, and still we go forward. Where? Damifino!

About noon we came to a bridge near CA DI MASO and the MP shook his head when we went by. We noticed several 105 [mm] batteries and some tanks dug into the mountainside, and all seemed to be firing missions. All of a sudden, the column stopped and before we knew it, there we were, all lined up hub-to-hub and some shells started coming in on the bridge 150 yards away where some Engineers were working. We all leaped out and fell into the ditch. I must admit that we were all scared as hell.

We went up to the 349th Infantry Hq. (88th Div.), stayed up there doing nothing, scared as hell for a couple of hours. The general idea is that the 365th is going to take over part of the (front) line for a prospective attack. We were finally told to report back to 88th Division Arty. Hq.

THE MULE TRAIN MASSACRE
It took about 1½ hours to get back down to the bottom of the mountain. Clark, Briggs, Vappie and I were in my car when we spotted an Italian mule train coming towards us about 100 yards away. Suddenly, the shells came in, landing right on the column. It was an awful mess. Mules and men were dead and dying but we couldn't stop and hold up traffic. As soon as it let up for a minute, we opened up and drove past the mess, but just before we got to a turn, they started coming in ahead of us. Vappie threw on the brakes and we smashed head-first in the muddy ditch. None of us was hit, however, and when it cleared up, we went on, finally found Div. Arty. Hq. (HBH/D)

We did not all leave the ditch on our own initiative. The driver of a 2½-ton truck from the 88th Division had driven through the bloody mud, apparently unperturbed, until he was blocked by our ¾-ton truck, abandoned in the middle of the road. He shouted above the noise of the exploding shells: "Get that G— d— truck out of the road!" After our driver removed himself from the ditch and started moving our truck, we had to run to catch it. I was one of the last to leave the relative safety of the muddy ditch because it took a while for my mental commands to be translated into physical action.

Dec. 3, 1944 (continued)—It (Div. Arty. Hq.) was in a hell of a spot; mud was three feet deep, and right above it was a battery of Long Toms [slang for 155mm M1 guns], so I know how hot it could get around there. (HBH/D)

When we arrived at 88th Division Artillery Headquarters, we found Colonel Derricks waiting. He took us to the firing battery position areas he had selected in the narrow valley beside the Idice River.

After spending the remainder of December 3 selecting positions for our individual howitzers and other battery installations, we rejoined Colonel Derricks to wait for the battalion, which was scheduled to arrive early the next morning:

Dec. 4, 1944—Left CP at 0130 hours to meet the battalion and guide them into the assembly area near Sv Btry. I stood out in the mud and cold for five hours before the battalion arrived. They were spread out, and it took some time to get them in. Returned to C.P. about 0830 and had breakfast with Lt. Col. Miller, CO 913th FA Bn—quite a character and a fine gentleman. I am told he is an author. Rest of day spent by battalion in occupying positions and improvement of same. All of my installations are shelled daily with a great intensity. The Massa front was nothing compared to this. (WTD/D)

Dec. 4, 1944—After a miserable night, reconnoitering for places in the river bed for three batteries, no sleep, shells coming in all night, we gathered at a road intersection to meet the batteries and guide them into an assembly area. When they came it was a most discouraging affair. Yorky was in command of C Battery and Jackson had the firing battery and from what Yorky said, they must have had a helluva time. Major Page had been left in charge of the battalion and, with little information to go on, he had brought it over. I think he did a swell job myself.

Yorky told me that the men had to pull out of position with no preparation or intelligible orders, no chance to properly prepare vehicles or other equipment for a long hard march. When they came out of position, in addition to all the discomforts, they got shelled. Yorky did a good job, too, even though I'm sure they left a helluva lot of equipment at Forte dei Marmi. Frank Williams' and Pendergrass' trucks broke down but Yorky transferred the gun to another truck and three guns came in. Pendergrass came in later during the afternoon. (HBH/D)

Later that morning of December 4, the 597th completed its movement into position on the floor of the forward portion of the Idice River Valley, in which most of the forward support installations of the 88th Division were located. The valley extended south about 4 miles from its intersection with the front lines and was called "Death Valley" because of the intense enemy artillery fire concentrated on the area. Knowing that our side was limited to gun positions in the valley and restricted to one supply route, which for obvious reasons was called "Purple Heart Road," the enemy could cause heavy damage anywhere he fired. He was able to deliver extremely effective fire on certain locations because several points on the road and in the gun positions, especially in the area of the 597th, were under direct enemy observation:

Dec. 4, 1944 (continued)—On the morning of the 4th we (Battery C) moved into position in the floor of the valley. To the left was the river bed, to our right ran what we later found was called "Purple Heart Road" and rightly so. Lee and the battery spent all night digging in the valley and I and my battery headquarters dug in on a slight reverse slope above them on the right, which looked safe enough. However, after we got in up there, all hell broke loose all around us. Shells came in diagonally so that they seemed to be coming directly from in front of where we were. One landed not 20 feet from where I was dug in with Private WBA Jackson and the only reason we weren't killed was because it must have been a dud and didn't go off. Needless to say, we unassed the hill and dug in along a ridge about 150 yards behind the firing battery. (HBH/D)

The ground in the position area was so muddy that the battalion's wheeled vehicles bogged down repeatedly and had great difficulty in towing howitzers into position. Therefore, it was necessary for one of the batteries of the 597th to borrow two M-5 tractors from the 339th, the medium battalion of the 88th Division Artillery, to get the job done. But even they were not successful in every case:

Dec. 5, 1944—Spent most of the day of the 5th digging in and getting into position. To our left in the dry river bed is a battery of 155mm howitzers, tractor-drawn. Yesterday when we had difficulty getting the guns in because of the mud they (339th) lent us two of their tractors but they not only could not make any headway ... Pendergrass and Frank Williams had to pull them out. Pendergrass and Frank did a magnificent job of pulling the guns in with 2½ ton trucks. Clark's battery [Battery A] is dug in right behind me, across the riverbed, 100 yards over, two of them on the forward slope of the hill. Clark's kitchen and CP are dug in on the reverse slope of the same hill. He thinks he's safe. (HBH/D)

Soon afterwards, I had an extremely close call. As Hargrove indicated, I had located my headquarters tent on the rear slope of a hill believing that it was in a relatively safe location. I had put it there because, based upon some calculations I had made, I concluded that the rear slope of the hill was steeper than the expected angle of fall of enemy shells. Therefore, if the shells cleared the top of the hill, they would fall beyond my tent, missing it by several yards. But after I had an even closer call with a dud than Hargrove, I discovered that my calculations were wrong.

It happened late one afternoon, just as it was becoming dark. I was having a meeting with the senior noncommissioned officers of the battery in the headquarters tent (which was also my personal quarters), when the Germans fired a large concentration in the area. In the midst of all the noises from exploding shells, we felt an earthshaking thud from a shell that had hit the earth but had not exploded. We started to search the area to find where the shell had hit; however, it soon became too dark to see, and we had to wait until the next morning to continue our hunt.

As soon as there was enough light the following morning, we continued searching in ever-widening circles for the point of impact of the dud. But we did not find what we were looking for until we returned to the area immediately around my tent. There we found a large hole underneath the corner of the tent where I had been sitting on my bunk at the time of the impact. The dud was still there; I had slept over it the night before. For obvious reasons, we did not try to remove it. Instead, I followed Hargrove's example and relocated my tent immediately.

The firing batteries spent several more days digging-in and improving their positions during the lulls between fire missions. The enemy continued the intense shelling of the battery positions and Highway 6531 with 88mm, 150mm, and 170mm artillery.

On December 6, Colonel Derricks attended a meeting at Division Artillery Headquarters and then had lunch with the Division Artillery commander, discussing plans for the operation that was scheduled to take place in a few days. This was the same Fifth Army operation, with the objective of taking Bologna and breaking into the Po Valley before winter set in, that had been discussed and then postponed while we were with the 92nd Division.

> Dec. 6, 1944—Improvement of position going along nicely. Attended a meeting at Div. Hq. & then had lunch with Gen'l Kurtz. Plans for big doings were made.

> Dec. 7, 1944—Position same. Conditions satisfactory. Krauts intensifying shelling of our positions and Hwy 6531. 88mm, 150mm & some 170mm shells are coming in. (WTD/D)

Only one building in the area was suitable for occupancy; the 597th Battalion Headquarters shared this with the 913th Field Artillery Battalion, one of the three light artillery battalions of the 88th Division Artillery. The remainder of the 597th dug-in everything, including kitchens, and was rewarded by a casualty rate lower than that for adjacent artillery units. Personnel of 88th Division were surprised at our digging:

> Dec. 7, 1944—The white boys have been amazed at how deep we dig. They amaze us more by the casualness with which some of them dig. Today, something happened which made me add at least two feet to the bottom of my dugout and two layers of logs and sandbags at the top. A white outfit had a kitchen tent right on top of the ground with two men inside. Yesterday, I remember seeing them watching Clark's men digging, with some amusement. Well, this morning at 1015, two shells, about 105's, dropped over the bridge. The third landed smack in the middle of the tent. What a mess! All such tents immediately disappeared and nobody else was amused at us. (HBH/D)

Liaison officers and forward observers were furnished to the supported units as directed by 88th Division Artillery and the 597th responded to calls for fire from the 88th Division Artillery, the 337th Field Artillery Battalion, and from its own observers with the front-line troops. The targets most frequently fired on were enemy personnel, machine guns, mortars, guns, tanks and self-propelled guns, and houses occupied by enemy troops.

The 597th also fired a number of propaganda missions to deliver the weekly edition of the *Frontpost* newspaper for German troops. The *Frontpost* for the first week in December included the following article, in addition to the news of the war:

Hitler's Silence

> A new explanation for the long silence of Reich Chancellor Hitler is offered by the Turkish Newspaper "*Ulis*": "Many people are saying," writes the newspaper, "that Hitler is ill". Perhaps that is true. But it is more likely that Hitler has nothing more to say.

> Until now everything that Hitler said has been proved wrong by events ... Hitler said in 1939 that Germany would win the war because she was fighting on only one front. Today there are three, or even four fronts ... Hitler said in 1940 that England would be "rubbed out" by the German Luftwaffe. Today Germany is being devastated by Allied air fleets. ... Hitler said in October 1941. "This opponent—i.e., Russia—is already broken and will never rise again." Today Russia has carried the War to German soil.
>
> In these circumstances, what could Hitler have to say to the German people? (*Frontpost*, Weekend Edition No. 6, Dec. 2, 1944)

On December 8, Colonel Derricks visited the 365th Infantry Headquarters. The next day he had a meeting with his battery commanders and staff officers at the 597th Battalion CP and discussed the plans for the 597th's participation in the big offensive operation scheduled to start in a few days:

> Dec. 8, 1944—Visited the 365th C.P. and was subjected to quite a bit of shelling but none came close. We hit the dirt many times and my old heart really beat fast.
>
> Dec. 9, 1944—Same position. Preparing for big push. (WTD/D)
>
> Dec. 9, 1944—1925—Shell Report. About 37 rds fell near A Btry, B Btry; C Btry, 200 rds. (597A Jnl)

Chaplain Diggs (who had been with the 597th in Forte dei Marmi) had not accompanied the battalion to the Bologna front, but had remained with Chaplain (Captain) Alfred G. Dunston, the senior Division Artillery Chaplain, to assist him in serving the other three 92nd Division Artillery battalions.

In his diary, Colonel Derricks noted the absence of the chaplain on the occasion of our second Sunday on the Bologna front:

> Dec. 10, 1944—The second Sunday on this front found us still about 10 miles south of Bologna and waiting for the big push. No chaplain here to conduct religious services. Read several days' lines in my prayer book sent me by my dad. (WTD/D)

During the next week, the 597th fired propaganda shells containing a periodic *Frontpost* supplement which, in addition to the news, contained the following information concerning the German V 2 bomb:

> The Stockholm "*Morgentidningen*" reports that every V 2 Bomb uses up 5 tons of oxygen and 3 tons of alcohol. For the production of 3 tons of alcohol, 30 tons of potatoes are necessary, the weekly ration of 15,000 Germans. (*Frontpost* Supplement, Dec. 44)

Enemy artillery was very active on December 10 and 11, as indicated by the entries in the battalion journal and the 88th Division G-2 Report for that period:

> Dec. 10, 1944—1335—A Btry & B Btry were shelled approx 200 rds—No damage. (597A Jnl)
>
> 1201–2400 Dec. 10, 1944—An intense 740 round concentration lasting about 15 minutes around 1800A along our MSR (main supply route) ... was the outstanding artillery event of the period. It has been established that this stretch of road is under observation from Hill 363

... and Point 343 ... The Krauts probably assumed heavy supply traffic would commence shortly after dark.

1201–2400 Dec. 11, 1944—Apart from another concentration along our MSR, the shelling was relatively light. As in the previous period, approximately 625 rounds were received about 1730A along the road. It would be inaccurate, however, to state that the road itself was the main target as every battalion of artillery in the division sector plus the 350th Regimental CP were hit during the concentration and harassed during the afternoon. (88Div G-2)

Dec. 11, 1944—
0945—Pvt Donald Jones was hit by fragments, Capt McCants reported.
1650—Pvt Phineas Bell of Btry A was hit by shell fragments.
1725—B Btry was shelled approx 100 rd. S/Sgt Willie Wyatt, Gun Chief was hit by fragments.
1725—Btry C had one 105 [mm] knocked out. (597A Jnl)

Colonel Derricks noted in his diary that the 597th had sustained its first battle casualties since arriving in the area:

Dec. 11, 1944—The first battle casualties (2) in the battalion received wounds when hit by shell fragments. It is believed that their wounds are not serious and that they will be returned to duty in a few days. The Lord has blessed us so far and I pray that He will find it in his plan to spare us from a large number of casualties. While writing this, the enemy fired a concentration of about 100 rounds near my A, B, and C batteries and near my CP too. Have received no report of injury to any personnel, but some of my ammo is burning, now ... Report just received that S/Sgt. Willie E. Wyatt, Btry B, has been injured by shell fire. I hope this is the last for today. (WTD/D)

Battery C got through the period without any personnel casualties but did have a busy night:

Dec. 11, 1944—Sgt Willie Wyatt, Battery B, was hit ... and Private Carolina and another soldier ran out and drug [sic] him into Lt. Lee's dugout, where he was given 1st aid, then sent back to the Aid Station. Corporal Fisher, when a pile of ammunition started burning near the gun position, ran to the burning pile and began throwing burning rounds into the water. I'm sure he saved many lives and I'm going to recommend all three of them for the Silver Star.

Boy! What a shelling. It was a concentration and it was right on us. Later on tonight, we got it again but not quite so heavily. All lines were out, but the wire sergeant got his gang out and kept the lines open every time they went out. The shelling gave us hell all night but we were lucky—no casualties. (HBH/D)

S/Sergeant Wyatt's injury was the last one sustained by 597th personnel for that day and for the remaining 25 days of the battalion's attachment to the 88th Division Artillery. The battalion continued to dig in even deeper than before and the men prayed a lot.

Some 88th Division personnel expressed amazement at the low casualty rate for the 597th. One of their battalions located in the same area (the 338th) sustained 21 casualties during the month, including two killed in action:

Dec, 11, 1944—It's hard to believe that with all these huge shell craters right in the area, there were no casualties in the battery. A white battery commander ... visited me this morning and was almost unbelieving when I told him we'd had no casualties. He couldn't understand it! WBA Jackson told him that prayer had something to do with it and the Captain said: "Well, I believe that now." (HBH/D)

Also on December 11, the battalion received the first mail delivery since leaving the coastal sector:

Dec. 11, 1944 (continued)—Received my first mail in two weeks today. It contained an air mail letter from my darling wife and letters from the following people: Charlie Brock; Rita; Theresa; Ann Jones; and a card from Maj Nat Freeman, who is also in Italy. A letter from WOJG Ralph Campbell was also received. Shall write him soon. He mentioned that the 1699th Eng (Comb) Bn is in England now. (WTD/D/12–11/44)

Dec. 11, 1944—The mail just came in and brought me a letter and a box from you. After 10 days without mail this is very welcome. The box is in perfect shape ... Tell all my friends hello for me. Having (not so) wonderful time. (Don't) wish you were here. I am now having my share of mud. My home is a hole in the ground. Everyone else has a home constructed along the same general lines. But you would be surprised to see the different types of holes that can be made. Long holes, short holes, wide holes, narrow holes—but all deep holes. (MC/FDC)

Meanwhile, back in the coastal sector, the 92nd Division G-2 Periodic Report included some startling information about what the enemy prisoners of war believed about the 92nd Division:

Dec. 12, 1944—The PWs knowledge about our side of the fence was very limited and not too accurate. They were told by their CO that the colored troops facing them had been relieved by other troops because they were unable to endure the present cold weather. In general, the German officers seem to create the illusion among their men that our colored troops have been recruited in Central Africa and we were unable to cure them of head-hunting and other cannibal practices. They have no idea that our colored troops are highly civilized Americans with a large number of college graduates among them. (Annex No. 1, to 92nd G-2 Periodic Report No. 38)

On December 13, in response to the enlisted men's requests for a visit by the chaplain, Colonel Derricks visited Batteries B and C with Chaplain (Captain) Austin of the 365th Infantry. He found the morale high in spite of the intense pounding from enemy shelling received by the battalion two days before:

Dec. 13, 1944—Visited B & C batteries this morning with Chaplain (Capt) Austin of the 365th Inf. Men of C battery had requested a visit from the chaplain. Morale high and men not as much afraid of shelling as I am. I don't believe that I can ever become accustomed to it. We are preparing for a big show and I hope Tedesche will not like our act. It should begin in a few days now. (WTD/D)

Dec. 14, 1944—
1230—FO #2 reports bombing in 953368. About 2 bombs dropped and there was strafing resulting in heavy clouds of black smoke.
1530—Heavy bombing and strafing on Hiway 9 all Day. Planes received heavy flak. (597A Jnl)

Several issues of the *Frontpost* and its supplements carried news about the 11 points contained in General Eisenhower's Proclamation to the German People (app. 8). Point No. 4 was of special interest to those of us who heard about it:

ALL ... ORDINANCES BY WHICH PEOPLE, BY REASON OF RACE OR NATIONALITY, HAVE BEEN SET AT A DISADVANTAGE, WILL BE ABOLISHED. (*Frontpost* Weekly Edition No. 8, Dec. 16, 1944)

Since we were fighting to make it possible for such a proclamation to be issued in order to benefit those who had been discriminated against in Germany, we wondered how long it would be before a similar proclamation would be issued in order to help those of us blacks who had been discriminated against in the United States.

CHAPTER TWELVE

Changes at the Top

Early on the morning of December 16, Colonel Derricks directed me to turn my battery over temporarily to Lieutenant Jacobs, my battery Executive Officer, and prepare for a trip back to Viareggio with the battalion color guard detail. There I was to represent the battalion in a parade and decoration ceremony scheduled for the next day in honor of the new Fifth Army commander, Lieutenant General Lucian K. Truscott.

Within an hour, after I had packed my traveling gear and met with Lieutenant Jacobs and the senior noncommissioned officers of the battery, I reported to battalion headquarters, where I found the color guard detail ready to go. There was also a message from Captain Quisenberry, the Service Battery commander, requesting me to stop by his place on the way out.

When we reached the Service Battery, Captain Quisenberry gave me a list of agencies to contact in the Viareggio area and a list of items to obtain from them. The list included: a piston and cylinder insert for a 1½ horsepower generator; two Christmas trees; several bottles of Cognac; cigarette lighters; a coat, etc.

Following my conversation with Captain Quisenberry, we continued on our trip to Viareggio, arriving there after nightfall.

Early the next morning, Sunday, December 17, I reported to the Commanding Officer, Special Troops, 92nd Division Headquarters, and was informed that the ceremony had been postponed for three days until Wednesday, December 20. Since I had been expected to return to the battalion on/ Monday, December 18, I sent the following message to Colonel Derricks:

> Dec. 17, 1944—Detail postponed. Tentatively rescheduled for Wednesday. Request Instructions. (MC/WTD)

In reply, Colonel Derricks directed me to remain in Viareggio until after the ceremony. Accordingly, I had two full days of "free time." After informing the color guard detail of the changed instructions, I decided to take advantage of my "free time" by finding out what had happened to the other units in the 92nd Division since the 597th left the area.

First, I made arrangements to pick up, after the ceremony, the items on Quisenberry's "shopping list." Then I visited a number of units from Viareggio forward to the positions of the 92nd Division Artillery battalions that were still in the coastal sector. I found only the 599th and 600th; the 598th was still in the Serchio Valley.

I also visited the 366th Infantry Headquarters in an attempt to locate an officer of the regiment who was the son of one of my high school teachers. I found the headquarters almost empty of military personnel but did meet two reporters there who were correspondents for black newspapers. It was from them that I heard the shocking news that Colonel Queen had been relieved from command during the preceding week, allegedly at his own request.

My visit to the 366th was a complete disappointment because the officer I was looking for was assigned to its 2nd Battalion, which was then in the Serchio Valley:

> Dec. 17, 1944—I again just missed seeing Mrs. Locust's son this week. As luck would have it, we had just left the area, when his outfit was first committed, and it came to where we had been. When I returned to the area, his outfit had moved someplace else.
>
> I was reading about all the snow back home. Well, we have snow some places, too. We only have to go a short distance to have a "white Christmas."
>
> Recently I spoke to two of our war correspondents (I believe they said they were from the *Defender* and *Courier*). They complained that they have a hard time getting their own papers over here. So we very much appreciate those clippings you send us. (MC/FDC)

Later, I met an old friend, the personnel officer for one of the 92nd Division units in the coastal sector. He told me that after Colonel Queen had been relieved as Commanding Officer of the 366th Infantry Regiment, the 92nd Division had requested Fifth Army to appoint Lieutenant Colonel Edward L. Rowny, Commanding Officer of the 317th Engineers, to succeed him. However, the Fifth Army did not approve the request because the 366th had been organized to be an all-black-officered unit and was only attached and not organic to the 92nd Division. Instead, the Fifth Army had appointed Lieutenant Colonel Alonzo Ferguson, the regimental Executive Officer, as the new regimental commander.

Although my informant had a reputation for reliability, I was somewhat skeptical concerning his statement about Rowny because he was a very unlikely candidate for appointment as commander of the 366th Infantry. My only official contact with Rowny had taken place in November 1942, when then Captain Rowny, as Assistant Division G-3, brought an instructor team to Camp Atterbury, Indiana, to conduct a "basic school" for junior officers and noncommissioned officers of the 365th Combat Team. I had attended the school as part of the first class and was then selected by Rowny as an instructor for subsequent classes. Notwithstanding my early limited favorable contact with Rowny, I could not disregard the opinions of other individuals who had been more directly involved with him or were more aware of his reputation; and that was not good in regard to his command of black troops.

There was a persistent rumor that conditions had been so bad in his 317th Engineer Battalion that an unsuccessful attempt had been made to kill him soon after his unit arrived overseas, and that after investigating the incident and its causes, the investigating officer had recommended that Rowny be relieved of his command.

My informant also stated that one white staff officer, upon hearing that Fifth Army had not agreed to the division's attempt to place a white officer in command of the 366th Infantry, was heard to remark: "If we can't say who will command the 366th, we can certainly fix it so that it will not operate as a regiment while it is attached to us, and maybe never again."

While there was no way that I could verify any of what my informant had told me, I was to recall our conversation two months later after two major disasters had befallen the 366th.

In the meantime, as noted in his diary, Colonel Derricks received an invitation to attend the Truscott decoration ceremony:

> Dec. 19, 1944—Received invitation to attend luncheon in honor of the new Army Commander, Lt Gen Truscott, at 92nd Div Hq on 20th and to witness the decorating of officers and men. Left my CP for trip to Viareggio about 1600 same day. Arrived at air strip about 2300 and spent the night with my pilots and observers. They were glad to see me and I enjoyed the visit very much.

> Dec. 20, 1944—En route from air strip to Viareggio stopped to visit Randall. He is ok and cheerful. Arrived at [92nd Division] CP at 1025 and found that instructions had been changed (as usual in the 92nd), and then proceeded to the area where the presentation was to be made. Saw a very colorful affair. A sergeant was decorated and commissioned a second lieutenant at the same time.
>
> After the ceremony, we retired to the mess (in a Casino) and had a very nice dinner. General Almond was unusually pleasant and commendatory of the battalion when he greeted me. Met the Army Commander and after dinner visited with Lt Harris and then attended to business with various supply agencies and about 1600, started on my return to the area. (WTD/D)

After the Truscott ceremony on the 29th, I picked up the items Quisenberry had requested and, with the battalion colors detail, started the return trip to the battalion. We drove most of the night and arrived there the next morning. Derricks, meanwhile, spent the night in Florence:

> Dec. 20, 1944 (continued)—Spent the night in Florence. Trip pleasant but cold.

> Dec. 21, 1944—Left Florence (Firenze) about 0930 and, after a cold crossing of the mountains, arrived at Service Battery about 1330. Had dinner there and then proceeded to my CP. Arrived there about 1400 [1600]. (WTD/D)

When I arrived back in my battery, I found some mail from my wife, including some recent newspapers. I wrote to thank her the next day:

> Dec. 22, 1944—I received the newspapers you sent last week. They meant a lot to all of us because it is seldom that anyone gets a newspaper from home less than two or three months old. I am having to pass them around so others can read them. (MC/FDC)

As winter set in, the 597th continued to carry out its support mission, and the enemy continued, periodically, to fire heavy concentrations into "Death Valley." According to an 88th Division G-2 Report:

> Dec. 23, 1944—Corps CB [counterbattery officer] now estimates a total of 400 guns opposing the Corps sector showing an increase of approximately 120 guns since last estimate about one month ago. These include all caliber field pieces as well as SPs (self-propelled guns) and AA (antiaircraft) guns capable of being employed as artillery. The bulk of this artillery is along Highway 65 and to the west. However, Highway 6531 between 35 and 42 northings does show a buildup comprised of 3 medium, 34 light and 12 AA pieces plus suspects of 4 × 150mm Infantry howitzers, 5 medium, 25 light and 12 Nebelwerfers [smoke mortars used to launch high explosive rounds]. To the northeast between 97 and 99 easting and 41 and 43 northings there is a buildup as follows: 2 light pieces, 11 AA, plus suspected 9 medium and 18 light pieces. One 210mm howitzer is believed to be in the 96–42 grid. (88Div G2)

Enemy artillery was relatively quiet on Christmas Day, which made it possible to enjoy a dinner of turkey with all the trimmings. There was even a Christmas tree at battalion headquarters, on which the battalion sergeant-major put a gift for all CP and FDC (Fire Direction Center) personnel (597A Hist):

> Christmas Day, Dec. 25, 1944—For the past few weeks, I have been in a rut with my writing, partly because of the lack of time and partly psychological. It has been hard for me to write to you or mother in a way that would let you know the extent of my involvement without worrying you too much. So, I haven't written much of anything.
>
> All of us who were on those pictures taken at Fort Huachuca are together today but in a situation that is much different from last Christmas. We still have a spirit of brotherly love toward most people, but there are some for whom we are going to make things as unpleasant as we can. They have already done that for us and we intend to do the same thing in return.
>
> I have been very fortunate in receiving my mail—especially Christmas packages. Unfortunately, many of the men in my battery have not received theirs.
>
> We are having turkey for dinner today and every member of the battery will get some no matter where he is. It is somewhat like Thanksgiving dinner, except that we have no civilian guests here while at Thanksgiving we had several. I recall how interesting it was then to see the people all dressed up sit down to a dinner which could have been interrupted at any time by enemy shells.
>
> The family life in Italy seems to be very close in these difficult times. Children will divide what they have with their brothers and sisters no matter how small it is to start with …
>
> The saying that "there are no atheists in foxholes" seems to be very true. Many men who previously showed no religious inclination are now found to be praying along with those who did before. I don't know how long this changed attitude will last after the danger ceases, but it is quite likely their experiences here will make an impression that will last long after they return home.
>
> The sun is shining momentarily—it makes the snow look very white. It is still cold enough to keep the snow from melting so I guess we will have it a day or two longer. (MC/FDC)

Colonel Derrick wrote of events at Christmas time too, but also commented on less festive matters:

> Dec. 25, 1944—Christmas Day and a pretty one. Received a visit from General Kurtz. Our Xmas at the CP was more pleasant than I had expected it to be and we had much cheerfulness all around.

Dec. 26, 1944—Received the report about the excellence of our fires on enemy installations.
Disloyalty and Deceit
The disloyalty and deceit of some of my staff is sickening, more so because they are the ones who are being fooled and are going to suffer for their folly. I will ignore it as long as I can but will take proper action if they force me. (WTD/D)

Meanwhile, having concluded that the Germans were possibly preparing for an attack in the 92nd Division sector, Fifth Army and IV Corps positioned certain units a few miles to the south of the 92nd's area of responsibility to back up the division in case such an attack occurred. However, the 92nd Division G-2 did not consider that an assault was imminent. Accordingly, the division did not properly redisposition its units, nor did it give adequate warning to the front-line troops, in weakly held areas to permit them to make necessary additional defense preparations:

Dec. 25, 1944—The information that the Germans were possibly preparing for an attack in this sector came from Headquarters higher than [IV] Corps. Div Arty S-2 information of enemy activity in the Coastal Sector during the past few days had not indicated that an attack was imminent, or that our front was anything but quiet.

Later in the morning … the Corps Artillery Staff joined General Colbern and the Div Arty staff in eggnogs. Maj General Almond, 92nd Inf Div Commander was also present for the eggnogs. IV Corps Arty Staff remained for a midday Christmas turkey dinner. (92A Hist)

***

Just before dawn on the morning of December 26, the enemy launched an offensive in the most thinly held part of the Serchio Valley sector of the 92nd Division. This sector was the easterly of two tactical fronts controlled by the 92nd Division, and was separated from the coastal sector by 13 miles of extremely mountainous terrain. The enemy's artillery, which had been quiet for some days, suddenly boomed forth and increased in tempo as the attack progressed. His troops penetrated some 6 miles in the division sector and occupied the towns of Bebbio, Sommocolonia, and Barga. On the 27th, the Commanding General, 8th Indian Division (British), took command of all forces in the Serchio sector, and during the following two days restored most of the territory that had been lost in the enemy attack. By January 1, the lines were practically restored.

This attack, coming on the heels of the enemy's unsuccessful Ardennes offensive in Northern Europe (Battle of the Bulge), created a tense situation throughout the Italian front, particularly in the area controlled by the 92nd Division. (Lee, 1966, 562–67; Goodman, 1952, 71–79; 92A Hist)

Back on the Bologna front, on the afternoon of December 27, 60 rounds of enemy artillery fell in the 597th Field Artillery Battalion position area within a period of 10 minutes. No casualties resulted.

A 105mm howitzer under camouflage net, Battery B, 597th, Serchio Valley, Italy, 1945. (OHS)

On December 29, the 365th Infantry assumed responsibility for the front-line positions previously occupied by the 349th Infantry, and the 597th resumed its mission of direct support of the 365th.

The following day, Colonel Derricks traveled to the headquarters of the 365th Infantry and visited the regimental commander and Captain Wesley B. Johnson, artillery liaison officer from the 597th:

> Dec. 30, 1944—Visited C.O. 365 and Capt Johnson at Dictate [365th Inf] C.P. While there heard of Randall's injuries. This news was rather depressing—had seen him just ten days ago. (WTD/D)

The 597th delivered another type of propaganda to the soldiers of the German 362nd Infantry Division, one of the two main formations opposing the 88th:

> You have the alternative:
> TO DIE FOR THE VAIN GLORY OF GENERAL GREINER OR TO LIVE TO SEE YOUR FAMILY
> Greiner's division
> Gets smaller and smaller
> Only one will be left in the end
> And that will be Greiner
>
> To the Solders of the 362nd Infantry Division
> You are commanded by one of the most reckless German generals: Greiner, the general with the incurable "throat trouble." [German infantryman slang expression—"the general whose neck itches for decoration"]
> Greiner has the distinction of having no less than three divisions shot from under him during this war.
> He is the CG who led your division into the Nettuno battle where so many of your comrades lost their lives.
> The few of you who survived the Nettuno campaign know what happened there: As usual, general Greiner refused to withdraw his troops in good time, in spite of the remonstrances of his subordinates. He said then: "I will keep my division in line until there are no more left than can be taken back in one single truck!"
> He tried his best to keep his word. The 362 I D was kept in combat until it suffered more than 50% casualties: until over two thirds of all divisional equipment was lost …
> … Soldiers of the 362 I D! Enough of this madness! Stop fighting! Put down your weapons! Withdraw from this suicidal struggle!…
> DO YOU WANT TO DIE FOR A LOST CAUSE?
> OR DO YOU WANT TO LIVE AND SEE YOUR FAMILY AGAIN? (Propaganda Leaflet, Dec. 1944)

There were varying reports of the level of activity as 1944 drew to a close:

> Dec. 31, 1944—Situation unchanged. A very quiet New Year's Eve. (WTD/D)

> 845 Dec. 31, 1944—Lookout reports paratroops landed just in front of our lines. Heavy traffic over radio by enemy. (597A Jnl)

The "Year End Report" for 1944 prepared by the 88th Division Artillery described the situation as follows:

> The positions along the IDICE VALLEY were crowded. Little protection could be secured from enemy artillery. Knowing that we were restricted to one main supply route, the enemy was able to concentrate his artillery and cause heavy damage ... At no previous time had artillery positions been so closely restricted and continually hammered by consistently accurate artillery fire. Heavy TOTs (time on target) of mixed calibers were received. Little could be done besides digging deeper and constructing strong dugouts. Damage to vehicles, weapons and other material around the positions was great. The road leading to the positions was pounded regularly. At several points it was under direct enemy observation as was the valley in which the batteries were emplaced. Movement in the positions and on the road was restricted to the utmost to minimize damage and casualties.

The situation from the perspective of the 338th Field Artillery Battalion was as follows:

> A resume of the month's (December) activity shows that we received a greater amount of fire on our positions this month than in any previous battle ... The reason for this undoubtedly was the fact that the enemy had a large number of guns defending the approaches to Bologna and that our positions were restricted to the Idice River Valley into which he could fire from all sides and did. (338A Hist)

CHAPTER THIRTEEN

A New Year and a New Assignment

In the United States, celebration of the New Year had been tempered by the shocking news of the December 31 railroad disaster in the marshlands near the Great Salt Lake, 18 miles west of Ogden, Utah. Forty-four persons, including military servicemen, had been killed when, in a dense fog, the second section of the Southern Pacific Railroad—Pacific Limited—smashed into the rear end of the first section. (World Almanac, 1946, 716)

In Northern Europe, during the first week of 1945, General George Patton's Third Army, having broken the siege of Bastogne on December 26, celebrated New Year's Day by continuing a drive as part of a pincer movement to trap the remaining German forces that had been committed to the Battle of the Bulge. (*ibid.*, 52)

In the Philippines, General Douglas MacArthur's forces, preparing for the January 9 invasion of Luzon, conducted operations on Mindoro to clear the northeast part of that island and deceive the enemy about Allied intentions against Luzon. (Williams, 1960, 365)

In Italy, Gen. Mark Clark, Commanding General, 15th Army Group, moved from Siena—which had been the headquarters of his predecessor, General Sir Harold Alexander—to a new command post in the woods beside the Arno River. (Clark, 1950, 415–16)

The Fifth Army had regained most of the ground lost on December 26 by IV Corps in the Serchio Valley, and the positions were about the same as they had been at the end of October. The German attack in the Serchio Valley had caused a serious dislocation of the entire Fifth Army. In addition, it led Allied commanders to realize that conditions were definitely unfavorable for the renewal of the offensive that had been planned in December, (Goodman, 1952, 79–80) The enemy seemed to have decided to hold fast on the Italian front. This fact—together with the continuing bad weather, the shift in the location of Fifth Army troops, and the depleted ammunition stocks—forced the postponement of the planned offensive until spring, when the troops would be rested and there would be enough ammunition.

Troops were directed to be prepared to resume offensive operations about April 1, with training and rest to highlight the activities until then. However, it was planned that two limited objective attacks would be made before then, one of which was Operation *Fourth Term*, to be carried out by the 92nd Division in February. (Lee, 1966, 567)

On January 1, 1945, the 597th was in the 29th day of its attachment to the 88th Division Artillery, in the Idice Valley on the Bologna front.

New Year's Day 1945 was one of the longest days of the war for me, although according to the weather section of the 88th Division G02 report, there was less than nine hours of daylight between sunrise at 0752 and sunset at 1642.

My day had started before midnight on New Year's Eve, as I directed the preparation of Battery A to deliver our share of the battalion's New Year's greetings to the enemy: a 12-gun volley delivered on target exactly on the stroke of midnight:

> Jan. 1, 1945—Our greetings to the Krauts was a twelve-gun volley on an area that they have fortified. Results of fire undetermined. (WTD/D)

The enemy delivered a noisy greeting in reply, but we had no casualties.

At midnight, I relieved my Executive Officer as battery duty officer for the midnight-to-dawn shift. All of my other officers were up front with the infantry, and my Executive Officer and I were the only officers present in the battery position.

My Executive Officer relieved me at dawn, and during the daylight hours of New Year's Day I worked on a multitude of administrative details which, as a field artillery battery commander, I was responsible for even in combat. As darkness began to fall, the battery Executive Officer came by the headquarters tent and we discussed our plans for the night. He returned to the Executive's post and I returned to my sandbagged and covered foxhole to take a nap before my next tour as battery duty officer, which would begin at midnight. However, although I had attended to all the items on my daily checklist and all the new items that had been brought to my attention, I had a nagging feeling that there was something else I should do before I slept.

Indeed, there was something else, as I found out when the telephone rang soon after I stretched out, fully clothed, on my bunk. It was Colonel Derricks and he came right to the point: "Clark, this is to remind you that it is a custom of the service for all officers of a unit to visit their Commanding Officer on New Year's Day."

My first reaction was complete surprise that this peacetime custom would be followed in the forward area of the combat zone. Had the colonel succumbed to battle fatigue? The colonel's voice on the telephone interrupted my train of thought: "I am going to make an exception for the other officers in your battery but you get back here as soon as possible."

I acknowledged the colonel's order and informed the battery Executive where I was going. It was only a few hundred yards back to the battalion CP, but I had to drive under blackout conditions and it took a few minutes to get there. I arrived there about the same time as the other two firing battery commanders, and found the colonel, his principal staff officers, and the Service battery Commander already toasting the New Year.

Our arrival was the occasion for another toast, then Colonel Derricks escorted me into his private office and closed the door. This was only my second strictly private official meeting with Colonel Derricks in the more than eight months that he had commanded the battalion. The first had occurred in June, when he assigned me as battery commander of Battery A. I had a slight feeling of awe because after all, I was only a first lieutenant (although I would be promoted to captain the following week) and he was the senior black officer in the 92nd Division.

Colonel Derricks came right to the point: "Within a few days, I intend to relieve you from command of Battery A and assign you to my staff. After I designate your successor, I want you to be prepared to turn over your battery to him, as soon as possible."

I was shocked and disappointed, for although the job of a battery commander in combat was very difficult, I preferred it to all other jobs in artillery. On a particularly selfish note, I knew that a battery commander could return to his battery any time, day or night, and find the mess sergeant waiting to ensure that a hot meal was ready. On the other hand, a battalion staff officer was treated almost as a stranger; the headquarters battery mess sergeant neither noted his departure nor waited for his return.

I considered my options. I could either accept the change without asking why, or I could attempt to determine his reasons for making the change. I chose the latter option and asked the colonel to explain his reasons: did he consider me unsatisfactory as a battery commander? Colonel Derricks replied: "On the contrary, you have been an outstanding battery commander and my reason for making the change is not related to that."[1] He went on to explain what his reasons were:

> To carry out my job properly as a battalion commander I need, above all else, to have confidence in the loyalty and trustworthiness of the members of my staff who assist me in making and carrying out my decisions. I do have confidence in your loyalty and trustworthiness—but I cannot say the same for some of the officers who are members of my staff now. Some of them do not share my views concerning how to conduct current operations in a manner best suited to enhance the future of the 597th. (WTD/MC/1-1-45)[2]

Derricks believed that I did share his views and, accordingly, had decided to make changes and restructure his staff, to the extent possible, with officers who shared—or at least did not oppose—his views.

I had been aware for some time that, among certain staff officers, there was an undercurrent of dissatisfaction with Colonel Derricks, stemming from a variety of reasons:

1. There was a continuation of old animosities between the elitists and non-elitists, the degreed and non-degreed, that had developed over the years while they were assigned to the National Guard in Chicago, before their unit was inducted into Federal Service. This included some lingering resentment that Derricks had been promoted from captain to lieutenant colonel on the date their National Guard unit was inducted into Federal Service, while their favorite elitist had only been promoted from captain to major.

2. He had caused some resentment when he assigned me, an "outsider," to a key position within the battalion. I was considered by some to be an "outsider" because I had not been in the National Guard unit with them, although I had been the first black officer assigned to the 597th and had been in the battalion more than twice as long as all except one white officer still assigned.

3. Derricks was blunt and direct in dealing both with officers within the battalion and with the white officers in adjacent units and higher headquarters. He made no attempt to ingratiate himself with the general officers within the division, the division staff officers, or the regimental commanders.

4. He did not have the physique considered ideal for a battalion commander; i.e. lean, mean, and over 6ft tall. Instead, he was slightly overweight for his height of about 5ft 8-inches, and because of the size and shape of his head the nickname "Railhead" was used by some of his detractors in their private conversations.

5. There was a perception that he lacked technical competence in detailed matters relating to field artillery. Since he had been an infantry officer for 20 years before he transferred to the field artillery in 1940 at the age of 44, he did not attempt to flaunt his personal knowledge. Instead, he attempted to assign competent officers to the jobs where competence in detailed matters was essential.

6. Some contended that he lacked courage because he limited his trips to the forward observation posts to situations he considered absolutely essential, and he did not hesitate to "hit the dirt" at the sound of an oncoming shell.

In my opinion, none of the conditions considered by Derricks' detractors were sufficient, either singly or in combination, to alter the fact that he was the only officer in the Army that could complete the mission that he was performing.

During the next four months, as the Battalion Intelligence Officer, I had frequent opportunities to observe Colonel Derricks when I accompanied him in many dangerous situations. Therefore, I can state from personal experience that he did not lack courage.

Col. Wendell T. Derricks (front and center). (OHS)

His limited visits to forward observation posts stemmed in part from the fact that climbing the steep hills on which the observation posts were located exacerbated his high blood pressure, a condition he was aware of before going into combat.

Derricks had recognized soon after he was assigned to the 597th that he was the only officer in the Army who could perform the unique service of maintaining the bridgehead that he had been permitted to establish. Accordingly, he disregarded his own health and physical wellbeing. When he took his pre-deployment physical examination, the battalion surgeon disqualified him for overseas duty because of high blood pressure. However, he succeeded in finding a doctor who certified that he was physically qualified, which enabled him to retain command and lead the battalion overseas and into combat:[3]

> Since I assumed command, the 597th has been like a Bridgehead for young officers like you because, unlike the situation that existed in the 597th before I arrived and still exists in the 598th and 599th, you can gain a foothold here for further progress. The Army is not going to be segregated forever and, in a few years, you are going to have to compete with white officers for jobs never before held by Negro officers. If you have creditable combat experience as a battery commander and battalion staff officer, you will have a distinct advantage over officers who do not have such experiences.
>
> You have been outstanding as a battery commander and, although I know you don't want to change jobs, I am going to give you an opportunity to serve as a staff officer to round out your experience.
>
> But there is an even more important reason. There is an attempt, traceable to the division staff, to counterattack this bridgehead by removing me from command of the 597th. The sickening thing is that the attempt is being supported by some members of my own staff, who believe that, if I could be forced out, another black officer, presumably one of them, would be placed in command and that promotions would follow.
>
> But they are being fooled. The 92nd Division will not assign another black officer to command the 597th if I leave, but will assign a white officer and eventually replace all black field grade officers and captains with white officers. One reason for this is that the presence of black officers above the grade of first lieutenant in the 597th reflects unfavorably on the way black officers are limited in the 598th and 599th. Also, many white officers in the division bitterly resent the fact that, as an all-Negro battalion, the 597th provides a greater opportunity than any other unit in the Army for our officers to prepare for future progress.
>
> For the sake of the progress of our officers in the field artillery, the 597th must remain all-Negro; but it will remain all-Negro only so long as I remain in command. Therefore, as long as I am physically able, I do not intend to be forced out.
>
> But I need help. I need officers on my staff that I can trust. I am transferring you to my staff because I know that I can trust you. Therefore, I need you on my staff more than I need you in Battery A. (WTD/MC/1-1-45)

I could find no valid basis for disagreeing with Colonel Derricks' assessment of the situation. Recent events in the 92nd Division provided grounds for even greater pessimism. When we had been in Viareggio two weeks before to attend the ceremony in honor of General Truscott, there was still a great deal of consternation among black officers concerning the departure of Colonel Queen, the senior black commanding officer in the combat zone.[4]

When we left the coastal sector in December, we had been disturbed to hear about the parceling out of the 366th Infantry in bits and pieces to other 92nd Division units all over the coastal and Serchio sectors. It was apparent that the 92nd Division had no intention of using the 366th as a complete tactical unit under a black regimental commander. Accordingly, we had been very pessimistic concerning the future of the all-black 366th Infantry, and since it had the only black infantry field grade officers in the division, about the future of all black field grade officers in ground combat units.

Our pessimism had turned to despair less than a week after we had returned to the Bologna sector when a disaster occurred at Sommacolonia, in the Serchio sector of the 92nd Division. Elements of the 366th and, before the situation was stabilized, the combat effectiveness of the 2nd Battalion, 366th, were almost destroyed.

Colonel Derricks was very critical of the intelligence evaluation made by the 92nd Division G-2 who had permitted Sommacolonia to be inadequately defended, in the face of overwhelming evidence that indicated an imminent attack by the enemy. The available intelligence information included the fact that an estimated enemy infantry regiment, artillery battalion, engineer battalion, and reconnaissance battalion were all brought into the Serchio sector within a few days preceding the attack. Although, on the basis of this information, IV Corps and Fifth Army had concluded that an attack was imminent, the 92nd Division Intelligence Officer concluded, on December 24, that there was not sufficient indication to favor the capability of an attack.

It had been an unusually long private meeting with Colonel Derricks, and the other officers seemed to be so involved in their toasts to the New Year that only one appeared to have paid any attention to our absence. He wanted to know what we had talked about. I evaded the question and, as soon I could make my excuses, returned to my battery to write a letter to my wife and get some sleep:

> My foxhole is an excavation resembling a shallow grave, cut into the almost perpendicular south (away from the direction of the enemy) side of the hill. It is just large enough to accommodate my canvas cot and my stove which is a large coffee can with a stove pipe sticking out of the top. My pup tent is stretched overhead to provide blackout protection at night and to provide some protection from the weather. The fuel for my stove is low octane gasoline, its volatility reduced sufficiently by the extremely cold weather that I can apply a lighted match to the exposed top surface of the fuel without fear of an explosion or even a flare up. After lighting it, I can expect an even burning flame to continue until all the fuel is consumed. This particular model of the stove does have two major problems. It smokes and it cannot safely be put out or refueled until all of the fuel in the can is consumed.
>
> As I write by the light of a candle stuck in the dirt wall, I hear artillery shells going overhead from left to right (south to north) and in the distance I hear the deep bass sound of the guns from whose throats they came. I know those shells come from a friendly source and I hope many more of them will go the same way. Then, from the opposite direction, I hear the flat sound of another gun and the eerie whine of a shell going over my head from right to left (north to south). I know that shell is unfriendly and I breathe a prayer of thanksgiving that it, like so many others of its kind, has passed me by.
>
> An artillery dialogue of response and counter response follows—and for a time it is impossible to distinguish the direction of the source or destination of any individual shell as the noises rise to a crescendo—then gradually die away.
>
> And now there is absolute silence—or so it seems—because of the contrast with the preceding violence.

In the distance, along the front line to the north, the harsh clatter of a heavy machine gun breaks the silence for a few seconds. It is answered by another more distant. The message of the first gun is repeated and is answered again. The first machine gun speaks a third time and has the last word.

A single 155mm howitzer fires and the sound of its firing is echoed and reechoed until the sound is lost in the distant reaches of the Idice Valley to the south. A few moments pass and the howitzer fires again. As the echoes gradually die away, I realize I am becoming very sleepy. Another quiet night is beginning. (MC/FDC/1-1-45)

Late on the afternoon of January 3, I watched as enemy bombers flew over my battery, then heard the sound of their bomb bays opening and the incendiary bombs as they plunged to earth and scattered incendiary fragments in our battalion Command Post area. Fortunately, the fires caused no damage, and apparently neither did the thousands of machine-gun rounds fired at the planes by our units in the Idice Valley. On the next morning, the casings of the bombs were found about 100 yards from the battalion CP.

> A flight of 4 JU 87's appeared over the 597th FA Bn area ... at 031730A. Two cut their motors and glided in from the south dropping 3 or 4 bombs which burst throwing out about 30 incendiary bombs about 10" long and 1–1/2" diameter. AA people say the larger "bombs" were the casings or containers of the incendiaries and hold from 10 to 60 each. No damage or casualties were reported. (88Div G2)

On January 4, I put my GI-issue watch in its box because its crystal had been broken, and placed it with other personal effects in my field bag. I did not have an opportunity to turn it in to Ordnance for repair because I expected to receive orders to move the battery to another combat sector.

On January 5, the battalion was indeed alerted to move to a new position, and at 2025 the order was given to close station. We were directed to ensure that all heavy vehicles and guns cleared the one-way stretch of road between the firing battery area and the Service Battery area before 2400.

Since another artillery unit was to move into our position as soon as we moved out, I left behind one of the battery officers to assist the movement of the replacement unit. In addition, because of the blackout conditions under which we were operating and the limitations of time, I left most of my personal equipment in a field bag for the officer to bring out with him the next morning.

Unfortunately, there was some confusion. A heavy snow was falling and our replacement unit started moving in before we had finished moving out. Accordingly, the officer did not find my field bag when he searched for it the next morning in the snow. The lost field bag also contained the two marble peaches that had been given to me by the sculptor in whose house I had lived in November.

CHAPTER FOURTEEN

In the Valley

By the second week of January, the situation in the Serchio Valley had been stabilized and most of the territory lost to the enemy during December had been regained. The 92nd Division had once again assumed command of the wide front that extended from the Ligurian Sea to the eastern slope of the Serchio Valley.

The 597th moved from the Bologna front to the Serchio Valley sector of the 92nd Division and continued in direct support of the 365th. Along with the other artillery units in the Serchio Valley, the 597th was placed under the operational control of the British 10th Army Group Royal Artillery (10 AGRA).

At 0645 on January 6, as part of the 365th CT, the 597th began to move out of the Bologna sector on the way to the Serchio Valley, where the 465th would relieve the 8th Indian Division, which had assumed operational control of the sector while restoring territory lost during the enemy attack in December. Snow and rain made visibility poor and travel difficult.

After a long cold march, the 597th arrived at 2100 in a new assembly area north of Lucca, and Colonel Derricks received orders for occupation of the position.

> Jan. 6, 1945—Bn moved out of Idice Valley on Bologna front to Serchio Valley rendezvous— arriving after a long hard cold march. Went into Bivouac. Saw Gen'l Colbern about 2130. Received orders for occupation. Took over installations of 596th. (WTD/D)

> Jan. 6, 1945—General Colbern arrived at the [598th] battalion Command Post on the 6th of January at 1745 hours. He discussed with the Battalion Commander the displacement of the Battalion and the 597th Field Artillery Battalion moving into the Battalion positions. Lieutenant Colonel Derricks, 597th Field Artillery Commander arrived at the Battalion at 2045 hours on 6th of January 1945 and also discussed the movement of his battalion into (598th FA Bn) positions.

> Jan. 7, 1945—On 7 January at 0943 hours, Lieutenant Colonel Derricks, 597th Field Artillery Commander with reconnaissance party arrived at [598th] Battalion Command Post. The members of the reconnaissance party discussed with the Battalion Commander and the Battalion S-2 the general situation and the location of the battery positions.

> … Brigadier Maxwell, 10 AGRA, arrived at the Battalion Command Post and discussed with the Battalion Commander and Lieutenant Col Derricks the displacement plan for each Battalion.

> The plan was that the 598th Field Artillery Battalion would displace by infiltration to an assembly area … The 597th Field Artillery Battalion would close into the 598th's positions as soon as the positions were clear. (598A Hist)

> Jan. 7, 1945—Bn [597th] went into position. Attached to 10 AGRA (British). Nice people. (WTD/D)

The 598th moved from positions on the east side of the Serchio River to new positions on the west side. The 597th took over the positions vacated by the 598th. The 597th was assigned the mission of direct support of the 365th and placed under the operational control of the British 10 AGRA.[1]

> Jan. 9, 1945—Visited [365th] regt and made recon for positions for Cannon 365 and 366 and B Btry. Put Cannon 366 into position. B moved about same time. (WTD/D)

> Jan. 9, 1945—1000A—General Colbern to all Bns and Attchd Units—Conserve ammo and shoot at only actual targets. (92A Jnl)

On January 9, as directed by Colonel Derricks, I turned over Battery A to First Lieutenant Albert A. Briggs, who had been Battalion S-2 (Intelligence Officer). I was transferred to the battalion staff to replace Briggs as Battalion S-2. In my new assignment I was responsible for assisting the Battalion S-3 (Operations and Training Officer) in the training and supervision of approximately 20 personnel in the Operations and Fire Direction Center Section; and for training and supervising, with the assistance of the Reconnaissance and Survey officer, approximately 19 personnel in the Instrument and Survey section.

Colonel Derricks informed me that I would be expected to supervise all personnel assigned to intelligence duties in the battalion and to serve as battalion historian. Specifically, I would be responsible for: collection, processing and dissemination of information; coordination of observation; collaboration with the Operations Section in intelligence matters; analysis of maps and photographs; advising the battalion commander on plans for future operations; maintenance of intelligence records; preparation of reports; preparation of monthly battalion history summaries; and preparation of a detailed battalion history.

In my capacity as one of Derricks' principal advisors, I would be required to assist him whenever he decided that the need for my services was greatest. For the time being, he had decided that I should give highest priority to the coordination of observation and liaison activities in support of the infantry. My most immediate task would be to ensure that the forward observers were properly positioned with the best possible fields of observation under the existing circumstances. And further, that they were reminded periodically by my physical presence that they were still a part of the battalion and would be rotated between front-line and battery area assignments on a reasonable schedule.

Regimental Headquarters, 1st and 2nd Battalions, and the cannon company of the 366th Infantry were in the Serchio Valley.[2] The cannon companies of both the 365th and 366th were attached to the 597th.

A 597th Battalion OP was established in Barga. According to the 92nd Division Field Order No. 6, issued on January 10, the mission of the division was "to defend present line; local offensives in coastal sector; follow enemy withdrawals; protect left flank IV Corps."

Jan. 10, 1945—597th FA Bn, with 365th Combat Team, moved into sector to right of Serchio River (having replaced 8th Indian Division Troops) came under 92nd Division control at 0900A. (92A Hist)

Jan. 11, 1945—A letter received at Battalion Headquarters 2050 hours 11 January 1945, Headquarters 92nd Division Artillery stated, "Verbal Instructions IV Corps Artillery Officer—10 AGRA. 10 AGRA is placed under operational control of 92nd Infantry Division for operational control of all artillery units in support of troops in the Serchio Valley. Light battalions in direct support, while attached to the Infantry Regiments will be under the operational control of 10 AGRA. 10 AGRA will furnish general support with its medium regiments. (598A Hist)

Jan. 11, 1945—Gen'l Colbern visited CP today and informed me of the promotions of Captain Clark and 1st Lt. Jacobs. Very pleased to hear of them. Brigadier Maxwell of 10 AGRA informed me of our attachment to them. They are nice people. (WTD/D)

In spite of disappointment at leaving Battery A, I was pleased with my new assignment, especially after I received official notice of my promotion to captain and the promotion to first lieutenant of Lieutenant Norman W. Jacobs, who had been my Executive Officer in Battery A.

Jan. 12, 1945—I am feeling much better than when I wrote you a few days ago. I am sitting in front of a large open fireplace in a very nice house. I am now on the Colonel's staff: not as much direct responsibility but I get around much more.

The general came by the other day and told me I had been promoted to Captain. I am taking his word for it (putting on my captain's bars). (MC/FDC)

Jan. 13, 1945—Certain staff officers of the 365th are attempting to cover up the deficiencies of the infantry by reflections on my battalion. The fools think that existing race hatred will permit them to accomplish just that.[3] (WTD/D)

Jan. 14, 1945—Today was fairly pleasant with snow in the mountains and just short of freezing in the valleys. I looked out into enemy lines from a high point near here and heard some of his artillery as it fired at us and our artillery as it answered him. Now I am back in a fairly quiet place in a fine house with a nice bed and a good fire in the fireplace. Today is typical of the past week but things can change rapidly in the war. The General was correct about my promotion; I received my official notice today. (MC/FDC)

Jan. 14, 1945—Attended church service conducted by Chaplain Diggs. He has been very dutiful to this battalion.

Jan. 16, 1945—Went to Viareggio to have my lower denture repaired—then visited Randall at Gen Hosp #33 at Leghorn. (WTD/D)

> Jan. 18, 1945—597th FA Bn had a good day's shooting by silencing mortars at 1730, which were shelling one of our patrols by shooting up a group of enemy at 1810, and covering the withdrawal of our patrol to TREPIGNANA with smoke. Propaganda shells were also fired at LAMA DI SOTTO, FOSCIANDORA … VALLECHIA, (10 AGRA OR)

The 92nd Division G-2 Reports indicated that the forces opposing the 92nd Division included, in addition to Germans and Italians, some Yugoslavs, Czechs, and even some Russians (who ran the supply trains). Propaganda shells fired by the 597th included safe conduct passes with English words on one side and translations in German, Italian, and Polish on the other:

> The soldier who carries this safe conduct is using it as a sign of his genuine wish to give himself up. He is to be disarmed, to be well looked after, to receive food and medical attention as required, and to be removed from the danger zone as soon as possible. (Safe Conduct Pass)

Colonel Derricks wrote that he was grateful for whatever comforts he could find near the front:

> Jan. 18, 1945—Inspected Air Section at air strip near Lucca.[4] Had a hot mineral bath at Bagni di Luca. My first bath of that kind. It was very refreshing. (WTD/D)

Bagni was a thermal establishment where once Mussolini and other renowned figures had relaxed in the famed mineral waters. It had a particular attraction for English poets such as Keats, Shelley, and the Brownings because of its mild climate, dense woodlands, and sedate village atmosphere. However, on December 30, 1944, just three weeks before Colonel Derricks visited Bagni di Lucca, a house once occupied by Keats and Shelley was demolished by the 8th Indian Division Engineers.

January in the Serchio Valley was much quieter for the 597th than December had been on the Bologna front, although the town of Barga—where the battalion Ops were located—was constantly subjected to artillery fire.

Captain White was assigned as Liaison Officer No. 2, replacing Captain Walter Macklin, who in turn replaced him as Assistant S-3. Promotions during the month included: First Lieutenant Henry Shorter, Battalion Surgeon, to captain; and Second Lieutenants James Christian, pilot, and Harold Connor, to first lieutenant.

In the coastal sector, some special radar equipment was installed:

> Special radar detecting equipment has been installed on the coast south of Viareggio by a British unit as a precaution against the rumor that the Germans are planning to launch V1 bombs from the La Spezia peninsula against the Leghorn area. (92A Hist/Jan 45)

Lieutenant Colonel Robert C. Ross replaced Colonel Marston as the Division Artillery Executive Officer:

> Jan. 31, 1945—1145A—Lt Col Ross, former C.O. 598th FA Bn, rptd for duty as 92nd Div Arty Executive Officer. (92A Jnl)

Major Clark in front of St Peter's Basilica, Rome, 1945. (OHS)

Jan. 31, 1945—92nd Division Artillery won the division basketball tournament. The 597th had five men on the team of ten.

Feb. 4, 1945—Heard that Randall is on the way home. (WTD/D)

Meanwhile, I made my first visit to Rome and was able to enjoy its historic sights:

Feb. 4, 1945—I visited Rome for a few days last week. I took advantage of the opportunity to see just about everything—on foot, I walked for miles, visiting St. Peter's Church, Vatican City, the Coliseum—in fact—all the historic places on the list.

Some of the places, like St. Peter's, are very beautiful; but others, like the Coliseum, are very old looking and dirty. But overall, Rome is a beautiful city.

Life there seems to be just about as normal as in many American cities except that the prices were abnormally high. I met several American show business people staying in my hotel. They were very nice. (MC/FDC)

CHAPTER FIFTEEN

Operation *Fourth Term*

For almost a month after the 597th arrived in the Serchio Valley, the sector remained relatively quiet. Then, early in February 1945, the 92nd Division implemented Operation *Fourth Term* by carrying out a diversionary attack in the Serchio sector four days before the main attack in the coastal sector. The attack was designed to draw enemy reserves from the coastal sector, hold maximum enemy troops in the Serchio Valley area, and advance our lines from the Serchio to the Lama di Sotto ridge, a hill mass that dominated the valley. (Goodman, 1952, 92; Lee, 1966, 568–73)

The 365th Infantry and 1st and 2nd Battalions, 366th Infantry, were the attacking units.[1] During the attack in the Serchio Valley, the 597th participated, for the first time, in artillery support of a significant offensive operation.

At the beginning of the operation, the mission of the 597th was direct support of the 365th Infantry. However, at the end of the following day, the 598th, which had been supporting the 366th Infantry, left the Serchio sector and returned to the coastal sector to support the main attack. The 597th was therefore assigned the additional mission of direct support of the 366th Infantry, thus providing direct support for two regiments at the same time. Throughout the operation, the cannon companies of both the 365th Infantry and 366th Infantry were attached to the 597th.

By the end of the operation, almost half of the officers of the 597th had been placed with the supported infantry, either as forward observers with the attacking companies or as liaison officers with the battalion or regimental headquarters.

On February 4, Colonel Derricks completed plans for participation by the 597th in Operation *Fourth Term*:

> Feb. 5 [4], 1945—Planning for attack on Lama di Sotto and ridge right and left of it. Gen Colbern visited CP to discuss attack plans. (WTD/D)

On the first day of the offensive, the 597th supported the attack by the 3rd Battalion, 365th Infantry, which was making the main effort, with a forward observer accompanying each attacking company. Hits were obtained on several enemy guns and strongpoints. The attack was initially successful, and all objectives had been reached by midday. Lieutenants Gayles, Johnson, and Conquest were with the forward elements. Colonel Derricks, Captain McCants, and I were at the Sommacolonia OP until the objective was reached. General Colbern visited Sommacolonia and Lama di Sotto during the day.

Colonel Derricks and Captain Hargrove described the preparation for and conduct of the attack:

> Feb. 6 [5], 1945—Left CP at 0500 hours for Sommacolonia (OP) to observe attack … Attack was successful but expensive in men and material. My guns have repelled all counterattacks so far. (WTD/D)

> Feb 5, 1945—Attack jumped off. C battery at Piana di Lama di Sotto above Sommacolonia. Received word that the battery knocked out one enemy gun about nine o'clock. Lt Burton adjusted the battery effectively on enemy mule train vie Treppignana. For most of the day we've been firing steadily—about two thousand rounds by four o'clock. The 365th has started up Lama di Sotto. I hear they have run into many mines and are getting a lot of machine gun and mortar fire. Casualties aren't too heavy, however, I hear, and they are moving up pretty steadily. We are getting calls for missions all over the front. Our battalion and the regiment of British mediums—the 10th AGRA—plus the Cannon Companies of the 365th and 368th Infantry Regiments are furnishing the artillery support. (HBH/D0)

On the second day, the 597th supported the attack by the 2nd Bn., 365th, which was making the main effort, with forward observers again accompanying each attacking company. Lieutenants Burton and McFadden were with the forward elements. Colonel Derricks was at the main battalion OP in Barga and Captain White and I were at the new left OP in Barga.

The attack was only partially successful; Hill 608 was taken but Hill 461 was not. The battalion broke up several enemy counterattacks with defensive fire. Three injuries were reported: Lieutenant Gayles, Corporal Griffin, and T/4 Mitchell, members of the forward observer party from Battery B, were injured in action on Lama di Sotto. Colonel Derricks and Captain Hargrove noted the results of the attack in their diaries:

> Feb 7 [6], 1945—2nd Bn jumped off with hills 906 and 461 as objectives. Attack not as successful as yesterday's. Battalion is doing excellent job of supporting the infantry. The men of the infantry are singing our praises. (WTD/D)

> Feb 6, 1945—We hear that one battalion of the 365th has units on Lama di Sotto but I hear the casualties are rather high. The men will be blamed if the thing fails but I believe the plan of attack is faulty. The troops are making a frontal attack with no feints at the flanks, and the enemy knows exactly where they are. York and S. K. Jackson are up there, and we've got a lot of missions from them all day. Lt. Lee, my executive, alternates crews on the guns and so far they've been doing pretty well. (HBH/D)

On that same day, the 597th was placed in direct support of the 366th Infantry for operations on the left (west) side of the Serchio. The double direct support mission required that almost half of the officers of the battalion be placed either as forward observers with the attacking companies or liaison officers with the infantry battalion and regimental headquarters.

Captain Johnson was placed on temporary duty with the Division G-4, Captain Macklin replacing him as liaison officer with 365th regimental headquarters. Captain Buchanan went to the 366th as liaison officer with the regimental headquarters.

On February 7, the 597th beat off several enemy counterattacks with defensive fire. One of Battery B's howitzers exploded, injuring two men seriously, and First Lieutenant Briggs went to the 2nd Bn., 366th, as liaison officer.

> Feb. 8 [7], 1945—Repeated counterattacks are holding up our forces. Artillery is beating them off—the enemy mortar fire is deadly. (WTD/D/2–8-45)

Battery C moved to a new position near Fornaci, while Hargrove reported to 1st Bn., 366th, as liaison officer:

> Feb. 7, 1945—Warning orders for my battery to move up to Fornaci … Lt. Lee is going to have to do it because I'm ordered up to Gallicano as Artillery Liaison Officer with the 1st Battalion, 366th Infantry. I hear the battery closed station at 1930 and made a good march. Now located … in Fornaci … in the north end of the town. Battery ready to fire at 2200.
>
> When I reported to Colonel Chase, I had Vapple and Herrin with me. The CP is right at the foot of hill 437 and the AT Company is two-thirds of the way up, and the Germans are on top. (HBH/D)

On February 8, the 597th successfully provided defensive fire for the 365th and 366th against enemy counterattacks. Nevertheless, after receiving three counterattacks from an enemy force estimated to be in battalion strength, two companies of the 365th Infantry were forced to withdraw from Hills 906 and 1048. Derricks recorded:

> Feb. 9 [8], 1945—Positions taken are very insecure. Defensive fires called for frequently. (WTD/D)

February 9 was hazy with intermittent showers of rain. Visibility was poor. Battery A, 600th Field Artillery, moved from the coastal sector and occupied positions near Ghivizzano to support the 597th.

During the preceding four days, my efforts had been focused on the positioning of forward observers to support the operations of the 365th Infantry on the east side of the Serchio River. My first task on February 9 was to position a forward observer party with Company B, 366th Infantry, located on Hill 408, a few hundred yards west of the 1st Bn., 366th, CP in Gallicano. The battalion, located on the west side of the Serchio, was commanded by Lieutenant Colonel Hyman Y. Chase.

The forward observer selected for the assignment was Lieutenant William G. Dix. We started out in separate vehicles, with me leading, until we reached the 366th Infantry Regimental CP in Bolognana. There, I had to park my vehicle and ride the rest of the way with Lieutenant Dix, since travel on the road between Bolognana and Gallicano was restricted to one vehicle each way, at intervals of

30 minutes. This restriction had been directed by Brigadier General John Wood, Assistant Division Commander, who was responsible for operations in the Serchio Valley. He had done so because the road was under enemy observation and subject to intense enemy artillery fire.

After seeing Lieutenant Dix and his party properly positioned on Hill 408, I walked back to the 1st Bn, CP in Gallicano to wait for a scheduled vehicle to take me back to my vehicle in Bolognana. When Colonel Chase found that I was waiting for a ride, he offered to immediately send his Message Center vehicle on an unscheduled trip to take me back. I respectfully reminded him that, in view of the traffic restriction imposed by General Wood and the fact that the general had been known to travel the road looking for violators, I did not mind waiting for the scheduled vehicle. But Colonel Chase insisted and I was soon on my way.

Halfway back to Bolognana, on an open stretch of road under direct enemy observation, I met General Wood. He waved for me to stop and, after I dismounted, he lectured me for five minutes. He would have continued longer if the sound of an incoming shell, impacting a few hundred yards away, had not reminded him that we were under enemy observation. Several times in the next few weeks, General Wood looked for an opportunity to continue the lecture, but was not successful.

Lieutenant Dix reported his arrival and location to Captain Hargrove, the liaison officer with 1st Bn., 366th:

> Feb. 9, 1945—Lt. Dix reported to me as FO. Put him on Hill 408 with B Company. Lt. Redd is CO. Got word that Hobson went back to Bn OP as FO.
>
> At 1600 hours I was setting up an OP when I picked up three Germans through the BC Scope coming over the top of Hill 437. I told Major Page but when he looked, he didn't see anything. I went forward to the CP, reported to Col Chase; he called Captain Errington Johnson. He reported that I must have seen some of his men. But about ten minutes later, all hell broke loose. We could look out the back door and see the fire fight up on the hill. I saw four enemy with their hands up coming down the hill. Lt. Dix reported that apparently a company was attacking the hill and he could see them coming over the hill. Lt. Knox, 81mm Mortar Commander, adjusted his mortars quickly in front of the enemy and Lt. Dix adjusted Charlie Battery on the rear, and between them we fixed old Tedeschi. Prisoners stated that over 50 men were killed in the attacking company and many wounded were left on the hill.
>
> The rest of the company surrendered bit by bit every day. They were from the Italian-German San Marco Division. The prisoners were dirty, hungry, ragged and, almost without exception, they were glad to give themselves up. Their story was that they had been forced to leave their homes and had been taken to Germany where they had been trained as a division for six months. All non-coms above the grade of Sergeant were Germans, and officers were either Fascists or Germans; the men were kept in the lines by these superiors and whenever they had a chance, they tried to give themselves up. (HBH/D)

Beginning at 0630 on February 10, the 597th supported the 365th Infantry, reinforced by the 2nd Battalion (less F Company) of the 366th Infantry, in an attempt to retake some of the high ground along the Lama di Sotto ridge which had been lost to enemy counterattacks. Captains McCants and Pickett, Lieutenant Briggs, and Captain White were liaison officers with, from right to left, 3rd Bn., 365th, 2nd Bn., 366th, and 2nd Bn., 365th. Lieutenants Burton and Conquest and Sergeants Simpson and Hobson were FOs with the companies making the main effort.

The 597th beat off several enemy counterattacks and at one time successfully held off the enemy with artillery fire when the supported infantry company ran out of ammunition. Although defensive machine-gun and mortar fire was heavy, the attacking troops drove through elements of the Italian 1st Berseglieri Regiment and returned to Lama and on to parts of the ridge southwest of the village, capturing 55 prisoners. But before nightfall, the Germans counterattacked and reentered Lama.

During the night of February 10/11, General Almond decided to halt the offensive operations in both the coastal and Serchio Valley sectors. On February 11, the enemy launched several counterattacks in the Serchio but all were beaten off by artillery fire.

The period of offensive operations had resulted in the surrender of many Italian soldiers, as highlighted by Captain Hargrove:

> Feb. 11, 1945—Captured four Italian soldiers who were from the company we had chopped up on the 9th, who said they had been trying to give up for days but every time they approached our outposts they were fired on. They finally killed their Lieutenant, a Fascista, and crept through the lines, staying in a house all night and giving up in the morning. (HBH/DO)

CHAPTER SIXTEEN

The Aftermath

The Serchio Valley quieted down after February 11. The Lama di Sotto ridge remained in enemy hands, but the outposts of the 365th Infantry had advanced their positions three-quarters of a mile.

In the coastal sector, the 598th and 599th had been in direct support of the 370th and 371st Infantry, respectively, and the 600th in general support with two of its firing batteries.[1] After the operations ended, the performance of the infantry units in the coastal sector was judged by the Army to be completely unsatisfactory, and was later cited as the primary reason for the reorganization of the division that took place following General Marshall's visit. (Goodman, 1952, 115; Lee, 1966, 572–75)

The 3rd Bn. of the 366th, especially, had been involved in a disaster of major proportions in the crossing of the Cinquale Canal as part of Task Force 1.[2] General Almond called off the operation after the 3rd Bn. had sustained casualties of 33 killed (including the battalion commander, Major Willis Polk), 187 wounded, and 48 missing.

When I heard the bad news, I recalled the conversation back in December with my informant in Viareggio concerning Rowny and the 366th. A few days after the operation ended, I saw my informant again. Referring to the befallen, the 2nd Bn. of the 366th on December 26 in the Serchio Valley and the 3rd Bn. in the Cinquale Canal operation on February 8–9, he remarked: "I told you so!"

A few weeks later, the Germans tried to exploit their defensive success in the Cinquale operation with propaganda leaflets intended for the soldiers of the 92nd Division:

MISSING IN ACTION!
HOW DID IT HAPPEN ON CINQUALE BEACH

Some weeks ago after JERRY had driven back the "BUFFALOES" to their base on the river-side?
Many hundreds of dead colored men scattered around the swampy grounds covering the German main defense line.
Burial was made impossible because of ceaseless American shell-fire.

Cinquale Canal. (OHS)

> Impressed by such misery the German commander got in touch with the American C.I.C. of that sector asking for an agreement to stop fighting for some time in order to fulfill human laws. AMERICAN G.H.Q. REFUSED!
> A "fine piece of humanity ..."

There was a much more favorable outcome in the Serchio Valley. During the period February 5–11, in addition to advancing their front lines, the infantry units supported by the 597th repulsed numerous counterattacks, took 288 prisoners, and neutralized an entire battalion of the 1st Berseglieri Regiment. They also inflicted heavy casualties of the 1st and 2nd Bns. of the 286th Grenadier Regiment of the German 148th Division. In making the main effort, the 365th Infantry sustained casualties of 52 killed and 249 wounded.

During this period, the 597th completed 265 fire missions, expending 7,231 rounds of 105mm ammunition, while sustaining casualties of four wounded.

A German officer captured during the period is reported to have remarked: "You don't need the infantry to hold the lines south of Castelnuova; your artillery can do it alone."

In spite of the performance of the units in the Serchio Valley and the capacity for success it revealed, it went almost unnoticed because it was considered only a diversion for the operation near the coast. (Goodman, 1952, 97) Of all the regimental commanders in the division, only the commander of the 365th felt that his troops had done well. (Lee, 1966, 572) However, his responses to a questionnaire from the division commander indicated that there was a reservoir of racial bias against blacks that could not be overcome merely by outstanding performance in combat:[3]

> *Question*: What percentage of the Negro officers of your command who were committed to combat would you say measured up well in all respects?
> *Answer*: About 90%.

> *Question*: Based on combat performance, what percent of your colored officers do you regard as of Field Grade potential?
> *Answer*: None.

> *Question*: Based on your observations and experiences what are your recommendations on the organization, command and use of Negro soldiers in a future emergency?
> *Answer*: While this Regiment apparently has done well, I am not convinced that it has good potential value despite the favorable comments of the Battalion Commanders as to the fighting ability of their troops. A possible use of Negro troops in a future emergency in addition to being used as labor troops, would be their employment in an antiaircraft organization. I do not recommend their use as combat troops. (CO 365)

In the sector of the 1st Bn., 366th, operations now returned to normal:

> Feb. 13, 1945—PW reported that there was a concentration of enemy troops in Flatone. Captain Clark, C Company 366th at Barca, reported that some PWs he had taken stated there were troops at Perpoli. He received mortar fire in his position which he believes was coming from Perpoli and Fiatone. We fire pretty often in those towns, mostly UF [unobserved fires], but even at that, anyone in those towns is catching hell.

> Feb. 14, 1945—Lt Dix reported that he observed 15 enemy with packs entering Malozzano. Adjusted effectively, using time shell. (HBH/D)

On February 14, the 597th beat off several enemy counterattacks in the 365th area with artillery fire. Meanwhile, Lieutenant Rogers of Battery A, 600th, relieved Lieutenant McFadden at Bn. OP, and General Colbern visited the battalion and commended all ranks for the support given to the infantry in the recent operations.

Also on February 14, General Marshall, the Army Chief of Staff, visited the 92nd Division.[4] While there, he approved, in concept, a plan to reorganize the infantry component of the division for the forthcoming spring offensive. The plan provided for the attachment of the white 473rd Infantry and the Japanese-American 442nd Infantry.[5] They would replace the 365th and 371st Infantry, which would be detached from the division for service elsewhere. The 370th Infantry would remain with the division but its composition would be changed to include the best men and officers of all three regiments (365th, 370th, and 371st). The 366th would be withdrawn from combat and converted to engineers. (Lee, 1966)[6]

Nine 3-inch guns that had been used by IV Corps artillery units for harassing missions were turned over to 92nd Division Artillery, the 597th establishing Battery E for the purpose of using the 3-inch guns:

> Three guns were assigned [to] each of the light Field Artillery Battalions … These guns are to be used for many of the night harassing missions. While normal-charge 3″ ammunition was limited to 40 rounds per battalion per day, reduced-charge 3″ ammunition was unlimited. (92A Hist/Feb 45)

In a letter to my wife, I avoided direct mention of the recent operation:

> Feb. 13, 1945—The effects of my "Roman Holiday" have worn off and I am back to work again …
> The standard civilian cars here seem to be about the size of the smallest cars we have in the United States and the roads are much narrower. (MC/FC)

Colonel Derricks, meanwhile, commented on everyday events during this quiet period:

> Feb. 14, 1945—Gen'l Colbern visited all batteries and complimented them on the work of the battalion and all echelons.

> Feb. 15, 1945—Attended dinner at Div Arty C.P.

> Feb. 16, 1945—Day-after effects from party not so good. (WTD/D)

On February 15, I enclosed a clipping from the February 12 issue of *The Buffalo* in a letter to my wife. I had been nominated as "Officer of the Week":

> Feb. 15, 1945—Enclosed you will find a clipping with a picture of me published in *The Buffalo* for 12 February. I was nominated as "Officer of the Week" in the division. (MC/FDC)

> Capt. Major Clark, S-2 of Lt. Col. Derrick's Destroyers, has been nominated as Officer of the Week because he "is an example of what a real officer should be like and because he is an inspiration to his men."
> A native of Haskell, Okla., Capt. Clark reached his present grade the hard way, having previously been an enlisted man.
> Before his appointment as S-2 he commanded a firing battery which had the reputation of being the best in the Battalion and today he is regarded as one of the best S-2's in Division Artillery. (*Buffalo*, Feb. 12, 1945)

During the remainder of the week, the 597th continued to fire on enemy strongpoints with good effect.

At the conclusion of the offensive operations, I made a survey to select the most suitable locations of observation posts to support the battalion's new defensive mission. We had just come through an experience during which our support of two regiments in offensive operations had stretched our personnel resources to the limit. Therefore, I was particularly concerned that our available personnel should be used in the most efficient manner during the relative lull in our activities. Accordingly, where there were other suitable locations from which the mission could be accomplished, I had advised Colonel Derricks that we should not send FO parties to certain locations requested by the infantry where the fields of observation were inadequate, and where the access routes and routes for maintaining wire communications were too exposed.

One of the unsuitable locations requested by the infantry was in the sector of the 1st Bn., 365th, near Albiano. I recommended to Colonel Derricks that we turn down the infantry's request for the establishment of OPs at Albiano because it was in an unsuitable location and because a more suitable location was available nearby.

On February 16 and 17, I was away from the 597th Bn. headquarters as I temporarily replaced Lieutenant Gayles as LnO with 2nd Bn., 365th. This was to permit him to perform a task that required him to go back to Viareggio. On the same day that I left, the infantry again requested that a forward observer party be sent to Albiano, and Colonel Derricks agreed to do so. Accordingly, Lieutenant M. I. Johnson and his FO party, in accordance with a decision made after I left the 597th Bn. Hq, reported to the 1st Bn., 365th, to establish an OP near Albiano.

The next day, the first fatal casualties within the 597th occurred when Privates First Class Herman Rochelle and Robert Curry, both of Battery A and members of Lieutenant Johnson's FO party, were killed instantly by an enemy mortar shell which landed between them while they were repairing the wire lines to the new OP:

> Feb. 17, 1945—After 92 days of combat, had first fatal casualties in battalion (2). Privates Curry and Rochelle of Btry A were killed by mortar fire in vicinity of Albiano, while working on telephone line. They were part of M. I. Johnson's party. Quite a blow. (WTD/D)

> Feb. 17, 1945—Lt M. I. Johnson, FO with Pickett, reported that Pfc Herman Rochelle and Pfc Robert Curry were killed by enemy mortar fire. Both were from A Battery. Time: 1030, vicinity of Piano di Ceragni, Italy. (HBH/D)

This incident continued to concern me for many years. My concern was based on the belief that, if my recommendations had been followed, the tragedy could have been prevented. Perhaps I should have been more convincing in my recommendations. Captain Hargrove stated:

> Feb. 17, 1945—General Wood seems to feel that the danger of Charley Clark's position at Barca has been greatly exaggerated. He wants Col Chase to take a patrol up there in daytime to inspect. He's sending his aide, Lt Newton, along. As soon as Col Chase told me, I registered C battery on Fiatone and Cannon Company on Perpoli—known mortar positions. Two rounds for each registration, Col Chase and I agreed if he radioed back, I'd fire on those points.
>
> They left about two p.m. and at about 2:12 the radio began to crackle. They were pinned down by German machine gun and mortar fire. I had the batteries standing by and within 60 seconds we were firing some fire into Fiatone and Perpoli. Col Chase reported that they walked right up to Barca and back with no more trouble.

> Feb. 18, 1945—Received lots of mortar fire in Gallicano all night. Fired several DFs in front of Foots Davis' A Company. (HBH/D)

On Sunday, Chaplain Duncan conducted religious services at Battery A in honor of Pfcs Rochelle and Curry:

> Feb. 18, 1945—Sunday—The Div Arty Chaplain is here to conduct services. We will have services for Curry and Rochelle at Btry A after regular service.

> Feb. 19, 1945—The visit by Chaplain Dunston was greatly appreciated by all the men. Morale has improved because of it. (WTD/D)

During that week, several changes were made in the assignments of liaison officers: Captain White relieved Lieutenant Gayels as LnO with 2nd Bn., 365th, Lieutenant Brown relieved Captain Buchanan as LnO with the 366th Regiment, Lieutenant Coles relieved Captain Hargrove as LnO with 1st Bn., 366th, and Lieutenant Dix relieved Lieutenant Briggs as LnO with 2nd Bn., 366th. Captain McCants reported back to the battalion as Big Battery Commander, and Major Page and Captains Quisenberry, Buchanan, and Hargrove departed for rest leave in Rome. Hargrove recorded:

> Feb. 19, 1945—Relieved by Lt Coles as LnO # 24–5. In spite of what they said about the 366th, they moved up tonight and took some more ground and held it—1 battalion—until relieved by the 473rd. (HBH/D)

Colonel Derricks and the 597th continued to receive compliments from the infantry units for the artillery support provided during the February 4 offensive operations. Derricks expressed his pride in the men of the 597th as a result of their performance during that offensive.

> Feb. 20, 1945—The situation is becoming static again. We are receiving compliments for the fine support we gave the infantry. They really believe in us now. All ranks and grades have nothing but praise for the 597th. I am humbly proud of all my people.

> Feb. 21, 1945—We have settled in defense again. I will take advantage of this opportunity to get my equipment in shape. (WTD/D)

Also during this week, Derricks served on a court-martial in Viareggio, and one of Hargrove's old acquaintances was killed by a mortar shell. The 597th fired the recently acquired three 3-inch guns of the newly established Battery E, and a motor vehicle inspection team from 92nd Division inspected the battalion's vehicles:

> Feb. 22, 1945—Went to Viareggio today to sit on a GCM (general court-martial). Postponed until 23rd. Stopped by air strip on way back. Italy is becoming more sunny daily and I enjoyed the ride. Saw Chaplain Beasley and Major Watkins. Beasley promised to write Ma [Mrs. Derricks] a letter.

> Feb. 23, 1945—Went back to Viareggio for the court. A very unpleasant case. (WTC/D)

Feb. 23, 1945—Foots company lost Vernon Woodland, Sgt. A mortar shell landed smack in his foxhole. I used to know him at Fort Devens when I was in A Company. He used to be a boxer. He was from Philly. He was killed on Hill 352. (HBH/D)

Feb. 24, 1945—Had command inspection of all vehicles. They are coming up fine. (WTD/D)

There were unmistakable signs that spring was returning to the Serchio Valley:

Feb. 24, 1945—Spring is beginning here. People are planting their gardens. The last of the olive crop is being harvested. A sheet is placed under the tree. The old man climbs the tree and shakes certain branches and the old lady and children pick up the olives.

The other night at dinner I met, for the first time that I can remember a Mr. (Warrant Officer) Garrett from Taft. We were in the 349th together at Fort Sill and we were in the 46th Brigade at Camp Livingston for two years—yet I had to come over here to meet him. (MC/FDC)

On Sunday, February 25, Derricks accompanied Chaplain Diggs on a visit to Battery C.

During that week, Lieutenant Gayles relieved Lieutenant Brown as LnO with 366th Regt, while Major Page and Captains Quisenberry, Buchanan, and Hargrove returned from Rome and Captain McCants, Lieutenant Lee, and Lieutenant Jones departed for Rome.

On February 24, the 92nd Infantry Division issued Field Order No. 9, which directed the division to operate in zone, holding maximum enemy forces in the coastal area.

Feb. 24, 1945—10 AGRA (597 F.A. Bn. Attchd) in direct support of the 365 and 366 Infantry Regiments until these regiments are relieved by 473 Infantry; then direct support of 473 Infantry. (92A Hist)

Meanwhile, the 473rd Infantry moved into the Serchio Valley sector:

Upon receipt of 92nd Division Field Order #9 on Feb 24th, immediate plans were laid for relief of the 365th Inf and 366th Inf 92nd Div in SERCHIO valley sector. Reconnaissance of this sector was accomplished on Feb 24th and on the night of Feb 25th, 1st Bn 473rd Inf relieved 366 Inf on the west side of the SERCHIO river ... One EM ... was injured by a mine during this relief.

At 0500 on the 26th 1st Bn 473rd Inf assumed responsibility for this sector and later that day moved its CP from BOLOGNANA (formerly 366th Regtl CP) to GALLICANO ... the 2nd Bn 473rd ... moved into an assembly area in vicinity of BARGA preparatory to relieving the 2nd Bn of the 366th Inf on the following night.

On the night of 27th Feb, 2nd Bn 473rd Inf completed relief of 2nd Bn 365th Inf ... At 2240 Regtl Hq being established in CATAROZZA and the 1st and 2nd Bn 473rd Inf having completely taken over their respective sectors, Col Yarborough assumed command of Regtl sector ...

10 AGRA with 597th under its operational control was placed in direct support of the Regt... (473Inf Hist/Feb. 45)

After the 1st Bn., 473rd Inf. had replaced 1st and 2nd Bns., 366th Inf. at the front, the 2nd Bn., 473rd Inf.'s Lieutenant Gayles was sent to 1st Bn., 473rd Inf.

as LnO and Captain White was assigned as LnO with 2nd Bn., 473rd. Upon the departure of the 366th Inf., including the cannon company, to a new position south of Viareggio, Lieutenants Dix and Coles were relieved as LnOs.

Although this was the first time in U.S. Army history that an all-black-officered field artillery battalion had been placed in direct support of a white infantry regiment, the attitude of 473rd Infantry personnel initially appeared to be favorable:

> Feb. 26, 1945—366th relieved by 473rd. We went into direct support (of 473) whether they like it or not. We found out almost immediately they didn't want us to leave. I don't blame them. Our observers are familiar with all the target areas and we have fired into almost every draw on the enemy side of the lines. (HBH/D)

Indeed, the departing 365th Infantry gave a favorable endorsement of the performance of the 597th to the incoming 473rd Infantry:

> Feb. 27, 1945—365 & 366 are moving out of sector and 473rd Inf is moving in. We remain support (direct). 365 told 473 that 597 can support anybody. (WTD/D)

Also during that week, the 92nd Div. G-2 and G-3 visited the 597th. During the week that included the end of February and the beginning of March, Sergeant Harrin relieved Lieutenant Rogers (Battery A, 600th) at Bn. OP; Battery A (597th) moved to a new position near Fornaci; the 597th Bn. CP moved from Ghivizzano to Fornaci; Service Battery moved from Bagnl di Lucca to Ghivizzano; and Battery A, 600th moved from the Serchio back to its old position near Forte dei Marmi.

On March 1, the 3rd Bn., 473rd, relieved 1st Bn., 365 Inf., completing the relief of the front-line units in the Serchio sector. Battery was lightly shelled by the enemy:

> Mar. 1, 1945—3 shells fell in front of battery position, 105s. One Italian killed. No soldier casualties. (HBH/D)

For several days, the grapevine traffic had forecast a forthcoming visit to the 92nd Division by Truman Gibson, Civilian Aide to the Secretary of War. Morale of the black enlisted men and officers, which had been extremely low in the light of the changes made and rumored following the just-completed February offensive operations, began to improve significantly. They believed that Mr Gibson, the highest-ranking black civilian in the U.S. Army, would straighten things out as soon as he determined the facts.

Gibson arrived in Italy on February 26 and visited Generals McNarney (MTOUSA), Clark (15th Army Group), Truscott (Fifth Army), and Crittenberger (IV Corps) at their respective headquarters. Then, with Major General Otto Nelson, the deputy theater commander, he visited the 92nd Division in Viareggio, where a dinner was held in his honor on the night of March 1. On the morning of the 1st, Colonel Derricks had informed me that I was to accompany him to the dinner:

Mar. 1, 1945—Change-over in sector now complete. Work on equipment going according to schedule. Will go to Viareggio this evening to attend dinner for Mr. Truman Gibson, Jr., who is visiting division, today. Will take Quisenberry, Page and Clark with me.

Visited C Btry to inspect their work on gun pits. Hargrove has the idea and is doing a good job now. (WTD/D)

As we rode together from our HQ in the Serchio Valley to Viareggio to attend a dinner for Truman Gibson, Colonel Derricks described a recent meeting with General Wood that had ended on a sour note. In one of his visits to the 597th Bn. CP, General Wood had remarked that, just as on previous visits, I had not been in the S-2 office where he thought I should be. Colonel Derricks had reminded the general of a unit commander's prerogative to use his staff to assist him where the need was greatest. During the February offensive operations, he had decided that my services were most needed for the task of coordinating the observation and liaison activities in support of the two infantry regiments.

I suspected that General Wood had remarked as he did because he wanted to find me in the S-2 office so that he could continue the lecture he had started on February 9 on the road between Gallicano and Bolognana that had been interrupted by the sound of incoming enemy shells.

After Colonel Derricks finished describing his response to General Woods, I started to remind him that, by being so blunt in explaining my absence, he was just causing the general to dislike him even more. But then I recalled that Colonel Derricks had been around long enough to realize that himself. Although he had been promoted to lieutenant colonel while Eisenhower was still in that rank, Eisenhower had advanced six grades to become a five-star general and Derricks was still a lieutenant colonel. Derricks realized that, although he was still just a lieutenant colonel, he was a black lieutenant colonel and his chief liability in the rank-conscious, race-conscious 92nd Div. could be attributed to the fact that he outranked all of the more than 500 other black officers and 230 of the 236 white officers.

He was in a vulnerable position, especially in the light of what had happened to Colonel Queen who, for the brief period of his attachment to the 99th Division, had been the only black officer senior to Colonel Derricks. commanding a ground combat arms unit in the combat zone. Because Derricks was now the ranking black officer, he was resented by more officers, including some black field grade officers, than any other officer in the division.

After the dinner, Colonel Derricks noted in his diary:

Mar. 2, 1945—Dinner was very nice. Saw many people and heard a real soldier talk, Maj Gen Nelson, Deputy Commanding General, MTOUSA. Saw Truman (Gibson). (WTD/D)

On March 3, I began my daily tour of forward observation posts but was interrupted about mid-morning by a call from Colonel Derricks directing me to report back to battalion headquarters for a special mission. When I reported to Derricks, he directed me to go to Viareggio that afternoon and report to the 92nd Division

Chief of Staff for the purpose of escorting Truman Gibson back to the 597th early the next morning.

I reported, as directed, to the 92nd Division HQ in Viareggio, spent the night there and, early on the morning of March 4, with Mr. Gibson and the driver in the front seat of my jeep and me in the back with the other paraphernalia, we started the two-hour drive back to the Serchio Valley. During that trip, I had what was considered to be an unprecedented opportunity for a black Army captain to talk directly to a high government official without the presence and interference of multiple echelons of superior officers.

After we arrived at the 597th Battalion HQ, Mr. Gibson met with Colonel Derricks and the other two 597th field grade officers, Majors Page and Turnley; then had a longer meeting with Major Page, who had been a classmate at law school. After that, Mr. Gibson visited the firing batteries, where he actually fired one of the howitzers, and met many of the other officers and men of the battalion:

> Mar 4, 1945—One Italian soldier (Fascist; Monte Rosa Division) walked right down the road into Fornaci—gave up. Armed with grenades, etc.
>
> Truman Gibson came to the GP, was astonished to see how near we were to the enemy. Talked to officers at Bn Hq. (HBH/D)

Finally, we turned Gibson over to the escort from the next unit he was to visit.

A few days after the 597th moved to Fornaci, I obtained a room in the home of a family located near the 597th Bn. HQ. The family, consisting of a father and mother and two young adult daughters, had remained in their home despite the daily shelling in the area. The parents' bedroom and the piano were on the first floor. My bedroom and the bedrooms of the two daughters were on the second floor. At about the same time I moved there, an enlisted man from the 473rd Infantry (an Italian from Brooklyn) began to "court" the elder of the two daughters.

For several nights, it was difficult for me to sleep before midnight because of the noise of the playing of the piano and the singing by the young ladies and the soldier. One night I did get to sleep by midnight, but then at about 0200 I was awakened by the noise of a violent argument. The father had discovered his elder daughter and the soldier coming down the stairs from her room.

During the second week in March, Generals Almond, Colbern, and Wood, and the 473rd Infantry Regimental Commander, visited the 597th CP, while Colonel Derricks and Lieutenants Brown and Burton left for Rome. Battery A started a training schedule, the OP at Albiano was discontinued, and Lieutenant Jackson adjusted fire on enemy troops with good effect, starting two fires. Lieutenant Lee also successfully adjusted fire on an enemy gun position, setting off some enemy ammunition. Lieutenants Connor and Burton, at separate Ops, obtained good cross-observation on a house occupied by 18 enemy troops and adjusted artillery fire with excellent results; at least five of the enemy were killed. Two direct hits were made on the house, setting it on fire. When the enemy ran out, waving a white flag, the battalion fired five propaganda shells with surrender passes.

Lieutenant Burton was relieved as FO after being out continuously since January 26, the longest uninterrupted tour as a 597th FO during the war. I instructed the observers at Sommacolonia OP to close their OP, and assigned their observation responsibilities to the observers on Hill 922.

One of Hargrove's noncommissioned officers reported that a white 473rd Infantry soldier had made some racial remarks to him at one of the OPs:

> Mar. 6, 1945—Sgt Hobson reported to me that some white soldier (473rd Inf) had made some (racial) remarks to him and he had reported it to the Company Commander. It certainly is ridiculous to know that those fellows would resent a man who was doing such good shooting for their protection just because he was a Negro. I guess a lot of them felt that way, but when we were ordered to move (a few days later), they asked that we stay with them. (HBH/D)

Enemy artillery was active, with rounds falling into the position areas of Batteries A, C, and E batteries:

> Mar. 8, 1945—At 1725 received four rounds in the position [Battery C]; no one hurt. 75s or 105s. (HBH/D)

The next day, 22 rounds of enemy artillery fire fell in Battery A's position, causing a slight injury to Corporal Fred Clay, and two rounds fell in rear of the Bn. CP area.

In a letter to my wife, I described the paradoxes of war in springtime in Italy:

> Mar. 11, 1945—From my window, I can look out at villages held by the enemy—each one with its church near the center—each church with a bell tower which the enemy uses as an observation post. I can listen to our artillery shells whistle by overhead and watch them as they explode in enemy territory. I can also listen to the enemy's guns and hear his shells as they come toward me—seeking to disturb our peace of mind.
>
> It is a beautiful spring day. Too bad there is a war going on to mar our appreciation of it. Today was Sunday and all the Italian people went to church this morning. In the afternoon, some chose to stroll about in the beautiful sunshine, seemingly unmindful of all the guns about them but jumping, nevertheless, every time one fired.
>
> Some of the houses are still elegant and untouched by the war; others have all windows broken. Some have huge holes in the side or roof where shells have come through; and still others have been reduced to rubble. (MC/FDC)

On March 12, Captain Charles White was fatally injured when the vehicle in which he was riding overturned on a bridge while he was en route between Fornaci and Barga at 0100. The driver, Private Norman Jenkins, was slightly injured. Hargrove had been at a party with Captain White at the officers' club in Ghivizzano only a few hours before his death, having left him singing there about 2030. (HBH/D)

On March 13, Colonel Derricks and Lieutenants Brown and Burton returned from Rome where they had been on leave. In the last significant entry in his diary, Colonel Derricks expressed his shock upon hearing of Captain White's death:

Mar. 13, 1945—Return trip started. Arrived at CP at 2145 hours or about. Learned of Capt. White's death. Quite a shock and a loss of a fine artillery mind to the battalion. (WTD/D)

Captain Buchanan temporarily replaced Captain White as liaison officer at 2nd Bn., 473rd. During the same week, Major Turnley made a patrol in the Air OP and adjusted fire on a river bridge near Castelnuovo, obtaining two hits. Another observer in the Air OP adjusted fire on enemy personnel and vehicles with good effect. Lieutenant Gayles was slightly injured when the jeep in which he was riding overturned.

During the following week, Battery E was deactivated and the 3-inch guns received one month before were turned in.

On March 14, 10 days after his visit to the 597th, Gibson held a press conference arranged in Rome by the public relations officer of the theater at the request of the war correspondents of the area. Following the press conference, there was some disagreement among the correspondents concerning what Gibson actually said. However, there is no disagreement over the fact that the statements attributed to him and widely publicized caused extreme resentment among black 92nd Division personnel and their supporters at home. Nor is there any disagreement over the fact that most black 92nd Division veterans will continue to resent the statements through their lifetime.

The statement attributed to Gibson that caused the greatest initial outrage among the infantry officers was that "Most of the casualties among the line officers have been sustained by Negroes under circumstances which might have reflected on their judgment but left no doubt as to their courage." A response to this statement was contained in a letter to the editor of *The Stars and Stripes* by Lieutenant J. Hubert, MC, published in the April 6, 1945 issue:

The recent article on the courage of the 92nd Division has been eating me for a week …

… The line officer is the guy who takes the same chances and endures the same hardships as the front-line soldier, in addition to leading and coordinating their actions in attack and defense. If he gets killed, let's not call it bad judgment that he didn't see the 88 shell coming, that he didn't catch the mortar shell coming, that he didn't catch the mortar shell when it dropped in his hole, that he didn't find the Schu [antipersonnel] mine until it went off.

The line officer, white or colored, has a job to do. Why call it bad judgment when he gets maimed or killed doing so.

I'm no line officer. I'm a medic treating what's left of those cases of bad judgment and doing what I can to make them feel their sacrifice was worthwhile. (*S & S*, April 6, 1945)

The reaction of Albert A. Briggs, who was commanding Battery A, 597th, at the time of the visit, is typical of black officers in the 92nd who talked to Mr. Gibson during his tour:

I want to say something about an incident because it besmirches the character of the 92nd Division and all black men everywhere.

It was one of the most distressing days of my life—and we were being shot at then—when I picked up the *Stars and Stripes* [and read] that the 92nd Division in a combat situation, specifically the crossing of the Cinquale Canal, had melted before the enemy and had shown cowardice, and all that stuff. This report had been made by a black man, Truman K. Gibson, Jr., and I want the record to show that I never forgave him for that. He was then the Civilian Assistant to the Secretary of War (Robert Patterson), and his job had to do with Negro soldiers' affairs and their problems. He was sent over there [to Italy] ostensibly to … inspect … But I believe he was sent specifically to render a bad report … on the 92nd Division.

[This, in spite of the fact that] our Division Artillery, especially, had been all over the theater and had been talked about as being some of the finest artillery that was. We had been detached from the regular unit and [been] sent other places to support other groups and we had often nothing but good reports.

The reason that I, personally, had such a bad feeling about it [is that] when he visited our battalion, Colonel Derricks brought him to Battery A. I don't know why he was brought to Battery A or whether he went to any other unit in the battalion or not. I am sure he went to battalion headquarters. But he came to Battery A to inspect. Somebody alerted me that the battalion commander was coming—it was just about twilight—and he wanted to look around. So he, Truman Gibson, came to the unit and I recall that they gave him a helmet and took him down to the battery area where the guns were firing … intermittently and … the next time we fired we let him pull the lanyard.

Then we had a two-hour meeting with him in a farmhouse and some of these same questions were raised. I remember the only white officer that came to that meeting was the major who commanded the tank battalion attached to the 92nd Division. I believe it was the 758th. When I saw him there … I wondered why, because I thought he [Truman Gibson] was just going to let the black officers in to try to get some answers from them about the situation. But the star of the show that night was this white officer who was very vehement in his denouncement of the white command structure of the 92nd Division.

Newspapers … say "an all-Negro division," but the 92nd Division was by no means all-Negro, you see, and especially in the area of planning and command. All command decisions and all operational decisions were made by white people in the 92nd Division. All the plans for that ill-fated Cinquale operation were made in General Almond's office … blacks had absolutely nothing to do with it. We also know that the supply situation was not what it was supposed to be. They didn't get the things to that engineer battalion which was trying to put a bridge across …

There were so many things wrong with that operation that we were there to complain about … We were very, very much disturbed about some of the ways in which the operation had gone, and [felt] that if we had had anything to do with it, things would have gone different.

When we let Truman Gibson know this, the white battalion commander documented some of the things—some of the orders—he had received that he thought were crazy, that would lend itself, that would help [us] in reaching our objective …

The reason that I was so personally disturbed about this is that we spent two hours with him … and he was writing, had his aid writing all this stuff down. And we made a *prima-facie* case, a good one, for him to go back and say that the evidence shows that we need to send over a real fact-finding commission before we make any conclusions …

But the reason I believe that he had already had his orders is because … it is apparent that all he had listened to is what the white folks said [before he visited us] … Although we talked to him until 9 or 10 o'clock that night … he didn't pay any attention to what we said. He wasted our time. (AAB/EVW; taped interview with Albert Briggs, October 25, 1983, by Edward Willette, on behalf of author)

On April 1, I mentioned the furore in a letter to my wife: "If you have read any of our newspapers you must have noticed the fuss created by the statements made by Mr. Truman Gibson at his press conference in Rome. I was his guide for a day while he was here and he gave no indication that he was going to make such statements." (MC/FDC) Her reply a few weeks later noted:

> I did notice the write-ups in response to this Mr. Truman Gibson. I misplaced the paper some time ago and just found it yesterday, at least only a portion of it ...
>
> In my opinion, this Mr. Gibson is evidently trying to become a big shot by blabbing something, anything, as a matter of fact, just because he was overseas awhile, and to start some new propaganda. (FDC/MC/4-22-45)

On March 15, additional organizational changes took place in the Serchio Valley sector:

> 10 AGRA relieved of operational control of 92nd Division at 1200A. 111 FA Regt (Br) assumed operational control of Artillery in the Serchio Sector. Weapons of the 111 FA Regt are 25 Pounder Gun-howitzers, P-Btry (17th Med Regt) was attached to 111 FA Regt. (92A Hist/Mar 45)

The mission of the 597th was changed from direct support of the 473rd to general support, reinforcing the British 111th Field Artillery (FA) Group. The 111th began gradually to assign their own personnel take over the LnO and FO duties with the 473rd Infantry. Information was received that we were going to move out of the area within the next 10 days to return to the coastal sector. This was confirmed at a meeting at Div. Arty. HQ which Colonel Derricks attended:

> Mar. 17, 1945—1030—Meeting of all Bn Comdrs at Div Arty CP with Gen Colbern. Present: Lt Col Derricks, 597th FA Bn; Lt Col Baumgartner, 599 FA Bn; Lt Col Ray, 600 FA Bn; and Lt Col Harvey, 76 HAA. Subject: Operations. (92A Jnl)

During our final week in the Serchio sector, the 597th Air OP continued daily to adjust fire on enemy vehicles and installations with good effect, and on one occasion was fired on by enemy antiaircraft guns. During this period, the battalion was visited by General Wood, General Colbert, and the Division Artillery Air Officer.

CHAPTER SEVENTEEN

On the Move

The plans for the 15th Army Group's spring offensive included provisions for phased attacks by the U.S. Fifth Army and British Eighth Army to break out of their winter positions, capture or isolate Bologna, seize Po River crossings, encircle as many as possible of the enemy forces of the 25 German and five Fascist divisions south of the Po, and then cross the Po and exploit northward. (15th Army Group History, 9–10)

Of importance to the main aim—the destruction of enemy forces in Italy—but independent tactically, was a diversion against Massa, on the battlefront's extreme left flank, at the mountains' edge and overlooking the route up Italy's west coast. The attack would keep busy the Germans in the west, and if it went well there was the possibility of exploitation toward La Spezia, the naval base 17 miles north, and on to Genoa. (*Ibid.*)

This task was entrusted to the 92nd, which was no longer a black division as its three infantry regiments now included one white regiment converted from antiaircraft units (the 473rd), the American-Japanese regiment (the 442nd), and a practically new black regiment with both black and white officers (the 370th). The 92nd, with its organic artillery and services remaining the same, operated under Fifth Army control for the initial stages of the attack. The 365th and 371st Infantry, detached from the 92nd and operating under IV Corps control, were scheduled to occupy the Serchio and Cutigliano sectors. (Lee, 1966, 580)

The west coast diversion began on the morning of April 5. The 370th, 442nd, and 473rd Infantry, supported by the 92nd's organic and attached artillery, attached tank and tank destroyer units, and with British and American air and naval support available, fought northward against stiff opposition near the coast and in the mountainous country just east of the coast (15th Army Group History, 12).

After Massa was taken on the 10th and Carrara on the 11th, the enemy opposition stiffened temporarily, and from the 14th until the 19th the advance was slowed as the Germans committed their available reserves. But the attack had achieved its purpose: the enemy on the division's front had been badly mauled and all the reserves the enemy dared use had been committed just in time to prevent their use against the main Fifth Army attack beginning on April 14. (Lee, 1966)

For the first two weeks of the offensive, the 597th moved three times and had two major changes in mission.

***

On March 22, Colonel Derricks and members of the 597th Bn. staff visited the 92nd Div. Arty CP for a conference concerning the forthcoming movement of the 597th back to the coastal sector. Following the conference, the detailed movement plan was formulated:

> Mar. 22, 1945—1815A—From 597 FA Bn—"B" Btry will move night of 23 Mar; HQ and 1 How Btry to move night of 24 Mar; Sv and 1 How Btry to move night of 25 Mar. (92A Jnl)

As the 597th prepared for the forthcoming move, Colonel Derricks and his party made a reconnaissance for new positions in the coastal sector west of Pietrasanta. The division G-4 published the route and schedule for the first convoy:

> Mar. 23, 1945—1040—From G-4, 92nd Div—"B" Btry, 597th FA Bn. 20 vehicles. Convoy No. 92W-111. Date of convoy 23 Mar 45. Rte: TP to bridge at Q223982 on Rte 1227 to 1226 at Camaiore. From Camaiore on Route 176 to Pietrasanta. Convoy leaves IP at 1920. Reaches Camaiore 2120. Arrives at destination 232200A. (92A Jnl)

Battery B closed its station in the Serchio sector and arrived at its new position in the coastal sector at 2320. An advanced Bn. CP was established east of Fiumetto on the road to Pietrasanta. During the following two days, the remainder of the 597th completed the movement from the Serchio Valley to the coastal sector.

> 597th Moved from the Serchio Valley during the night of 24–25 March … The arrival of A Btry, 597th in the Coastal Sector marked the first time all organic units of the 92nd Div Arty had been under the direct command of General Colbern since this headquarters arrived overseas. (92A Hist/Mar 45)

The 597th Bn. CP was located northeast of Fiumetto on the Fiumetto–Pietrasanta road. The firing battery positions were a little less than a mile generally north of the Bn. CP, about 500 yards apart, with B Battery on the left, C Battery in the center, and A Battery on the right. Service Battery was about 5 miles south, in Lido di Camalore, returning to where it had been located in November.

> Mar. 24, 1945—Moved from Fornaci to vicinity Crociale, Italy–95835–92710. Lt. Lee and Chief of Sections were there already. Yorky rode with me. Marvelous march, excellent cooperation by MPs. Got in without any trouble.
> Bn went into support of Coastal Sector at 2330. The dugout the palsans fixed for me was just about complete; good one; two layers of logs, three layers of sandbags and big enough for me and Yorky to sleep inside and set up a stove and radio.
> Everybody is still digging; it's too dirty around the houses, so I'm not going to let any of the men stay in them. It's safer in the dugouts anyway. (HBH/D)

The 597th was assigned the mission of general support of the 92nd Division, reinforcing the 598th, with Bn. Ops established in Capriglia on the right and Forte del Marmi on the left.

During the first day in the new position, several shells fell in the Headquarters Battery area, seriously wounding three Italian civilians. On the second day, General Colbern visited the Bn. CP and stayed for lunch with Colonel Derricks.

A few days after we returned to the coastal sector, I revisited the village where I had been "headman" during the preceding November:

> Mar. 27, 1945—I saw Hubert Locust the other day. He was ok.
> The flowers here are very beautiful, especially the roses—which are the most abundant. I saw the three little girls in "my village" for the first time since leaving this area last year. They remembered me and, as before, lined up in stair-step order to greet me. (MC/FDC)

On March 28, a premature explosion of a howitzer shell injured two men in Battery B:

> No. 1 piece, B Btry 597th FA Bn was put out of action at 1107A as a result of a muzzle burst. Two enlisted men of the crew were injured. (92A Hist/Mar 45)

> Mar. 28, 1945—Battery B had a premature burst of an M54 shell, injuring two men. This [Battery C] was the best organized position and the best dug-in we've ever had. Plenty of logs and sandbags. Even the kitchen was dug in deep enough for men to walk around in and cook in comfortably. Sgt Spikes had the best gun pit I've yet seen. (HBH/D)

On Easter Sunday, April 1, I attended a memorial ceremony at the US Military Cemetery at Castelfiorentino, southwest of Florence. The ceremony was in honor of the men of the 92nd Division who, after sacrificing their lives in defense of our nation, had been buried in that cemetery:

> Apr. 1, 1945—Today was Easter. All the Italian people dressed up today and had a big celebration even up on the front lines. I left the front for a few hours today and passed through a lot of Italy and it was the same all over. The celebrating will continue until tomorrow.
> I was in charge of a detail of ten enlisted men to represent the 597th at a ceremony at a military cemetery to honor the division dead. The division commander placed wreaths on the graves of one officer and two enlisted men. One of the graves was that of Pfc Robert Curry of Battery A, 597th, killed in action near Albiano, Italy, on 17 February.
> ...
> Hubert Locust's outfit (366th Inf) has had continuous bad breaks since last December—but I think they will be in a less difficult situation now, although the Courier and Defender will be most unhappy about it. I saw Hubert the day before they were changed to Engineers.[1] (MC/FDC)

During the first week of April, as preparations continued for the offensive which was to begin in the coastal sector on the 5th, the 597th furnished three FOs to the 370th Infantry, two FOs to the 371st Inf., and three FOs to the 442nd Inf. Captains Pickett and McCants were sent to the 371st Infantry and 598th FA Bn., respectively, as LnOs.

On April 4, General Colbern and Fifth Army Artillery Officer, General Kurtz, visited the Bn. CP. Then, late in the afternoon, the 597th registered on targets which were to be fired on in support of the forthcoming operation.

The operation was to be supported by heavy bombing by the Army Air Force. Prior to the bombing, propaganda leaflets were distributed to warn the Italian civilians:

> ITALIAN CIVILIANS
> THE ALLIES WARN YOU TO PROTECT YOURSELVES AGAINST THE HEAVY BOMBING THAT IS PLANNED TO DESTROY THE ENEMY.
> SEEK SAFETY BY FOLLOWING THESE INSTRUCTIONS:
> Keep away from gun lines and defensive positions. If your house is near such defense, dig holes in the fields to shelter each person safely.
> Keep dispersed, Keep off all roads.
> THE ALLIES WILL SPARE YOU ALL THEY CAN BUT YOU MUST HELP IN YOUR OWN PROTECTION.

On April 5, the offensive started with a 10-minute artillery preparation that began at 0455 and ended at 0505. The 370th Inf. was on the left, with 442nd Inf. on the right. The mission of the 597th was general support of the 92nd Division, reinforcing the 598th FA Bn. in support of the 370th Inf.:[2]

> The first phase of the preparation began promptly at 0455 continuing until 0505. The second phase was fired between 0515 and 0520. While the light artillery concentrated on the known or suspected front-line dispositions and mortars, the mediums laid on known enemy batteries, concrete emplacements and strong points ... Close support was given to the attack in all sectors by units of Div Arty through forward observers, AOP's and other methods of observation. A total of 22,824 rounds—the largest amount of ammunition fired in one day during the campaign—was fired between 0400 and 0500. (92A Hist/Apr 45)

> Apr. 5, 1945—D-day for Coastal Sector. H-Hour at 0500. Artillery preparation started at 0455, ended at 0505. We are in general support of the 598th. Visibility good. We can see everything! The battlefield is right in front of us. I can see our artillery killing Krauts and I can see our men getting it. Our ranges are from 3,400 yards up to 11,000. The P-47 dive bombed, fired rockets, machine gunned all day long. One went down and didn't come up; the other came up to about 5,000 feet, wobbling crazily, then the pilot tipped it over on its back, flipped out and came down in a chute. The last I saw of the plane, it was over the sea, upside down. Private Will Crumpton reported MIA. (HBH/D)

In an operation that took place in the vicinity of our old basepoint, Castle Aghinolfi, Second Lieutenant Vernon J. Baker, the only black officer in Company C, 370th Infantry, earned the Distinguished Service Cross by an extraordinary act of heroism. In spearheading the attack of the 1st Bn., 370th Inf., Company C had reached a position far in advance of the other units of the battalion. However, because of a series of unfortunate incidents, the position became untenable. Baker volunteered to remain in the position to cover the withdrawal of Company C back to the line of the 1st Bn.

In another part of the first day's operation, Lieutenant Rose, 597th FO with Company L, 370th, in the vicinity of Strettoia, was wounded in action but carried on with his duties until relieved and evacuated to hospital. (92A Hist)

At the beginning of the operation, the 473rd Inf., less one battalion in the coastal sector in division reserve, was in the Serchio sector, supported by the British 111th Field Regiment.

The second day of the offensive began with a five-minute preparation from 0555–0600. Captain Buchanan relieved Captain McCants as LnO with the 598th. Captain McCants became LnO with 2nd Bn., 370th.

> Apr. 6, 1945—D+1 for Coastal sector ... We fired Arty preparation from 0555–0600. Visibility good. Crumpton located; had found and attached himself to Lt. Burton's party. Made us all feel better. From my OP, I have a beautiful front seat view of the battlefield. Alaska is 3,500 yards away; I can see our men moving up. They should have it before nightfall. (HBH/D)

> Apr. 6, 1945—Trouble began to be experienced with smoke interfering with artillery observation. The smoke resulted from [smoke] generators which the division employed to hide troop movements, our own artillery smoke shells as well as that generated by the enemy. This problem requires a command decision weighing the advantage of improved artillery support resulting from observation against the veiling of troop movements. (92A Hist)

Troop movements. (OHS)

On the third day, the German position known as "Alaska" was captured after some hard fighting:

> Apr. 7, 1945—Alaska is taken, also the large hill mask beyond it. Negro soldiers took it and they took it the hard way. I can see them taking a terrific pasting from mortars and artillery, but they are sticking it out. I can see a group bringing prisoners back. A P-47 just dropped some fire bombs in a large grove of trees just behind a ridge to the left. There are some guns (or were) dug in along this ridge. I think Dix knocked two of them out. Boy, are those fire bombs terrific! The whole woods are on fire! Any Germans still in there are catching hell!! There comes almost a whole company! "El Homo" is taking them prisoner. Fire is dying down and I can see a patrol moving through the grove. They are on the other side and threw grenades into the house and fired Tommy guns into the window. They are bringing out two–three prisoners. Digging in all over the hill and it's a good thing, too. God! The whole hill is being covered by Jerry mortar fire! Thirty minutes of it! But El Homo is still there! And now there goes all our artillery! Somebody must have picked up something. They've stopped the mortars, too. (HBH/D)

On the right, meanwhile, the 442nd Inf. captured Mt. Belevedere.

After the battalion of the 473rd Infantry in division reserve on the coast had been committed on the April 7, the remainder of the regiment, less one battalion, also moved to the coast. There, on the 8th, with elements of 370th attached and the 598th in direct support, the 473rd assumed command of the sector of the 370th. The 597th continued to reinforce the 598th.

At the same time, the 370th, less elements remaining on the coast, moved to the Serchio sector and, with one battalion of the 473rd attached—and with the 111th Field Regiment in support—assumed command of that sector:

> Apr. 8, 1945—1400B—Meeting of all Bn comdrs and atcd unt comdrs at Div Arty CP. Present: Lt Col Derricks, C.O. 597 FA Bn; Major Lane, C.O. 598 FA Bn; Lt Col Hansen, C.O. 766 FA Bn; Col Harvey, 76 HAA Bn; Lt Col Clayton, C.O. 530 FA Bn. Subj: Present situations and future operations. (92A Jnl)

Following the meeting, the battalion commanders went on reconnaissance in the area north of the Cinquale Canal, during which Lieutenant Colonel Harvey, C.O., 76th HAA (Heavy Antiaircraft Artillery, British), was badly injured by a mine explosion and evacuated.

On the morning of April 9, General Colbern ordered the 597th, 598th, and 329th (from 85th Division Artillery) to move to positions between the Cinquale Canal and Frigido River. One battery of each battalion was ordered into position to register during the day; afterwards, the remainder of each battalion was to move by infiltration.

> Apr. 9, 1945—0845—From Gen Colbern to S-3—597, 598 and 329 FA Bns to move 1 btry to goose/eggs[3] before noon today. Remainder of 597th as fast as possible by infiltration and 598 infiltrate to new positions this afternoon. Remainder of 329 move to new pos[ition] right after dark. 500 FA Bn get 1 How to new pos and register before dark. Remainder of Bn move after dark. (92A Jnl)

Colonel Derricks led the 597th battery commanders to the assigned "goose egg" to select individual battery positions:

> Apr. 9, 1945—Went on reconnaissance north of Cinquale. Went up as far as 500 yards from a fire-fight. Near our selected positions there were several tanks and TDs [tank destroyers] stopped, one sitting on top of 4 mines and all of them scared to move.
> Colonel Derricks pointed out our positions … Mine was right out in the open. B Battery's was being shelled. No one knew whether there were mines or not. Lt Mundy and I went to my position, made a thorough reconnaissance. Anders, Vapple were with me. We went back [and] moved the battery across the Cinquale Canal; had to go into new positions, could not get into the ones selected. Fortunately, we met General Colbern who picked some positions quickly and told us to move in. (HBH/D)

The Bn. CP was located about 900 meters north of the Cinquale Canal, some 1,000 meters inland, along a road that ran generally northeast from its intersection with the coastal road. The firing battery positions were located about 700–900 meters north of the Bn. CP, with Battery A on the left and Battery C on the right.

Many of the forward gun positions were occupied under enemy small-arms, automatic weapons, and mortar fire, and under intense shelling from enemy artillery, particularly the guns on Punta Bianca. At nearby positions, the 600th FA Bn. suffered one enlisted man killed, several wounded, and the loss of a tractor with other items of equipment. Between this time and the evening of April 10, the only cover in front of the forward artillery battalions consisted of a company of infantry and a few tanks. At least once, all battalions were alerted for a possible German counterattack from the vicinity of the Frigido River.

During the night of April 9/10, the 370th Inf. established elements approximately 300 yards south of the Frigido River. Harassing of forward battery positions from enemy small-arms fire, automatic weapons, and artillery fire continued.

By midmorning of the 10th, all of Massa south of the Frigido River had been taken by 473rd Inf. Captain Pickett reported to 2nd Bn., 370th, as LnO. In the firing batteries of the 597th, a high priority was given to the continued improvement of positions:

> Apr. 10, 1945—Still digging in. Alerted for enemy patrol. Enemy artillery active, especially the big stuff from la Spezia (Punta Bianca). Infantry still moving up. From where we are, we can see the Castle and some of our men have an OP set up there. It's directly to our right. Colonel Derricks has his CP back on the road … there are no more houses anywhere. Macklin was going to use a pillbox just behind my CP. I didn't want it and sure enough it turned out to be booby-trapped. Snoopy John Gales set it off. He was lucky!
> Massa was taken! (HBD/D)

On April 11, after Massa was cleared of the enemy, Colonel Derricks, Captain Pickett, Lieutenant Mundy, and I went there on a preliminary reconnaissance. The battalion continued to dig in:

Apr. 11, 1945—Still digging in. Shells are coming in all over. They say the bridge across the Cinquale gets harassing time fire constantly. Sent Hines back after ammo and he had to come back around through Porta—or what's left of it. (HBH)

Also, on the 11th, the 442nd, advancing through nearly impassable mountain terrain, reached and occupied Carrara. They found the Partisans in control, as later reported in the *Stars and Stripes*:

PARTISANS PRAISED
HELPED U.S. TROOPS

WITH THE 15th ARMY GROUP … Exploits of a daring band of Italian Partisans who cleared Carrara of Germans and Fascist sympathizers before the entry of the 5th Army troops earlier this week have been recognized officially by the 15th Army Group.

Military authorities released the story of the Partisans—a story of five months of raids and sabotage, planned in and conducted from caves in the famous marble quarries north and east of the coastal town.

These roving bands of guerrilla Patriots made Carrara untenable for the Nazis and their collaborators. In the final phases of their campaign, they helped U.S. troops reach the town by disrupting German communications and denying the enemy troops refuge in the high ground which dominates the municipality. (*S&S*, 4–17–45)

Late on the afternoon of April 11, I returned to the old CP near Fiumetto to get some items which had been left behind when we moved. I took longer than expected because of difficulty in locating some of the items, and it was after dark before I started back to the new position. Then I encountered another delay because of a traffic bottleneck as I approached the bridge across Cinquale Canal, which was being shelled heavily by the guns on Punta Bianca. Some of the shells had time fuses which were set to go off just high enough above the bridge to cause the greatest possible number of personnel casualties.

While I was waiting to cross, I had a new experience. For the first time at night, I was looking at the exact spot in the air where a time shell exploded, at the exact instant of the explosion. I saw the white-hot outline of the shell in the first brief millisecond of the explosion and then observed as the shell became a multitude of individual hot fragments. Some spent fragments fell around me but I was not hit.

On April 12, Colonel Derricks and his party went on reconnaissance north of Massa and the battalion moved to their new position after 2000. In moving to the new position, the battalion crossed a ford on the Frigido River without incident. However, when the 600th FA Bn. crossed later at the same point, one of its vehicles struck a mine:

Apr. 12, 1945—Three officers and an enlisted man of the 600 FA Bn were slightly injured and their jeep damaged at the entrance to the ford over the Frigido near Massa on the night of 12 April, when their jeep hit a mine. It was a peculiar accident since much traffic, including the 597th FA Bn had already passed over the ford that night. (92A Hist)

Apr. 12, 1945—Orders were received at 2000B to displace one battery forward to the vicinity of Carrara, Italia. While crossing a ford on the Frigido River, the reconnaissance party riding in a ⅓-ton vehicle, struck a mine injuring Capt Claude C. Clark, Capt Clifford Moore, 1st Lt Ossie G. Alexander and Sgt Wilfred W. Avery. (600A Hist)

Apr. 12, 1945—Made reconnaissance vicinity Castagnola near Massa. Rough!! Shelling, snipers, machine guns. C Battery ... ready to fire at 2330. On my way back, met Alexander, Moore and Clark (600 FA) at the (Frigido) river crossing. They had hit a mine (apparently antipersonnel), so I piled them in my jeep and took them back to their aid station. On my way back to my new position, Major Wimp, Strayhorn, with C Battery, 600th FA lined up the road at the same spot, so I showed them how to get across. They're lucky they didn't get shelled while they were lined up on the road.

Apr. 13, 1945—Captain Buchanan (LnO) called for Arty fire to break up enemy counterattack (850–057). Good effect. They won't do that "no" more. Went to Partisan headquarters, met Il Corsaro, the leader, and invited him and his staff over to my CP for chow. They came, we talked; I liked and respected him. One of his officers is a woman from Carrara whose family was wiped out at Santa Anna, August, 1944. They practically had Massa cleared out when the Allies came in. They're plenty tough. I gave them a couple of cases of C rations. (HBH/D)

On April 14, General Colbern visited the Bn. CP. The 597th was assigned the mission of direct support of the 758th (L) Tank Bn., while continuing to reinforce the 598th FA.

In spite of the requirements to deliver high explosive shells on enemy troops and equipment, the 597th still had time to deliver *Frontpost*, the newspaper for German troops. During the week following the death of President Roosevelt, *Frontpost* included the following item:

Roosevelt's Testament

President Roosevelt, who died of a cerebral hemorrhage on April the 12th, had written a speech which he was to have delivered on the radio that evening.

In this unheard speech, the President wrote: "more than an end to war, we want an end to the beginnings of wars—an end to this brutal, inhuman thoroughly unpractical method of settling differences between governments ... Mere conquest of our enemies is not enough. We must go on to do all in our power to conquer the doubts, fears, ignorance and greed which made this horror possible."

On April 16, Colonel Derricks and his party went on reconnaissance for new positions northwest of Carrara, to which the battalion moved later that day:

Apr. 16, 1945—Was snatched out of battery on very short notice to go on reconnaissance near Carrara; party ran off and left me, I caught up with them near Carrara. Came back and got my battery and moved up that night. Rough, coming and going. Tough position to get into. Lost Pendergrass' truck coming in; went back after it leaving Boutte in charge. While battery was digging in, we received about fifty rounds in and in front of the position. Apparently an SP-88 or 75. Nobody hurt.

Apr. 17, 1945—This morning I checked all installations and everything was coming along pretty well, I thought. Page came down and ordered two of the pieces moved—said minimum elevation would be too high. So what! The guns were behind a thick stone wall and the dug-out sandbagged, which gave the crews added security and protection. Everybody knows that minimum elevation has nothing to do with keeping a howitzer from being effective. My chiefs of section are doing a good job in a tough situation. Lt Boutte is the only officer with me and he is doing ok. I let him lay the battery last night.[4] (HGH/D)

On April 17, Lieutenant Gayles fired the battalion against enemy guns and SP with good effect, destroying one completely, and the next day captured some enemy maps. Private Robert Evans, of Battery C, broke his leg when it was hit by the howitzer trail during a fire mission. Hargrove was assigned as LnO No. 1:

> Apr. 18, 1945—Colonel Derricks phoned to tell me that I was to be LnO #1. I reported to the CP, checked all my equipment and my section and made preparations to go forward on immediate notice. Then I bought two bottles of Grappa, went to my section's quarters and got pleasantly high.
> Carrera is famous for its marble workers; there were many partisans here; they have come in from the surrounding mountains, long hair, chicks, and everything! Beautiful women, and although the German and Fascist propaganda had pictured American Negroes as quite awful people, they were beginning to be more and more friendly. There is still a lot of shelling going on and not much activity in the streets, however.
> I just heard that Pvt Evans (C Btry) broke his leg in an accident at the guns; they have had no casualties up to now. (HBH/D)

I spent most of my time during this period either observing from one of the battalion's two observation posts or making a reconnaissance for a better forward location for our rearmost OP. It was my practice to leapfrog each OP forward as soon as possible to ensure the best observation possible of the area in front of our supported units. Among the locations used during this period were Marina di Carrara, Nicola, Ortonova, and Hill 1212. Since my OPs were consistently the best in the area, I shared them from time to time with observers from other artillery units and with high-ranking officers from all the units in the area. Among the visitors at my OPs during the period from April 10–20 were General Colbern, Colonel Miller—who was the Regimental Commander of the 442nd—and Colonel Derricks, who at one time was accompanied by the 597th battery commanders to observe a special fire mission.

One day, while at our most forward battalion OP, I observed some unusual enemy activity in front of our supported unit: guns being pulled out of position in daylight and moved toward their rear. I assumed that they were being moved so that they could be used in another location. Accordingly, I transmitted a fire request to the 597th fire direction center and, within three minutes, was successful in reducing the enemy's inventory by at least one gun and a truck.

On April 19, Captain Buchanan, LnO with the 598th, moved to a new position southwest of Fossola.

CHAPTER EIGHTEEN

The Enemy Withdrawal Becomes a Rout

92nd Division units continued to move and change missions as necessary to maintain pressure on the retreating enemy. On April 20, Colonel Derricks made a reconnaissance for new positions near Castelnuova di Magra and the 597th moved later in the day to the positions selected. The 597th's mission changed from direct support of the 758th and reinforcing the 588th to reinforcing the 599th in support of the 442nd Infantry.

Captain Macklin was assigned as LnO with the 599th, while Captain Hargrove relieved Captain Buchanan as LnO with the 598th:

> Apr. 20, 1945—I relieved Captain Buchanan as LnO with 598th. I reported to them near Fossola. Bn relieved from reinforcing firs of 598th w/473rd Inf to reinforce 599th w442nd Inf. Arrived at 1900 at 598th CP reporting to Major Starbuck, notified him of bobby-trapped body of dead German soldier. Made myself comfortable. Just talked with Dusty; he's getting ready to go up front. It is pretty rough over here and the 598th is getting a lot of calls for fire. Major Starbuck called for an FO; I called Colonel Derricks and he sent Burton. Received orders to report to the 599th. General Support mission. (HBH/D)

On April 21, Captain Hargrove relieved Captain Macklin as LnO with the 599th:

> Apr. 21, 1945—I relieved Captain Macklin as LnO with 599th. Relay station and switching central at Fort Bastione 838–108. Collins and Turner manned my phone there. Communications went out; I got in touch with Collins and told him to get out on the line immediately. They did; meanwhile I communicated with Bn through the relay station. Boutte and his party came up but had no assignment for them so I had them wait with us in Castelpoggia.
>
> Saw Sanders today; he told me about some narrow squeaks. The 599th FDC is noisy. The men are pretty good but the white officers think *they* [author's italics] are the great ones. They'll probably get all the awards and decorations, too. They don't think much of me or the 597th which doesn't surprise me. I haven't found any white folks who do even before they've seen us perform. (HBH/D)

On pages 149–52 of *Journey to Washington*, Senator Daniel K. Inouye (D—Hawaii) describes an action by the 442nd Infantry that took place on April 22, during which he lost an arm. Inouye, then a first lieutenant in Company E of the 442nd, led a successful attack against the Germans on Mount Musatello, for which he was awarded the Distinguished Service Cross. At the time of the action, the 597th was reinforcing the 599th and furnishing two FOs in support of the 442nd.

For the first time, as the war began to wind down, 597th personnel had the chance to act as liberators:

> Apr. 22, 1945—We are still chasing the Germans but it looks as if he is just about done for. For the first time I get to actually play the role of liberator. There is something about riding into a town that the Germans left just a little while before, and having all of the townspeople lining the streets, throwing flowers, cheering and waving. Some of them may not mean it, but all of them have had enough practice to make it look genuine. (MC/FDC)

On April 22, Colonel Derricks and members of his staff made a reconnaissance for new positions in the vicinity of Castelpoggio and Gragnana. Later, the battalion moved to positions near Gragnana, where, upon arrival at the position, Battery B, 597th, was assigned a new mission of direct support of the 2nd Bn., 370th Inf., and Captain McCants was assigned as LnO. This battalion had remained in the coastal sector throughout the April offensive but was then en route on a cross-country forced march from the Mount Folgorito ridge through Gragnola to join its parent unit coming from the Serchio sector. The ultimate mission of the 370th was to contact the 442nd Inf. at Aulla by an extremely wide enveloping action from its position in the Serchio Valley.

On April 23, a radio relay was established at three points for communication with 2nd Bn., 370th, while Lieutenant Jacobs—who except for me had the longest service in the 597th as an officer—was transferred to the 598th.

The situation along the 92nd Division front had become so fluid by April 24 that no front line in the usual sense existed. Only pockets of resistance were left, but it was expected that the Germans would fight a delaying action until pressure forced them to capitulate.

Although less than a week of the war remained, the 597th experienced some of its greatest difficulties during that short period. For example, the 473rd Infantry had taken the high ground north of S. Stefano on the Sarzana–Aulla highway on April 23:

> Apr. 24, 1945—By 0900, 24 April, S. Stefano was occupied and elements of the 1st Bn which had been moved to the left flank attacked to seize high ground north of S. Stefano and Albiano. By 1700, the 1st Battalion had been withdrawn from sector and waited [for] motors to move west of La Spezia. The 3rd Battalion had occupied the high ground northeast of S. Stefano and was also withdrawn to move to La Spezia. (598A Hist)

The 442nd Infantry was approaching Aulla from the southeast and east, while the 597th was reinforcing the 599th in support of the 442nd. The 92nd Division was still operating on the basis of Field Order No. 10, which provided for it to advance in the coastal sector. Colonel Derricks had been directed to reconnoiter for positions south of and as close as possible to Aulla to reinforce the 599th in their support of the 442nd. The positions he selected were just beyond the S. Stefano area from which the 473rd had just withdrawn.

At 1230 on the 24th, Colonel Derricks led a reconnaissance party through Sarzana to Isola, a small village north of S. Stefano, just beyond the area from which the 473rd Infantry was withdrawing. It was located along the Sarzana–Aulla highway at a hairpin bend in the Magra River, about 3 miles southwest of Aulla. Although the stretch of the highway between Isola and Aulla had not yet been traveled by any of our units, it was assumed that it would become a main supply route for any advance to the north and would receive engineer support commensurate with that status.

After selecting the position area for the battalion, the party returned to the old area, arriving there at 1830. Colonel Derricks issued instructions for the battalion to prepare to close station at the old position by 2230 and begin the move to the new position.

In the meantime, according to the 92nd Division Artillery history, Field Order 11 was issued:

> Apr. 24, 1945—At 1600B a telephone call from Division (to Division Artillery) changed the entire operational picture—the Fifth Army had ordered the Division to take Genoa ...
> The mission of the 92nd Division under Field Order 11 was to seize Genoa; to pursue the enemy north on Highways 62 and 63 to Cisa and Cerrata and to prepare for further advance.
> CT 473 was given the mission to pursue the enemy in the direction of Genoa.
> The mission of CT 370 was to pursue the enemy in zone north to the oie [sic] Cisa pass–Cerreta Pass.
> 442nd Inf was to constitute the Division Reserve
> 597th FA Bn was attached to 370th Infantry.
> 111th Field Regiment was attached to the 597th for operational control. (92A Hist)

Examination of the 92nd Division Artillery Journal discloses that, at 1730, one hour before Colonel Derricks and the 597th reconnaissance party arrived back in the old area, the Division Artillery Executive received additional instructions pertaining to the 597th:

> Apr. 24, 1945—1730B—From Lt Col Ross—[DivArtyExec]
> (1) 597 FA Bn to occupy positions close to 599 FA Bn ... CO 597 to go to 599 FA Bn and locate the 599 FA Bn btry positions and occupy them when 599 FA Bn withdraws. 597 to send Ln O's and FO's to 370 Inf immediately.
> (2) 599 to stay in position until 442 Inf clears Aulla. (92A Jnl)

Under the circumstances, the division plan for the 597th to occupy positions in the area to be vacated by the 599th was the most feasible solution to the problem caused by the change in mission. The 597th could move over the same roads used and maintained as the main supply route by the supported unit, the 370th Infantry, to which it was now attached. It could move, without difficulty and in a relatively short time, to the 599th's positions near S. Terenzo, about 5 miles northwest of the present position of the 597th.

There is nothing in the available 597th or 92nd Division Artillery records to indicate that Colonel Derricks ever received the movement instructions included in the division plans. If he had done so, I am confident that he would have canceled the planned movement to Isola, and would have moved to occupy the positions vacated by the 599th instead.

In the meantime, Hargrove reported to the 370th Inf. as LnO:

> Apr. 24, 1945—Bn from reinforcing 599 to support of 370 as part of CT 370. Bn moved to positions near Isola. I was ordered to report to 3rd Bn, 370 Inf, as Ln O. It was dark when I got my orders from the Colonel by radio. He didn't know where to tell me to report to. But, by questioning 599th, I learned there was a rear CP in vicinity of Pallerone. Had Vappie, Boutte, A. Williams, Pugh (FO) in my party. Found Pallerone, left part of my party there, moved up to vic [vicinity] Quercia where the Bn CP was. Went along with the mule train, left both jeeps at Pallerone, on foot. Rough. Couldn't contact Bn. Cpl Johnston and Cpl Collins with me. (HBH/D)

One hour before the battalion began the move to Isola, a meeting of unit commanders was held at the Division Artillery CP to discuss future operations. The 597th was not notified of the meeting and there was no representative present from the 597th:

> Apr. 24, 1945—2130—Meeting of unit commanders at Div Arty CP with Gen Colbern. Present: Lt Col Baumgartner, C.O. 599 FA Bn; Col Stancisco, CO. 428 FA Grp; Lt Col Crockett, Div Arty S-3; Major Sharp, Div Arty S-Z. Subj: Future Operations. (92A Jnl)

Lacking instructions to the contrary, the 597th began the move to Isola as planned, a movement that turned out to be one of the most difficult and unnecessary made by the battalion during the war. A portion of the move was made through a railroad tunnel and I still have a distinct memory of the discomfort as we bumped over each cross-tie. We started about 2200 hours, and although the distance was only 10 miles as the crow flies, we did not complete the move until 0700 hours the next morning. When we arrived in the new position, the troops were exhausted and the vehicles were in need of maintenance and repair.

Shortly after arriving in the new area, I had my first opportunity to consider the impact on our operations of the change in the division's mission, especially the new organization for combat which made the 597th a part of CT 370. Now that we had been detached from Division Artillery, I was especially disturbed at the possible difficulty of providing continuous support to the infantry, since to do so would require us to move our howitzers rapidly over roads that the retreating enemy had made impassable for vehicles.

Without pausing to rest, I started immediately to reconnoiter for routes to move the battalion toward Aulla and beyond to support the advance of the 370th Infantry. The most direct route was northward up Highway 62/63, but after a brief reconnaissance, I discovered that the route was impassable because the bridges had been destroyed and the likely bypasses in the adjacent streambed had been extensively mined.

We had moved into a cul-de-sac and would probably have to travel back a long way to get out.

Since Colonel Derricks was getting some well-earned rest, I reported the situation to the battalion operations officer and to members of my S-2 section. I instructed them to disseminate the information about the mines to the battery commanders and the other staff personnel. Then I started again for Aulla, taking a round-about route, suitable for my jeep but unsuitable for larger vehicles.

When I reached the outskirts of Aulla, which had been taken by the 442nd Inf. only a few hours before, I encountered General Colbern. He was making his last reconnaissance in the area before joining the main elements of the 92nd Division in the race to Genoa up Highway 1.

I could not hide from General Colbern the fact that I was not full of "vim and vitality." He guessed correctly that my only sleep within the last 24 hours had been while sitting in my jeep. Accordingly, he ordered me to go back to my battalion headquarters and get some rest on my cot. Before I left, I informed him that the battalion had moved into a cul-de-sac and could not take a direct route northward out of the position until the engineers swept the mines and repaired the road. General Colbern stated that he recognized the problem but the division was spread out over a very large area in which the Germans had been very thorough in destroying the bridges and mining the bypasses. Priorities had to be established for the available engineer support since there was just not enough of it to take care of everything at once. Since we were now a part of CT 370, we would have to look to the 370th for that kind of support although it, too, was spread out and had to use its Regimental AT Co., Replacement Co., and the POWs to keep the road net open in its area.

I returned to the battalion headquarters at Isola, reported my discussion with General Colbern to Colonel Derricks, and attempted to get a couple of hours' sleep. But before long, my sleep was interrupted when two men were brought into the aid station next door. They were suffering from wounds inflicted by mines they had set off in the streambed adjacent to the highway; mines that I had discovered and reported only a few hours before:

Apr. 25, 1945—Reported to Lt Col Daugette in the morning and moved out with him. Still couldn't contact Bn. Bn went into direct support of 3rd Bn, 370 CT. Marched up Highway #62, reached Terrarosa, picking up several PWs on the way. Saw several German supply columns which had been messed up by our Air Corps. Entered Terrarosa, saw about 15 Chinese PWs who had worked for the Germans. They sure looked awful. I contacted Bn, registered on checkpoint. Notified Bn and received acknowledgement of message that I must reach Pontremoil in order to support 3rd Bn properly. But when we ran into trouble at Annunziata the next day, the Bn could do us no good. The drivers brought up the jeeps. Good for them. Didn't even have to send for them. (HBH/D)

Apr. 23, 1945—The 370th continued to move forward in the mountains northeast of Aulla and on the road north of Aulla. Little resistance was encountered. The 597th was not called on to fire in support of the 370th Inf—the Battalion only fired 3 registration missions during the day. (92A Hist)

Meanwhile, back in Isola, I finally went to sleep. But when I awoke, I was faced with some more bad news: Division Artillery had not issued us a new set of maps before they left the area. The last maps were issued in expectation that we would continue to follow the enemy withdrawal up Highway 1 northwest along the coast, but it did not include any tactical maps appropriate for our advance northward up Highways 62 and 63.

Therefore, early on the morning of the 26th, I left Isola for the new Division Artillery CP, somewhere up Highway 1 toward Genova, to obtain a set of tactical maps for use as firing charts for our changed axis of advance. En route to the Div. Arty. CP, I passed the still-smoking remains of some of the 92nd Division vehicles that had been destroyed by a German artillery concentration the day before, as indicated in accounts in the 473rd Inf., 92nd Artillery, and 598th Field Artillery histories:

> Apr. 25, 1945—At dawn of the 25th April 473 CT pushed off in the drive that would carry them in approximately 60 hours, some 110 miles up the Ligurian coast to Genoa ... The infantry rode tanks, jeeps and trucks, wherever possible, dismounting when held up by enemy resistance ... Working in this manner, the CT reached SESTRI LEVANTE by 1500 and continued up the coast road toward CHIAVRI. The speed of the advance caught the enemy short, and the Regtl I and R Platoon, out ahead of the main body of troops SE of CHIAVARI, ran flush into enemy artillery and infantry at ENTELLA (9284347), part of which was already in "March Order" and was making frantic efforts to withdraw. The enemy now had no choice but to fight and this he did viciously during the following 5 hours. Heavy enemy coastal guns at Porofino took the highway from SESTRI LAVANTE to CHIAVARI under devastating fire and the CT lost 12 jeeps, several 2½ ton trucks, some equipment and suffered casualties as a result of this fire. The infantry and tanks and D/S artillery deployed rapidly, engaged the enemy, inflicted heavy casualties on him, silenced his artillery near CHIAVARI, reorganized and prepared to continue the attack at dawn (473 Inf Hist)

> Apr. 24, 1945—The 473 CT attached one Btry of the 598 F A Bn to each of the Infantry Battalions for the advance toward Genoa. One Battalion of Infantry was motorized and with this column went B Btry, 598 FA Bn, commanded by 1st Lt Borden. It moved rapidly toward Genoa against sporadic resistance. In the vicinity of Chiavara (P28–37), on a straight stretch of road across a flat, the column was heavily hit by well emplaced 152mm and 105mm guns at 1500B, causing several casualties and loss of several vehicles. B Btry immediately dropped trails[1] and aided in silencing the guns. By 2300B Partisan patrols confirmed that the Germans had withdrawn. (92A Hist)

> Apr. 24, 945—At about 1500, the 2nd Bn met enemy resistance in vic Chiavari. Enemy 105[mm], and 152mm Arty hit the column (motor) hard and harassed the road vic Cav. Lt. Borden returned to move his battery into firing position and the Bn Comdr remained forward to organize the observation and firing of the tanks and cannon. The Regtl set up in Cavi when advance was stopped. B Btry was put into position ... to fire and silenced one enemy 152mm battery. (598A Hist)

I found the Division Artillery HQ, obtained a new set of maps, and began my return trip to the 597th in Isola. By the time I reached there late in the afternoon of the 26th, Colonel Derricks had selected new positions near Fillitiera and the 597th had started to move there. However, before the batteries left the old positions, several more men had been injured by mines.

The 370th Infantry was still pursuing the enemy:

> Apr. 26, 1945—Moved out early next morning [26 April]. Saw a mile-long column of dead horses and Germans' wrecked material. Air Corps again. Had just done it the day before. Just north of Terrarosa, moved out of range of relay station. Bn had not moved. Left Jeep at Villa Franca. Contacted relay station here. Told them again they would have to move to help us. Sent back message to Reg't for Col Daugette. Nearing Annunziata, greeted by flower throwing civilians. Fired on as leading elements entered Annunziata—mortars, artillery, snipers. Stopped for the night. Received permission from Col Daugette to go back to try to get Bn up. Met Col Sherman on way back and did he raise hell! Bn had not even left Isola … B Battery got in position and fired at 0500 next morning. (HBH/D)

By April 29—with the 370th at the Cisa and Ceretta passes, the 442nd and 473rd north and northwest of Genoa, and the British Eighth Army and American Fifth Army north of the Po River—the shooting war in Italy was over. The formal surrender took place on May 2. (Goodman, 1952, 173–75; Lee, 1966, 588) From April 20 until the shooting stopped, the 597th had moved six times and had three major changes in mission.

Part V

The Long Way Home

CHAPTER NINETEEN

Two Down and One to Go

On May 1, Colonel Derricks and I left Pontremoli with a small reconnaissance party en route to Genova to find an assembly area there for the 597th and prepare for the events of the following day, which was expected to be especially eventful.

May 2 was indeed eventful. It marked the official end of hostilities in Italy, Colonel Derricks and I attended a 92nd Division victory parade in Genoa, and the 597th arrived in Genova from Pontremoli and was guided to the assembly area we had selected.

The victory parade included a detachment of Italian partisans, and a battalion each from the 442nd and 47rd Infantry Regiments. However, most of the organic elements of the 92nd Division were represented only by their massed colors:[1]

> May 2, 1945—To honor the Partisans for their part in the liberation of the Ligurian coast, a Victory Parade in which the 2nd Battalion and elements of the Cannon Company represented the regiment, was held in Genoa on 2 May 1945. The troops and a large Partisan detachment were reviewed by the Commanding General, 92nd Infantry Division and G-5, 5th Army. Citations were presented to outstanding Partisans for their efforts. (473Inf Hist)

The victory parade was followed by a decoration ceremony during which Colonel Derricks was awarded a Bronze Star Medal.[2] After the ceremony, Derricks and I rejoined the 597th, then arriving in Genoa after the trip from Pontremoli. Captain Hargrove had traveled with the battalion from Pontremoli:

> May 2, 1945—left 0100 to move with Bn to Genoa. Rumor has it that the Germans have surrendered. We have served 167 consecutive days and have fired 55,822 [artillery] rounds.
> Villa Soldi—Via Pisa—Genoa. Arrived Genoa, 1500, via Sarzana, La Spezia, Chiavari, Rapallo. Officers put up at a former coffee merchant's house. We heard that Colonel Derricks received the Bronze Star in a decoration ceremony.
> Genoa is quite a place; everybody is quite happy to see us and we can get just about anything we want. Our 92nd Recon troops were the first Allied soldiers in the city but the 473rd tried to get credit for it. It's a beautiful city, kind of beat from bombings (Allied) and shellings. (HBH/D)

For the first time in several days, I found time to write a letter to my wife:

May 2, 1945—Events have moved so swiftly in the past two weeks that I have only now caught up. As part of a victorious Army, we have covered a lot of territory. You have read by now, I'm sure, that we took Genoa. It is a very nice city—surprisingly modern.

Everywhere we have gone, we have been welcomed by cheering crowds, flowers, etc. These people have plenty of practical experience in doing this sort of thing because, according to them, the Germans and Fascists made them do it. We have observed what years of practice can do—because they can really put on a show—but now they say they do it voluntarily. (MC/FDC)

On May 3, the 597th moved to Bolzanetto, about 5 miles north of Genoa. As usual, I had to go back to a previous position (the assembly area in Genova) to check for items left behind, and I could not participate in the initial competition for a place to stay. Since I was a staff officer with only a small section, I had nobody to look after those requirements. Accordingly, when I returned to Bolzanetto after my trip, all the choice accommodation had been taken.

A partisan found out about my problem and insisted on helping me to solve it. When I first met him, he was still wearing the colorful costume he had worn during the May 2 parade, and he had a submachine gun hanging by a sling from his shoulder.

As the first step in solving my problem, I complied with his request and accompanied him to the finest apartment building in the city, where he confronted the manager and demanded that he find a room for me. The manager replied that all apartments in the building were taken and there was not a single room available. The partisan ordered the manager to show us, requiring each apartment to be opened for inspection. We found occupants in all of the apartments except one, in which we found only furniture and personal items.

The partisan asked for the name of the individual who leased that apartment. When the manager supplied the name, the partisan noted that the individual was a Fascist "fat cat" whose office was in a Genova skyscraper and who had a family and a fine home elsewhere in the city. The apartment was obviously used for his extramarital adventures.

The partisan cradled the machine gun in his right arm and, standing about a foot away from the apartment manager, explained that we were going to leave for about 30 minutes, but when we returned we expected to find the apartment empty and available for me to move into.

When we returned to the building, the apartment was indeed empty, most of the furniture and personal items were in the hallway, and the manager was making room for them in some of his storage rooms. A few minutes later, the apartment leaser arrived, having been summoned from Genova. He greeted me pleasantly, showed no ill will, and assisted the manager in finding a place for his property.

On May 6, Chaplain Diggs held religious services in the new battalion area, during which Colonel Derricks addressed the congregation.

May 6, 1945—The people around here were not hit as hard by the war as those to the south. It appears that life has gone on here not too different from life in America except that just about everything is rationed. Also, the people seem to ignore race.

The young people I have met all say they want to go to America. One woman said she wants to go to America to divorce her husband because she cannot get a divorce here.

The coast line of Italy is very beautiful. Beginning at Viareggio, there is a continuous beach all the way around to Marinello di sarzana. The land is flat along the coast for about four miles inland; then it rises abruptly up into the mountains. Most of Italy's towns seem to be on or around hills. (MC/FDC)

The next day, it was reported that hostilities in northern Europe had ceased:

May 7, 1945—The radio is really giving the details of the San Francisco [United Nations] Conference and the coming of VE Day. I only hope and pray it will mean your coming home soon. (FDC/MC)

On May 11, the 597th participated in a practice division artillery parade in the Gonova [Genoa?] Stadium. A week later, the formal parade took place in the same stadium and was reviewed by the division commander, British naval officers, and local partisan officers. At this ceremony, Staff Sergeants William L. Hobson and Booker T. Simpson, both of the 597th, received their commissions as second lieutenants.

During the night of May 19/20, the 597th moved to Varazze, a seaside resort along the Ligurian seacoast, about 20 miles west of Genoa:

May 23, 1945—Battalion moved to Varazze on the Italian Riviera. Each battery is housed in a special hotel. The officers are located in a beautiful small hotel, the Astoria, overlooking the Ligurian Sea. It is a beautiful town and the people are reasonably glad to see us although I suspect there are quite a few Fascists and German sympathizers left. (HBH/D)

The unit now wound down from the grueling pace of the preceding month of combat by starting a training program built around information and education activities.

597th Field Artillery Battalion, Varazze, Italy, June 13, 1945.

The tactical mission of 92nd Division Artillery changed from combat operations to one of administration and training. The division accelerated the program of sending officers and enlisted men on rest leaves and furloughs to facilities established by the Fifth Army and 92nd Division. Each battalion in the 92nd Division Artillery initiated a practice of holding frequent parades and ceremonies (NA RG 407, 18305, May 45, 1), which were conducted for the purpose of presenting decorations and awards to personnel who had earned them during combat.[3]

Col. Wendell T. Derricks in Varazze, Italy. (OHS)

> This training program was built around I and E [information and education] activities, competitive athletics, basic military and artillery training. The program was scheduled for one month.
>
> A survey was made of the scholastic desires and educational background of the men. Each Battalion organized its own individual I and E training featuring literacy training, on-the-job-training. In some battalions, Unit Schools were established, making use of local Italian school facilities. However, due to the temporary nature of the program, emphasis was placed on counseling men, helping them to get straightened away on post-war school plans and enrolling them in USAFI correspondence courses. Weekly orientation was carried on, concentrating primarily on Redeployment and discussion of the Japanese War. In connection with the Redeployment discussion, the US Army film, "Two Down and One to Go", was shown to all available men. (92A Hist/May 45)

Selected personnel participated in an inventory of the battlefields covered during the April offensive operations. After the 597th moved to Varazze, Lieutenant Harold Connor and I returned to our recent battle area in the vicinity of Aulla and Carrara to carry out an inventory of small arms, artillery material, and ammunition abandoned by the enemy. We found a great deal of ammunition, as well as many artillery pieces which had been disabled by the enemy before he withdrew. I took advantage of the opportunity to visit the former enemy gun positions on Punta Bianca to see the guns, which they had used so effectively against our forces in the coastal sector. I confirmed that their tubes had been rendered useless by the enemy before he retreated:

92nd Division returns Columbus's ashes to the city of Genoa. (OHS)

May 23, 1945—During the past week, I went back over the entire area that we operated in during the last two months. People are repairing their houses and working in their fields. The roads are full of people going in both directions—going back home. (MC/FDC)

The division artillery chaplains aided the battalions in conducting memorial services for the men lost in combat. (93A Hist May 45)

> May 27, 1945—Bn Memorial Service in Cinema Margherita for Bn deceased (personnel) attended by Gen Colbern and Lt Col Ross. (597A Jnl)

On May 28, the 597th held a retreat parade and decoration ceremony on the Battalion Parade Ground in Varazze, with General Colbern as Reviewing Officer. Bronze Star Medals were presented to Major Turnley, Lieutenants Connor and Simpson, and Corporal Griffith, while Air Medals were presented to Lieutenants Eskridge, Conquest, and Moore. Good conduct medals were awarded to over 300 enlisted men of the battalion.

The men of the 597th found Varazze a very pleasant place to stay, with excellent recreation and athletic facilities. Among the principal forms of recreation in Varazze were bathing and boating in the Ligurian Sea:

> May 29, 1945—We have a nice beach here. Every afternoon it is full of people. When the sea is "quiet," there are also many people boating.
> The Town "belongs" to us, for all practical purposes. The people are impressed with the conduct of the soldiers and they especially like our frequent parades and ceremonies. (MC/FDC)

On June 1, General Colbern left 92nd Division Artillery for assignment elsewhere. He was replaced by the Division Artillery Executive, Lieutenant Colonel Robert C. Ross, who was promoted to colonel on that same date. This was considered necessary because Colonel Derricks outranked Ross as a lieutenant colonel.

The next day, Battery C left Varazze and traveled by motor vehicle back to an area south of Viareggio to begin a training program in preparation for deployment to the Pacific theater. The personnel of the remaining batteries of the battalion continued to enjoy their stay in Varraze:

> Jun. 3, 1945—Sunday—I just returned from the beach. Today is a beautiful Sunday and it seems that everybody is out on the beach, swimming or boating. The sea is very calm—even babies are in the water. We are participating in things that were only possible to read about years ago. I have been told that Monte Carlo and Nice are only about three hours drive; Switzerland and Austria about six; and Venice about eight. (MC/FDC)

The Sunday afternoon baseball game between the 597th FA Bn. and the 317th Engineer Bn. was won by the 597th by a score of six to five.

A special division ceremony was conducted in Genoa on June 6 to return the ashes of Christopher Columbus to that city.[4]

CHAPTER TWENTY

A Special Mission Carried out From Varazze

During World War II, the success achieved by each field artillery battalion was judged in terms of missions completed, rounds fired, enemy casualties inflicted, damage to enemy equipment and facilities, and decorations and awards earned.

More than 600 US Army field artillery battalions took part in the war. (Sawicki) On the basis of the foregoing criteria, many may be judged more successful and some less successful than the 597th. However, on a mission-by-mission basis, no other battalion can match the type of success achieved by the 597th in one special mission. During that mission, not a single howitzer was placed into position; not a single round of ammunition was fired; no casualties were inflicted on enemy personnel; and no enemy equipment or facilities were damaged. Yet the results achieved by that mission were far more gratifying than anything accomplished by the 597th in any of the previous 1,864 missions.

Toward the end of May, in order to aid in the establishment of the Allied military government and the initiation of civil relief measures in the province around Genoa, armed sector patrols, consisting of one officer and at least 10 enlisted men, were sent out daily by the Division Artillery units to visit outlying towns and villages. The mission of the patrols was to contact local civilian and partisan authorities to obtain information considered essential for the reestablishment of law and order in the area.

The patrols did not have authority to issue orders to partisans or to interfere with the Italian officials. Daily reports of the situation were sent to Division Headquarters.

The 597th Battalion Intelligence Officer organized and commanded the patrol for his battalion. During the last week in May, the patrol began to carry out a mission which required it to visit about 30 towns and villages at least once each week in an assigned sector about 25 miles west of Varazze.

Although the war had ended a month before, the 597th Field Artillery Battalion had to accomplish one last tactical mission. On May 28, a directive was issued by the 92nd Infantry Division Headquarters:

May 28, 1945—The 92nd Infantry Division has established its forces in the Ligurian Area, and portions of the contiguous areas thereto, as a military occupational force for the elimination

597th sector patrol in small Italian village, June 1945. (OHS)

of German or Fascist Italian formations and the re-establishment of law and order among the civilian population ...

... Each senior tactical commander will operate visiting patrols within his zone so that all towns and areas where there is no AMG (Allied Military Government) will be visited. (92nd InfDivLtr)

As one of the senior tactical commanders in the division, the 92nd Division Artillery commander issued 92nd Division Artillery Operations Instructions No. 1, dated May 30, to comply with the division directive:

May 30, 1945—Each battalion operates a DAILY PATROL (Minimum of 1 Officer and 10 EM) in assigned sectors to visit each of the following towns as often as practicable—At Least ONCE EACH WEEK. (597th FA Bn Sector)

This was followed by a list of 34 towns and villages in an area about 20 miles long, running generally north and south, and some 5 miles wide. The center of the area was about 20 miles west of where the 597th FA Bn. Headquarters was located in Varazze.

Patrols will contact Recognized Local Civil and Partisan Authorities; Obtain Information required by the Sector Report ... but will ISSUE NO ORDERS or interfere in NO [any] way with these Italian officials. (92A 01 No1)

As the Battalion Intelligence Officer and commander of the 597th Field Artillery Battalion Sector Patrol, my specific mission was to contact local civilian and partisan authorities in our assigned area to obtain information such as evidence of sabotage; unusual occurrences; unauthorized military personnel or vehicles; armed partisans; curfew hours; Germans or fascists in the area; and the attitudes of civilians and ex-partisans.

We operated our first patrol on Thursday, 31 May; the second on Friday, 1 June; and skipping Saturday and Sunday, operated the third patrol on Monday, 4 June. (597A Hist)

During the June 4 patrol, there was an incident considered significant enough to be noted in the Monthly 597th Battalion History Summary:

June 45: Patrol 040830 to Bormida ... Casseria, Carretto, Ville and Ferriera. Bn S-2, from Bn Hq and one officer and eleven enlisted men, from Btry B. ... Mrs. Frederick de Billier, in vic of Cairo, claims that she is an American Citizen. AMG (Savona) already notified. Patrol in at 1830. (597A Hist)

It was also significant enough to be mentioned in a letter to my wife:

Jun.11, 1945—Last week I met four members of a family who have had some remarkable experiences since 1940. One of them is an American citizen, Ms. Marry Hammond de Billier, of the Hammond family of New York ... Her nephew is John Hammond, one of Duke Ellington's good friends ...

Her daughter is married to a marquis, who is in the Italian diplomatic service. I met two of her daughter's children: Gloria, about 20; and Bobby, about 12. I took Gloria and Bobby on a jeep ride (she claimed it was her first), and they seemed to enjoy it ...

The Marquis is in Rome preparing for his next diplomatic assignment.

Two years ago they were living in Germany but they have had many difficult experiences since then, which caused them to change their family name and move to the old farmhouse where I found them. (MC/FDC)

Before the incident occurred, the patrol activity had been relatively uneventful—but instructive. I was beginning to understand how three towns in the general area (two of them in my sector) could be named Bormida and two named Rochetta. I had been told that the towns of the same name were in different communes (small administrative districts), and that the name of the commune was added when it was necessary to distinguish the towns from one another.

After completing our visits for the day, we started back to Varazze along the same route we had taken on the preceding Thursday and Friday. We were in a hurry to get back to the battalion area in Varazze to begin preparations for the two parades scheduled in Genoa on Tuesday and Wednesday. However, about a mile northwest of Cairo, our return trip was interrupted by an Italian boy, estimated to be about 12 years of age, who ran out into the road and waved his arms to attract our attention. He later recalled:

I ... stood by the roadside and shouted, "I, too, speak English," and [had a] feeling of relief when you stopped. (RFR/MC/1-2-86)

I had signaled the drivers to stop, partly out of curiosity, because it was unusual for young people in that area to speak English. The boy told me that his name was Bobby. His mother had watched us go by on one of our previous patrols, and when

Ms Marry Hammond de Billier and family, the Italian family saved by the 597th. (OHS)

she saw us approaching this time, she had sent him out to invite us to come by their house.

We followed Bobby to an old farmhouse, some distance away from the road, and one of the most unusual experiences of my career began to unfold. When we reached the house, I met three ladies, each one of a different generation. The youngest was Bobby's sister, and since she appeared to be about 20 years of age, I estimated his mother to be between 40 and 50 (she was actually 57 on her next birthday) and his grandmother to be between 60 and 70 (she was 79).

Bobby's sister was Gloria, his mother was Marchesa Virginia Ferrante di Ruffano, and his grandmother was Mrs. Mary Hammond de Billier. His brother, Giovanni, was not at home but was working as an interpreter in the Ferrania camera and film factory a few miles away.[1]

Mrs. De Billier told me an amazing story about her family. Her father, John Henry Hammond, had been the youngest general during the Civil War and General William Tecumseh Sherman's Chief of Staff. One of her brothers, Ambassador Ogden Hammond, was a well-known member of the U.S. diplomatic service. Another brother, John Henry Hammond, was a New York lawyer and financier, married to Emily Vanderbilt. Her first husband had been Lincoln MacVeagh, son of Isaac Wayne MacVeagh—who had served as Attorney General under President Garfield—and nephew of Franklin MacVeagh, who had served as secretary of the Treasury under President Taft. Her son, John Hammond MacVeagh, was an officer in the Army Air Force who had been in the U.S. Foreign Service for many years between the world wars. Her second husband, Frederic Ogden de Billier, had been a retired member of the U.S. diplomatic service. Her nephew, John Hammond, was the foremost discoverer of jazz talent in the United States and counted Lena Horne, Billie Holiday, Count Basie, Teddie Wilson, Lionel Hampton, and other prominent black entertainers among his friends.

Several years before World War II, she and Mr. de Billier had moved to a house in Cherbourg, northern France, where he died in 1935. She continued to live there until the house was taken over by the Germans as a military headquarters after the fall of France in 1940. Then she moved to Dresden in Germany, where her daughter's husband, Marquis Agostino Ferrante di Ruffano, was the Italian consul-general.

Mussolini had been Italy's dictator from 1921 until July 1943, when the Fascist Grand Council refused to continue to support his policies. As a result, King Victor Emmanuel III had dismissed him and placed him under arrest. However, Mussolini was freed two months later by a daring German rescue party, and he became head of a Fascist puppet government set up in northern Italy by Hitler.

Because the Marquis and his family were still loyal to King Victor Emmanuel, Mussolini dismissed the Marquis from his diplomatic post and the family was interned in northern Italy. A few months later, they escaped and moved, incognito, to the old farmhouse where I found them.

The Allied victory had restored the diplomatic status of the Marquis and, at the time of my visit, he had gone to Rome to prepare for his next diplomatic assignment.

The time seemed to pass very swiftly as I continued the fascinating conversation with the Marchesa and Mrs. de Billier, but finally we had to stop. I returned to Varazze with my patrol and reported the situation to my battalion commander, Lieutenant Colonel Derricks.

Colonel Derricks wanted to know if the family had any difficulty obtaining certain staple food items, which were not generally available to the civilian population in that area because of the shortages created by the war. I reported to him that, based upon my observations, they were having difficulty obtaining certain foods because they were still in short supply.

After a brief discussion, Colonel Derricks stated that, until Mrs. De Billier was repatriated or until civil relief measures were adequate in the area, we would consider her family to be unofficially attached to the 597th. Accordingly, he directed me to obtain whatever could be spared from the battalion's kitchens that could help to relieve the family's food shortages. Afterwards, I was to return to their home to see if our offer of food would be accepted.

I complied with his directions and returned to the old farmhouse with the items obtained from the battalion's kitchens. The family accepted our offer of food with gratitude. Since we were scheduled to leave the area in a few days, we furnished them with a supply which we hoped would last for several weeks. We invited the family to attend a dinner in Varazze as special guests on June 10, which was our last Sunday dinner before we moved from the area. Other guests included some members of the "Wings Over Jordan" choir, then touring the area:

> Jun. 11, 1945—Yesterday I brought part of the family to Varazze as guests for our Sunday dinner. They all speak several languages and are related to a lot of the European nobility. (MC/FDC)

The Marchesa, Gloria, and Bobby attended the dinner, but Mrs. De Billier, then over 79 years of age, declined our invitation. We were unable to obtain a sedan for the trip and she did not feel up to taking the long trip over poor mountain roads in the types of military vehicles available to us.

The outcome of our last mission was more gratifying than any of our previous missions because it involved a short period of contact with the most remarkable family any of us had ever met. Although we had only a short period of contact with the family, they were gracious enough to remember us long after memories of our other missions had faded into the dim shadows of the past.

A week after the war in the Pacific was over, Marchesa Ferrante di Ruffano wrote a letter to me on behalf of her family expressing their gratitude for the help provided by the 597th:

> It is so wonderful the war is over. I want to congratulate you that the nightmare of having to continue fighting in the Pacific is no more before you. You will be leaving Viareggio very soon, I think, and I want to express to you in the name of each of us, our deepest thanks for the infinite trouble you have taken to help us. We are still enjoying the good things you procured for us, and Bobby, especially, will continue to think of you for many months, maybe years!!—unless he grows too quickly.
> … My husband is still tied down in Rome …
> Good luck to you and may you have a pleasant crossing. My mother and Gloria, particularly, join me in sending you our most grateful thanks. (VFR/MC)[2]

I made my last visit to the Ferrante family about September 17 and, as I indicated in a letter to my wife about a week later, Mrs. De Billier was getting ready to return to the United States:

> Sep. 24, 1945—I wrote you that I was going on leave to Milano—but it was changed to Venice, instead. This time I got to know the place very well. While I was there, the Noble Sissle show, "Shuffle Along" came to Venice and stayed in my hotel—the Palazzo Al Mare, on the Lido di Venice.
> I cut short my stay in Venice and, in one day, made a trip all the way across Italy from the Adriatic to the Ligurian Sea to revisit the family I have mentioned in other letters. It was lucky that I did so, because they will all probably be gone before I get back.
> Mrs. De Billier was scheduled to sail yesterday, 23 September, on the *GRIPSHOLM* (the diplomatic ship), from Naples. She was very excited about it and invited me to visit her in New York …
> I was told that the rest of the family expected to go to Caracas, Venezuela, where the Marquis will be assigned. (MC/FDC)

A quarter of a century passed before I began, as part of my research for this book, to check the status of this family. When I contacted John Hammond in 1971, he stated that his Aunt Mary was dead. However, several years before her death, when she returned to the United States after the war, she had told him of an extraordinary occurrence in Italy in 1945. After I provided him with the details of my experience with the family, he indicated that he was convinced that she had been referring to the same thing.

In 1946, Mrs. de Billier had moved from New York to Santa Barbara, California, where she died in 1956 at the age of 90. (*Santa Barbara News Press*) My next contact was with Baroness Gloria Gasparini, who wrote to me later in 1971:

> Jul. 23, 1971—Both mother and father remember your great kindness at the end of the war and if my grandmother were still alive, she too would want you to know how grateful we all are to you …
> … Wishing you much luck in the publication of your Book. (GFR/MC)

Marquis Agostino Ferrante di Ruffano and his wife, Marchesa Virginia di Ferrante di Ruffano, moved to Santa Barbara in 1952. Marchesa Ferrante di Ruffano died in 1973 at the age of 85, followed a year later by Marquis Ferrante di Ruffano at the age of 90. (*Santa Barbara News Press*)

Robert Ferrante di Ruffano received a BS Degree in Economics from Georgetown University and then graduated from the American Institute of Foreign Trade in Phoenix in preparation for a career in American business abroad. (*Santa Barbara News Press*)

***

On June 13, three days before leaving Varazze, the 597th held a retreat parade and decoration ceremony with awards presented by Colonel Ross. Bronze Star Medals were presented to Lieutenant Marion L. Johnson, T/4 Ladson Livingston, Corporal Carl E. Proctor, and to me. Oak Leaf Clusters to Air Medals were presented to First Lieutenants Chauncey Eskridge and James S. Christian, Jr. The "Wings Over Jordan" choir were again among the visitors. (597A Hist) I mentioned the event in a letter home:

> Jun. 16—Here are a few pictures I took recently. Last week I received the Bronze Star Medal for meritorious achievement in combat. The Wings Over Jordan Choir was present for the ceremony and for supper afterwards. Some of them appear in the pictures. Reverend Settle is next to Colonel Derricks. (MC/FDC)

About two weeks after we moved back to the Viareggio area, I received responses from my brother and my wife concerning the news of the June 13 decoration ceremony in Varazze:

> Jun. 23, 1945—GOOD GOING on the BRONZE STAR! (WJC/MC)

> Jun. 26, 1945—Congratulations Captain on your receiving the Bronze Star for meritorious achievement in combat. (FDC/MC)

CHAPTER TWENTY-ONE

Preparing for Redeployment

On June 15, the 597th conducted the last sector patrol in its assigned area and made final preparations to leave Varazze, and the following day moved by motor vehicle convoy back to the area between Pisa and Viareggio. There it joined Battery C and began a training program to prepare for redeployment to the Pacific theater.

A Special Service Theater was constructed – the new 597th FA Bn Area as a memorial for PFCs Robert Curry and Herman Rochelle.

On August 6, the first atomic bomb ever used was dropped on Hiroshima, Japan. This was followed by a second bomb on August 9, this time on Nagasaki. After Japan surrendered on the 14th, World War II was over and the remainder of the training program for the 92nd Division was cancelled. (Goodman, 1952, 181)

On June 15, the 597th operated the last sector patrol in its assigned area west of Varazze, and on June 16 the remainder of the 597th moved by motor vehicle convoy from Varazze back to a tent camp in the area between Pisa and Viareggio to join Battery C. (597A Hist)

Shortly after we arrived, I wrote a letter to my wife recounting some recent events:

> Jun. 16, 1945—We have moved from Varazze and are now in a tent camp south of Viareggio very near where we started. The citizens of Varazze were very sorry to see us leave.
>
> … Since the war stopped, many white soldiers have come into the area and tried to enlighten the people about how things are in America concerning our race, and articles have appeared in print. However, it is difficult for them to change the people's attitude about us in an area where our soldiers have stayed for ten months and we will probably be gone before that happens.
>
> We only stayed in the Genoa area a few weeks. That area had been occupied for years by the Germans whose views on race were well known. Then it was arranged that most of the soldiers who went first into Genoa were white. They had several days to enlighten the people there, but it appears that they were not effective. (MC/FDC)

On the same date, I wrote a memorandum to all batteries in the 597th, advising them of what I had been told by the 92nd Division Historical Committee:

> Jun. 16, 1945—In the near future the 92nd Division will publish a book with a brief history of each unit in the division. This history will include pictures of unit activities and personnel.

> It is desired that the 597th FA Bn have the best possible representation in this Division History. (MC/597)

We were extremely disappointed when the Division History was published a few weeks later because it included only 50 words about the 597th, and there was no mention of Colonel Derricks' name anywhere in it.[1]

> On 25 June, Division Artillery began a training program ... to prepare the Division Artillery for redeployment to the Pacific Theatre through the United States. (92A Hist)

On June 27, Colonel Derricks began a seven-day period of leave and Major Turnley assumed temporary command of the 597th while Derricks was absent. On the afternoon of the day of Derricks' departure, a serious motor vehicle accident occurred on Highway 1 between Pisa and Migliarino. Technician Fourth Grade Sammie C. Johnson, Medical Detachment, and Sergeant Joseph Coles, Headquarters Battery, 597th, were fatally injured. Johnson died immediately; Coles died in the hospital on June 30. (597A Hist)

On June 30, I had the sad duty of representing the battalion commander at the funeral for Johnson held at the U.S. Military Cemetery at Vada in central Italy. The entire 597th Medical Detachment and a representative from each battery attended. On July 3, I returned to Vada for the funeral of Sergeant Coles; all of Headquarters Battery and representatives from each of the other batteries attended. (597 Hist)

The following day the 597th participated in the division Independence Day ceremony:

> July 4, 1945—Independence Day ceremony at the Division Review Field ... Wings Over Jordan Choir sang four numbers and a 48-gun salute was fired by "B" Battery, 597th Field Artillery Battalion. (92A Hist)

My brother, William, a communications specialist in the 332nd Fighter Group Headquarters, had written to me that he wished we could get together before he left Italy to return to the United States:

> Jun 23, 1945—I just returned from Rest Camp where I met the 365th. I heard where you were located but it was much too far unless I had a direct ride.
>
> I am at Cattolica Air Port. This is just south of Rimini. We are almost on the Adriatic Sea ...
>
> I wish you could come over here and visit with us [332nd Fighter Group] a few days. I am expecting to go home on rotation as soon as they call the 95-point class. Do you expect to stay with the Army, and how many points have you? I have seven battle participation stars. (WJC/MC)

About a week later, while Colonel Derricks was on his seven-day leave, he visited the 332nd Fighter Group and met my brother.[2] Derricks told me about the meeting with my brother when he returned to the battalion on July 4, but did not tell me that he had made arrangements for my brother to visit me. As a matter of fact, I did not find out about that until my brother described the meeting and the arrangements in a letter he wrote to me many years later:

I had a pleasant meeting with Colonel Derricks at the headquarters of the 332nd Fighter near Rimini, Italy, in July 1945. Despite his numerous ribbons, medals and service stripes, he made me feel that he was just another soldier. His (buffalo) shoulder patch led me to ask him if he knew my brother, Captain Clark. He replied that he did … Before I excused myself from his presence, I expressed my desire to see my brother.

Within a week, without further effort on my part, arrangements were made for me to do so. On the specified day, the Executive Officer of the 332nd, Colonel Nelson S. Brooks, drove me to the air strip and directed me to ride the mail plane to the air strip at Pisa, where a motor vehicle from the 597th was waiting to transport me to a happy reunion with my brother. (WJC/MC/6-7-84)

Major Clark's reunion with his brother, William Clark. (OHS)

During this period, medals were presented to Captain Charles L. Pickett, First Lieutenant Leon E. Burton, Staff Sergeant John L. Carter, Private First Class Otis E. Foster, and Private David McAlliaster. (597A Hist)

On August 8, the 597th held a special retreat parade and decoration ceremony on the battalion parade ground at Migliarino. Colonel Derricks presented Division Commander's Commendations to First Lieutenant James R. Mundy, Battalion Headquarters; Staff Sergeant Isreal Payton, Technician Fourth Grade Thomas E. Williams, and Technician Fifth Grade James D. Coker, Headquarters Battery; Private Waverly Fitzgerald, Medical Detachment; First Sergeant Raleigh Bowen, Battery A; Corporal Davis Edwards, Technician Fifth Grade Robert Meeks, Private First Class Otis Foster, and Private George Smith, Battery B; Technician Fourth Grade Earl L. Vappie, Battery C; and First Sergeant Cleveland Rutledge, Service Battery.

Early in July, General Almond directed that an award orientation program be implemented for decorated personnel in the 92nd Division and attached units:

1. All decorated personnel of your command will be individually informed and instructed in the significance and details of the particular operation for which he received his award.
2. This will include locating in detail the exact locations, explaination [*sic*] of the mission and scope of the operation on the Regimental and Division level.
3. If possible, he will be taken to the area so he may examine the terrain over which he was fighting.
4. This will be considered as a part of the time allotted for I & E Orientation. (92nd Div Mem 7-8-45, Subject: Award Orientation)

I developed a plan and a detailed schedule for the orientation of the decorated personnel in the 597th, and made a preliminary visit to most of the applicable locations:

Jul. 13, 1945—I went on a picture-taking trip back over the area we occupied earlier this year. Many were taken in Sommacolonia where the trouble occurred on 26 December 1944. (MC/FDC)[3]

In a somewhat prophetic letter to my wife, I described some of the continuing dangers to personnel caused by mines that the enemy had left behind:

Jul. 13, 1945—The weather is hot here even on the seashore. The beaches are full every afternoon, although there are still some places that mines have not been removed and each day one is reminded of that by hearing that somebody else was blown to bits. (MC/FDC)

Five days later, an explosion in the vicinity of the Enlisted Men's Red Cross Club in Viareggio caused the building to collapse. Twenty-three Army personnel were killed, including Private First Class Robert L. Montgomery, of Battery C. Private Herbert T. Cheltenham, also of Battery C, was injured along with several other Army servicemen. (597A Hist)

First Lieutenant Norman Jacobs, a former member of the 597th, arrived at the scene of the disaster soon after it happened:

After General Almond issued an order that the beaches had to be cleared of mines to prevent accidents, several units removed mines from the beaches and stored them next to the E.M. Service Club.

On 18 July I was on my way into Viareggio with a small group of my men when I heard an explosion and saw smoke on the horizon in the direction we were going. When we arrived in Viareggio, the dust of the explosion was settling.

We saw some persons walking around bleeding; they were dazed and confused; the MPs and some medical personnel were rounding up the wounded. At first, no one seemed to know what caused the blast—but then it was revealed that the mines were responsible and the MPs began to clear the area for fear of more explosions.

I had offered my help and that of my detail when I arrived. After about half an hour with no one seeming to be in charge, I took my men and moved into the rubble ... Dust was everywhere and we could hear moaning within the debris. We began to clear the rubble with our hands and tools from our truck. I cautioned my men about wires and the possibility of more explosions as they began to clear the stones and the broken mortar away. Others began to join us. We found one body—but he was dead, crushed by falling stones. Someone found a girl who was crying and appeared to be badly hurt.

By this time, others began to arrive with tools, wrecking bars, shovels and bolt cutters. We helped them until it started to get dark. We found no more bodies but others did find some, most of them dead.

I called my men together and returned to Torre del Lago. I never did know how many were lost in this disaster. The girl we found was working in the Club. I hope she recovered. The others I saw were not so lucky. The war was over and yet our men were still dying!!! (WJ/MC/10-24-76)

On July 30, the emphasis on training was switched to preparation for Army Ground Force Tests to be fired in October. (92A Hist Jul 45) The Montecatini Redeployment Training Area Artillery Range was designated for the conduct of service practice

Red Cross Service Center after land mines exploded in July 1945, killing several black soldiers and civilians. (OHS)

by the battalions of 92nd Division Artillery. However, this phase of training lasted less than two weeks, during which only two service practices were conducted by the 597th. The first was conducted on August, with Battery C firing, and the last on August 6, with Battery B firing. (597A Hist)

The service practice on August 6 was the last conducted by the 597th during World War II, because on that same date the first atomic bomb ever used was dropped on Hiroshima, Japan. This was followed by a second atomic bomb on August 9, this time on Nagasaki. After Japan surrendered on the 14th, World War II was over and all training programs were cancelled. (Goodman, 1952, 181; 597A Hist)

As the war was ending, Colonel Derricks left for a 10-day leave in Switzerland and Major Turnley assumed temporary command of the 597th during his absence.

CHAPTER TWENTY-TWO

Three Down and It's Over

After Japan surrendered, deployment operations were suspended throughout the world and plans were made to return the troops that were not needed for occupation duty to the United States for discharge. Men would be discharged individually rather than by units. A point system would be established to determine the order in which they would be discharged. Since the War Department planned that the occupation forces would be composed as much as possible of volunteers, many service personnel with sufficient points to return to the United States volunteered to remain overseas. These were transferred to units designated as occupation forces.

Personnel shifts were made within the 92nd Division Artillery to transfer out those personnel who were remaining in Italy, either because of a lack of points or as a result of having volunteered to remain for occupation duty. Personnel from the 598th and 600th were transferred either to Headquarters, 92nd Division Artillery, or to the 597th or 599th Field Artillery Battalions. Afterwards, there was a consolidation of units, reducing to two the active field artillery battalion headquarters for the voyage home.

***

On August 17, Division Artillery held a formation at the theater named in honor of Curry and Rochelle, the two men from Battery A killed on February 17, 1945. Colonel Ross, Colonel Lane, and Colonel Ray addressed the soldiers.

On August 31, Colonel Derricks entered the 64th General Hospital and remained there until September 4, Major Turnley again assuming temporary command during his absence.

In periodic letters to my wife, I described some of my activities following the end of the war:

> Sep. 3, 1945—Last Thursday I went to Venice … but stayed parts of only 3 days. On Saturday morning, I gazed out over the Adriatic Sea. At 1000 hours, I left Venice and headed westward to Padua and then took Highway 11 through Verona, Vicenza and Brescia to Milano. From Milano,

Venice, Italy. (OHS)

I took Highway 35 to Genova where at sunset I watched the sun go down over the Ligurian Sea. I completed the trip back to Viareggio before midnight. (MC/FDC)

During September and October, the 92nd Division completed the remaining decoration ceremonies in the series that had started in May. Late in September, a parade and decoration ceremony was held on the Division Artillery Parade Ground. Colonel Derricks was among the persons to be decorated, scheduled to receive the Oak Leaf Cluster to the Bronze Star instead of the Legion of Merit that had been recommended initially by General Colbern. When General Wood, the acting division commander, started to make the presentation, Derricks refused to accept it.

After the ceremony, Derricks explained to the officers of the 597th that he had refused to accept the award because of his exceptional pride in the performance of the 597th. In his opinion, the level of the award made to the battalion commander was considered by the troops to reflect the Army's recognition of the performance of the battalion as a whole. Since two commanders of 92nd Division Artillery battalions (whose performance had not been superior to that of the 597th) had already received the Legion of Merit, it was felt an insult to the 597th to present a lesser award to their battalion commander.

***

The procedure for returning troops to the United States was outlined in a report to the Secretary of the Army by Gen. George C. Marshall, Chief of Staff of the U.S. Army:

> The day Japan capitulated orders were issued by the War Department to suspend redeployment operations throughout the world. Theater commanders were immediately directed to devote all facilities not required for the movement of occupational troops to the demobilization of the Army.
>
> It was decided to discharge men individually rather than by units. An Army-wide survey was conducted to determine the consensus among enlisted men as to the basis for determining discharge. The opinion was that those who had served the longest, fought the hardest, and who had children should be permitted to leave the Army first. As a result, the point system of returning men for discharge was established.
>
> This system gave credit for length of Army service, overseas service, certain decorations, battle stars and up to three dependent children under 18. The points were computed as of 16 September 1945. Originally a minimum requirement of 85 points was established. Subsequently, the point system was revised downward as necessary to keep the demobilization steady and orderly. (Marshall 1945, 225–226)

The 597th prepared for return to the United States by the transfer of men out of the battalion who did not have sufficient points for discharge as well as those personnel, including several officers, who volunteered to remain in Italy with units designated for occupation duty. It also accepted personnel into the battalion from the 598th and 600th. These battalions were being placed on an inactive status as the result of consolidation of 92nd Division Artillery units for return to the United States.

On August 16, 152 men were transferred out of the 597th. I wrote to my wife that, because of continuing racial discrimination, I was undecided about returning to the United States right away:

> Aug. 21, 1945—Most of the men are transferred to organizations which may stay over here a little longer ... I haven't decided yet whether or not I will stay in the Army ... I hear that the civilian job outlook in the US is not good at the present because there has been no real change in the policy of accepting whites first in all of the best jobs. (MC/FDC)

During the first week in September, Captains Charles L. Pickett, Battery C, and Lester McCants, Liaison Officer, were transferred to the 679th Tank Destroyer Battalion; Captain James Quisenberry, Service Battery, was transferred to Headquarters Battery as LnO; and Lieutenant Rose assumed command of Service Battery. Lieutenant Leonard Jackson was transferred to Battery C as Commanding Officer, and Lieutenant George Richardson was transferred to Battery B.

In mid-September, Captains Albert A. Briggs, Battery A, and Hondon B. Hargrove, LnO, were transferred to the 226th Engineer Service Regiment. First Lieutenant William Dix assumed command of Battery A.

During the last week in September, the black officers and all of their remaining men of the 598th and the officers and men of the 600th moved into the 597th area and were transferred to the 597th effective October 1. This resulted in the assignment of all of the black field grade officers in the 92nd Division Artillery, except one, to the 597th.[1]

The 597th received a total of 22 officers and 150 enlisted men from the 600th and seven officers, one warrant officer, and 115 enlisted men from the 598th. Some of these personnel subsequently were transferred to units remaining in Italy, and as a result, when the 597th sailed for the United States about five weeks later, a total of only 265 personnel remained in the battalion.

Captain Henry F. Shorter, Battalion Surgeon, and First Lieutenants William J. Cleveland and Tully Hickman, Liaison Pilots, were transferred from the 597th to Division Artillery Headquarters.

On October 11, the Italian Cross of Merit was awarded to the entire division in a special ceremony near the division headquarters. Colonel Derricks received the Italian Military Cross for Valor from Crown Prince Umberto, Lieutenant General of the Realm.

On October 14, Captains Wesley B. Johnson, Otis Buchanan, and I, together with three officers who had been transferred into the 597th from other units, were transferred to PBS units remaining in Italy:

> Following offs orgns indicated are reld asgmt and dy those orgns and are asgd as indicated …
> … Capt Wesley B. Johnson … 92nd Engr GS Regt …
> … Capt Otis Buchanan … 480th Port Bn …
> … Capt Major Clark … 92nd Engr GS Regt. (92Div SO 270 10–14–45)

> Oct. 27, 1945—Many changes have occurred in the past few weeks. The division was originally scheduled to sail about 1 November, but was delayed because of the lack of ships. All Class A Volunteers (like me) have been transferred out of the division to PBS units remaining here. I was placed in command of E Company, 92nd Engineer Regiment (no connection with 92nd Division), one of the first units to come to this theater. (MC/FDC)

Finally On November 6, Colonel Derricks led the "altered" 597th on the voyage back to the United States, boarding with 264 officers and men the Liberty ship *William T. Barry* at Leghorn. The move was reported:

> BUFFALO DIVISION REMNANTS WILL SAIL IN THREE GROUPS

> LEGHORN—3 November 1945—The 92nd Buffalo Division, only U.S. all-colored division to combat the German armies, will sail for the States in three groups starting November eighth.
> The first ship carrying 500 troops, will be followed by two others to leave the tenth port here on the 15th and 16th of November. Each will carry 1950 troops.
> Although, in name, the 92nd is leaving Italy, actually men are high point replacements. Many of the original 92nd men, lacking points, remain in Italy. (Penbase Press)

> BULLETIN!

> LIVORNO, ITALY—10 November 1945—Beginning return of the entire division after seventeen months overseas, the first contingent of Negro troops of the Ninety-second (Buffalo) Infantry Division sailed from this port for the United States Tuesday. (*Pittsburgh Courier*)

The 597th Field Artillery Battalion returning to the U.S.A. aboard the Liberty ship *William T. Barry* in November 1945.

I wrote to my wife that I and several other black officers had decided to stay in Italy and had persuaded many black enlisted men to reenlist in the Regular Army to enhance the chances for black representation in the peacetime Army:

> Nov. 13, 1945—Tomorrow the last units of the 92nd Division will begin leaving here to board the ship at Leghorn, the same place where we landed last year. As you know, I will not be leaving with the division because I volunteered to remain in the Army until 1947. For the time being, I am here in Italy but before long, I may be sent to France or Germany.
>
> There are about 50 of us Negro officers with enough points to return to the United States who decided to remain here to see how long we would be retained in the grades we hold. We have persuaded a large number of Negro soldiers to reenlist in the Regular Army to ensure that we have adequate representation in the peacetime Army. (MC/FDC)

The last units of the 92nd Buffalo Division left Leghorn Port for United States on November 17:

> Leghorn—17 Nov—Last units of the 92nd (Buffalo) Division embarked from Leghorn's 10th Port Monday for the United States with three of the theaters top ranking officers present at shipside ceremonies to see them off. Flanked by aides and a 92nd MP guard of honor, Lt Gen Matthew B, Ridgeway, Commanding General of MTO; Brig Gen John E. Wood, 92nd Division Commander and Brig Gen Francis H. O, Commanding General 1 PBS, briefly addressed the 1750 officers and men who for the past three hours had been loading of the SS *Eufala [Eufaula] Victory* ...
>
> Actually, the 92nd leaves Italy in name only, carrying high point replacements. (Penbase Press)

During the next week in Italy, I returned to some of the former combat position areas of the 597th:

Captain Major Clark, Leghorn, Italy, 1946. (OHS)

> Nov. 29, 1945—Last Thursday was Thanksgiving. I went back to some of the places that I passed by last year and early this year.
>
> People have begun to engage in their peace-time activities again. The train runs again over the railroad through Viareggio, Pietrasanta, Forte dei Marmi and Massa; however, people are still hitchhiking.
>
> I am sending you some pictures from my historical file. I intend to publish a history in a few years and I am compiling data now.
>
> In group 1 are some pictures taken about 6 August from a church steeple in Ortanova about 6 miles from Lucca. I was range officer for the battalion (which was firing service practice that day) and I used the church steeple (with permission) as a range tower to watch the range to the be sure that no civilian was in the restricted area while we were firing …
>
> Picture No. 2 should give you an indication of the mountainous country we were just in last winter. The picture was taken one Sunday last summer on the Fornaci–Barga road looking west toward Gallicano across the Serchio River.
>
> No. 3 was taken on Highway 1 near La Spezia on last June 16, while we were moving from Varazze to Migliarina …
>
> No. 4 is a picture of the factory (I still don't know what kind) where we stayed from 3 to 19 May. It is near Bolzanetto about 5 miles N of Genova.
>
> No. 5 is a view looking east down Highway 1 which runs through Varazze. We were coming from a parade on 12 June.
>
> No. 6 is a view looking up at what was once a church steeple in Sommacolonia. It tells its own story. That is where the trouble occurred last 26 December.
>
> No. 7 is a view of Hill 908 near Sommacolonia. The two bumps indicate where the Germans had two of their observation posts from which they could observe our positions in the valley. (MC/FDC)

The 597th disembarked at Boston on November 23 and was inactivated at Camp Myles Standish, Mass., on November 24. On November 28, the 92nd Division was inactivated at Camp Kilmer, New Jersey.

***

After the inactivation of the 597th Field Artillery Battalion on November 24, 1945, Colonel Derricks went home to Chicago for several weeks of military leave. When he returned to duty early in 1946, he was assigned to the Training Center at Fort McClellan, Alabama, as Assistant Executive Officer. He served in that capacity until August 10, 1946, then returned to Europe. There, on September 12, 1946, he was assigned to command the 349th Field Artillery Battalion at Grafenwohr, Germany.

The 349th had both black and white officers assigned to key command and staff positions, and Colonel Derricks thus became the first black officer to command a field artillery battalion with a mixed staff. Several weeks after Derricks arrived in Germany, Mrs. Derricks was authorized to travel overseas to join her husband. Shortly after the 349th Field Artillery Battalion was inactivated on January 20, 1947, Derricks became ill and was hospitalized in Bayreauth, Germany. The decision was made to return him to the United States on a hospital ship, but Mrs. Derricks could not accompany him. She had to wait and return on the next ship available: "When we returned, I met Colonel Derricks in Battle Creek, Michigan and he was separated there at Percy Jones Hospital. He came back to Chicago and tried to take up some of his work there. He started a real estate agency with his good friend, Attorney Eugene Jones. We bought a home on the west side of Chicago. Soon, the Colonel began to show his illness and, in less than a year, he was hospitalized at Hines Hospital in Hines, Illinois."

At his own request, Colonel Derricks was transferred on July 2, 1948 to the retired list, Illinois National Guard, with the rank of colonel. After a final period of hospitalization, he passed away on April 14, 1949.

Part VI

Beyond Derricks' Diary

CHAPTER TWENTY-THREE

Derricks' Legacy

Colonel Derricks had the foresight to plan for the time when black field artillery officers would serve in an integrated U.S. Army where black and white officers would be required to compete directly on the basis of merit. He realized that, without combat training and experience in key command and staff positions, black officers would be at a serious disadvantage in that competition. Since the 597th had a greater potential than any other unit in the U.S. Army to provide combat experience for black field artillery officers in senior command and staff positions, Derricks had made the most of the opportunity and had periodically rotated his officers in such positions, as they exhibited the necessary potential. Accordingly, more officers were permitted to gain such training and experience in the 597th than in any other unit in the Army.

This was the bridgehead that he had maintained and protected from the time he assumed command on April 13, 1944 until the 597th was inactivated on November 24, 1945, thereby becoming the only black battalion commander of a ground combat arms unit to command the same unit continuously, from the time it began preparation for overseas service until it returned to the United States after successfully completing combat operations.

He had provided a protected window of opportunity into an area where black officers could prepare themselves for future progress, and which could be used as a springboard for the final offensive to refute the myth of inherent inferiority.

Although some of the beneficiaries of "Derricks' Bridgehead" left the Army after World War II to become outstanding achievers in other fields of endeavor, many remained in the Army, and during the transition to a desegregated military establishment were able to serve and compete with white officers for positions never before held by black officers.

In 1946, we experienced the first results of Colonel Derricks' foresightedness. Many of those beneficiaries who remained in the service experienced the initial results in Germany. In February 1946, I was transferred to West Germany, assigned to the 350th all black enlisted men and an integrated staff ... blacks assigned to key command and staff positions commensurate with their backgrounds.

In his Black History Month Special Feature, *LISTEN TO THE BLOOD— The Meaning of Black History* (Ebony, 1981), Dr. Lerone Bennett, Jr., paraphrases the postscript to the *Gift of Black Folk* by Dr. W. E. B. Du Bois with the question, "What shall our sufferings and trials and triumphs mean?" Dr. Bennett's answer to the question included the following statement:

> For peoples, races and nations advance on the shoulders of succeeding generations. One generation runs as fast as it can then passes the baton on to another generation which runs as fast as it can and then passes the baton on, *ad infinitum.*

Captain Major Clark at Hampton Institute.

Because of happenstance—not planning by the Army—the black officers of the 597th were able to carry the baton faster and farther than others of their generation. The 597th provided combat training and experience to more "senior" black field artillery officers (captains and above) than any of the other 16 black field artillery battalions during World War II, and together with the 600th to more than the combined total of the other 15 battalions.

Because of qualifications gained as a result of their unique experience in the 597th and 600th, some of the officers of those battalions were assigned during the first decade after the war as professors, and assistant professors, of military science and tactics at the artillery college ROTCs where the first black field artillery ROTC officers in the U.S. Army were commissioned following World War II:

Cartwright, Roscoe C.—Assistant PMS&T (Professor of Military Science & Tactics), West Virginia State College;

Claude, C.—Asst. PMS&T, West Virginia State College (later PMS&T, Florida A&M College);

Clark, Major—Asst PMS&T, Hampton Institute, VA;

Gray, Ben—Assistant PMS&T, West Virginia State College;

Johnson, Marion I.—Assistant PMS&T, West Virginia State College;

Page, Orion—PMS&T, West Virginia State College;

Washington, Robbin, E.L.—PMS&T, West Virginia State College.

Thus, we were in positions to pass the baton at institutions which provided most of the black junior artillery officers for the Korean War and for the NATO commitments in Europe during the 1950s and early 1960s.

Some of the other officers were assigned to ROTC units of other branches. For example:

Ray, Marcus—PMS&T, Central State College;

Smith, La Von E.—Asst. PMS&T, Prairie View A&M College, Texas.

***

All 17 of the black field artillery battalions with World War II campaign credits were inactivated after the war. These included the only all-black-officered field artillery units, the 597th and 600th. However, 10 of the field artillery battalions, including the 597th but not the 600th, were reactivated during the period from 1946–51. Four were restored in 1946 and 1947 and six in 1950 and 1951. The first four were World War II Regular Army battalions, and three of these—the 349th, 350th, and 351st—changed their numeral designations to 96th, 98th, and 503rd, respectively.

The other six were Army of the United States World War II battalions, which were reallocated to the Regular Army before they were reactivated. Three of these, including the 597th, which was assigned to Fourth Army and activated at Fort Hood, Texas, on November 20, 1950, were reorganized as armored field artillery battalions.

Several former 597th officers were assigned to the 349th and 686th Field Artillery Battalions in Germany, which were inactivated in 1947. Later, black World War II field artillery personnel were assigned, along with second-generation black field artilleryman, to other units in Germany and to units in the United States, Japan, and Korea.

96th	Fort Sill, Oklahoma	Korea
98th	Fort Bragg, N. Carolina	
159th	Japan	Korea
503rd	Fort Lewis, Washington	Korea
593rd		
594th		
595th		
597th		
598th		
571st	Fort Riley, Kansas	
969th	Fort Lewis, Washington	
999th	Fort Benning, Georgia	Korea

Segregation was still practiced during this period in certain cities near military installations. For example, the situation in Manhattan, Kansas was reported to be as follows:

> Colored persons are allowed in all of 4 of the Manhattan theatres, however, must sit in the balcony in the theatres where there are balconies.

> Colored persons are not allowed in the restaurants; the U.S.O. Douglas Center located at 900 Yuma will maintain a "snack bar" for colored troops.

> Colored troops are not allowed in the beer parlors or recreation clubs, except the Savoy, 812 Pottowatomie Street, and the Casa Monterey, 610 South Juliette. (Letter, Chamber of Commerce, Manhattan, Kansas, to Major Arthur La Capria, Headquarters 10th Inf Div., Fort Riley, Kansas, October 4, 1948)

The Race Continues

After World War II, and particularly during and after the Vietnam War, the U.S. Army made outstanding progress in the utilization of black officers in key command and staff positions in the field artillery. Also, just as it had been directly involved in that progress during World War II, the 597th continued to be a factor

Fort Bragg Field Artillery ROTC Summer Camp. Front row (squatting), Rogers is third from left. Next row (standing), Major Ben Gray is fourth from left, Major Claude Clark is sixth from left, Captain Major Clark is seventh from left. (OHS)

in the progress that followed. This involvement included significant interaction between some of the former members of the 597th and the post-World War II generation of black artillery officers, and the perpetuation of the history and traditions of the World War II 597th by the 597th Armored Field Artillery Battalion.

Immediately following World War II, senior ROTC units for artillery were established at Hampton Institute (antiaircraft artillery) and West Virginia State College (field artillery). At the same time, the Army began a program to combine the ROTC programs of instruction for field artillery and antiaircraft artillery officers, but soon reverted back to divided programs. During this period, certain officers from the 597th and 600th, including me, were assigned as Assistant PMS&Ts

Charles Rogers, 1968 recipient of the Congressional Medal of Honor for services as a Battalion Commander in Vietnam, and in 1973 the first black Corps Artillery Commander. (OHS)

at one or the other of these institutions, and attended the Fort Bragg ROTC Field Artillery Summer Camp each year with the field artillery students.

By the beginning of the Vietnam War, the outstanding achievers among these former students as commissioned officers were prepared to compete in the mainstream and become field artillery battalion, group, and finally corps artillery commanders.

One of these outstanding achievers, Charles C. Rogers, was influenced both by the former members of the 597th and by his subsequent service in the 597th Armored Field Artillery Battalion. As a West Virginia State College ROTC student, Rogers had attended the 1950 Field Artillery ROTC Summer Camp at Fort Bragg, North Carolina, during his Junior Year. He was assigned to Battery C, where I and several other black field artillery veterans of the World War II generation were his instructors.

We passed the baton to Rogers and the next generation of black field artillery officers attending the camp. As we did so, we hoped that our momentum was sufficient to give them an equal opportunity to successfully compete in the race, if they ran as fast as they could. Rogers did run as fast as he could, and despite some obstacles placed in his path along the way, continued to "sprint and outrun the pack."

Lieutenant Rogers was commissioned in the Regular Army on June 15, 1951 upon graduation from West Virginia State College, number one in his ROTC class. On November 1, 1968, while he was assigned to command the 1st Bn., 5th Artillery, 1st Infantry Division in Vietnam, he earned a Congressional Medal of Honor for conspicuous gallantry in action at the risk of life beyond the call of duty.

In 1973, as a brigadier general, Rogers was assigned as Commanding General, VII Corps Artillery in Germany, thus becoming the first black officer to be assigned as a corps artillery commander, the highest organizational command level in the field artillery.

The 597th Armored Field Artillery Battalion

Since neither the 366th Infantry nor the 600th Field Artillery Battalion was reactivated after World War II, the 597th was the only former all-black-officered color-bearing ground combat unit restored to active status. Accordingly, the 597th Armored Field Artillery Battalion established significant milestones when it was activated in 1950 and integrated in 1952. In each instance, it became the first and only color-bearing ground combat unit, in the history of the U.S. Army, to perpetuate the combat history, traditions, battlefield participation credits, and honors earned by an all-black-officered unit in a previous war.

But notwithstanding the unique status of the 597th during World War II as an all-black-officered unit, the 597th AFA Bn. was activated in 1950, as it was in 1942, with black and white officers and black enlisted men. Also, in the period between its activation in 1950 and integration in 1952, the plight of the black officers was very similar to what it had been in the 597th during the period 1942–44 before Colonel Derricks assumed command.

One of the non-commissioned officers who helped to activate the 597th was Sergeant John T. Ferguson of Fort Worth, Texas, a World War II combat veteran of the 349th Field Artillery Bn. Sergeant Ferguson was platoon sergeant of the right platoon of Battery A of the 597th. He recalled that, in December 1951, a little more than a year after the battalion was activated, a black second lieutenant, Charles C. Rogers, reported to the 597th and was assigned to Battery A as his platoon leader. During the period June–October, Rogers completed the Basic Course at Fort Sill and, after a brief assignment to another unit at Ford Hood, Texas, was assigned to the 597th. He recalled:

> My first unit was the 73rd Armd FA Bn at Hood, but that was interim to my assignment to the 597th which was on orders to reassign to Germany.
>
> My only memory of the 73rd Armd FA Bn touches me even today and impacted on me throughout my military career. I was assigned briefly to Btry B; on the afternoon of my arrival the B.C. [Battalion Commander] was orienting me on the unit and the Army in general; he looked at his watch, noted that it was near 1700 and said, "Come with me." We got into his car and we drove to Division Hqs (1st Armd Div.) Retreat was about to be played. Then, as the flag was slowly lowered, we saluted. The next morning as I arrived at the battery for

reveille, he once again took me in his car to Div Hqs; as the flag was raised, we saluted. After the ceremony he looked at me and said, "Rogers, that's why we are in the Army—to protect that—the flag." I was greatly moved, and throughout my career, through the grade of Lt Col, I always took my newly assigned officers to the Hqs and repeated this old ceremony. Love for the flag was always foremost in my mind throughout my career.

I joined the 597th in December 1951 with great pride, because they had just completed the Bn Test with the highest score ever shot at Fort Hood. What was most dramatic about that was that about 8–12 months earlier, the 2nd Armd Div had left Hood being reassigned to Germany. They had weeded out their worst soldiers—most black—and these soldiers were reassigned to the units remaining at Hood. After all the moaning and groaning was over, the commanders of these units began working with these "rejects," and found to their great surprise, that these rejects—with good leadership—could become great soldiers. I suppose they were already "good soldiers," but even good soldiers need—and deserve—good leadership.

That's my first memory of the 597th—i.e., that good leadership can bring even "rejects" into the winner's circle. Thereafter, in the three batteries and two battalions commanded, I always, much to the dismay of my subordinate comdrs, took the rejects and developed them into good soldiers.

The 597th, under [command of] Maj Fred White … shipped out of New Orleans in Feb 1952, and after three rough weeks in the North Atlantic, landed in Bremerhaven, where we unloaded and shipped to Fussen, Germany in Bavaria—a temporary location while our barracks in Hanau, Germany were being renovated. We remained in Fussen two months, and moved to Hanau, where the unit remained until 1956 before shipment to Fort Sill.

The Color Barrier in the 597th

Now a bit about the battalion. Upon my assignment, all our soldiers were black, all officers captain and above were white, most of our lieutenants were black. All of the desirable lieutenant jobs—i.e. Btry Ex O, FDO, Asst S-3, etc., were occupied by white lieutenants. We as black officers experienced the unpleasant experience of knowing we were needed—but not wanted. Many white officers treated us quite well and were very friendly and helpful; many others were openly racist and frequently used such expressions as "nigger" or "you people," "those people are dumb." They felt that serving in a black unit was a penalty and openly showed resentment of blacks. Many, however, were compassionate and fair. We as blacks however, were always uncertain as to where we stood. We were suspicious of all the friendly nice ones as well as those openly hostile. We knew for certain that a black officer would always be dealt with more harshly. On efficiency reports, we were always rated lower than our white counterparts and were only compared with other blacks, e.g. "Lt Rogers is one of the finest colored officers in the battalion." Those were the realities of life in the 597th and other black battalions at that time. The experience was belittling, the rewards few. (CCR/MC)

In October 1952, the 597th was integrated. This summary of the implementation of the integration program is based on the 597th's Command Report for 1952:

On 2 September, thirty white EM were assigned to the 597th from replacement companies. These men were apparently assigned through an erroneous assumption by replacement centers that racial integration had been completed in the battalion. However, they were released from assignment and transferred elsewhere by 20 September.

Detailed instructions for the implementation of the racial integration program were received from headquarters Seventh Army on 3 October 1952. During the second week in October, major personnel changes began to take place, followed by the first of many large-scale shipments of men to the United States for separation from the service. On 12 and 13 October, the battalion shipped five (5) packets of men (to white battalions) in compliance with these instructions and on 14 and 15 October, seven (7) packets were received (from white battalions). The major portion of integration was completed on 25 October with the exception of small increments of one or two men which continued to arrive until the latter part of December.

The racial integration and rotation program caused an approximate 80 percent turn-over in enlisted men and an approximate 60 percent turn-over in officers. This turn-over in personnel, while not affecting the basic organization of the battalion, did in effect result in a "re-organization" in so far as administration and training are concerned.

Major Fred White commanded the battalion from March 19, 1951 until October 17, 1952, when Lieutenant Colonel James G. Kalergis arrived and assumed command. He commanded the 597th until June 1954, retiring in 1975 as a lieutenant general. During the integration program in October, Captain Richard V. Stockwell replaced First Lieutenant Max Rector in command of Headquarters Battery. Captain Ralph W. Hampton commanded Battery A.

Rogers was one of the very few black officers remaining in the 597th after it was integrated:

Integration of the 597th in October 1952 was traumatic. While we were still all black in Fussen, some commanders told us they did not favor blacks with German girls and "tacitly" prohibited black officers from bringing German girls to the Officers' Club. I say "tacitly" because there were never any written directions, only oral statements and facial expressions of hatred if some black officers violated this unwritten dictate. Officers who had no intention of making the Army a career brought girls to the club, others did not.

When the battalion integrated in Hanau in 1952, one of the white battalions which integrated with us was a Mississippi National Guard battalion loaded with personnel who made no secret of their disrespect for blacks. On the other hand, some officers and soldiers of this battalion were genuinely friendly and helpful. The most common expression one heard was that having blacks in units would greatly reduce the combat readiness of the battalion. How quickly they had forgotten that the all black 597th had a year earlier shot the highest Bn Test score ever shot at Hood …

Incidentally, I neglected to mention that the 597th shot the highest Bn Test Score in Europe in its first two years there …

Wanted to Resign

… In 1954, I … put in my resignation—not out of dissatisfaction but because I planned to study for the ministry. When I didn't get a response from the Army, I was sending a tracer in, but my Bn CO, Lt Col James A. Kalergis (now Lt Gen Ret) called me in and told me that he had not forwarded my resignation to Washington because he believed I was making a mistake. He said he had observed the integration of the battalion and had seen that many whites and blacks simply could not get along together and were a hindrance to integration. He said, however, that he and my commander had observed that I got along well with whites and blacks alike and was the kind of officer who would make integration work. (I was a bit irritated that my resignation had not gone in, but as things panned out, I'm pleased I stayed in.)

Why did I stay in? Because every time I'd think about getting out, I got another job I liked! It's hard to walk away from work you love. I finally did, however, after 33 years of service, and now I'm doing that which I always knew I'd do. I'm studying for the ministry—presently at the Ludwig-Maximillian Universitat, Munchen.

Rogers remained with the 597th until 1955. After the battalion was integrated, he observed some remarkable changes in race relations:

> By late 1953 the overt racism was hardly evident—we had good sensitive commanders and good NCOs. Of course, what helped a lot was that a lot of officers and NCOs who had fought in integrated units in Korea, were coming to Germany and they had seen—in combat—what Blacks could do. Covert racism continued—as it does to a much lesser degree today, but it was quite clear that we were making progress in race relations. Good leadership—officer and NCO—can solve any problem. This problem, of course hasn't been solved, but it has been greatly responded to and attenuated.

In April 1956, the 597th was transferred from Germany to Fort Sill, Oklahoma, where on June 25, 1958 it was inactivated and replaced by the 2nd Howitzer Battalion, 37th Artillery.

***

At the conclusion of my four years and seven months (1956–60) of service on the Army General Staff, I was convinced that Colonel Derricks' efforts had been successful. Black field artillery officer veterans of World War II had convinced the U.S. Army of their ability to serve with distinction in any staff position to which they might be assigned, and the assumption that black officers lacked the technical competence to be field artillerymen finally had been put to rest.

CHAPTER TWENTY-FOUR

A Look Both Ways

The order directed me to proceed to Room 3E648, the Pentagon, and report to Lieutenant General John C. Oakes, the Deputy Chief of Staff for Military Operations, at 1400 hours, September 30, 1960. I reported to General Oakes as directed and, in about 15 minutes, my final official Army mission was accomplished successfully, with a minimum of effort on my part. However, I did stand at attention for about three minutes while an officer read the citation for my Army Commendation Medal and General Oakes pinned the medal above the right pocket of my uniform coat. My citation read:

> Lieutenant Colonel Major Clark, General Staff (Artillery) distinguished himself as a staff officer in the Missile Training Section, Training Division, Organization and Training, during the period 25 September 1956 to 30 September 1960.
>
> For more than two years, Lieutenant Colonel Clark was the only general staff officer available to the Missile Training Section. He initiated, coordinated, and obtained approval of key actions which contributed very materially to the creation and development, on a high priority basis, of Army missile and special weapons training programs. His initiative, thoroughness, diligence, sound judgment, and tireless devotion to duty were vital factors in the ability of the Army to meet pressing missile deployment schedules in the continental United States and overseas.
>
> His outstanding work on Nike and Hawk training contributed immeasurably to the air defense of the free world. Through his detailed knowledge of air defense operations, he was able to effect numerous improvements in the training and processing of air defense package and replacement personnel and thus made an outstanding contribution to the early combat readiness of missile units ...
>
> His long and outstanding service, his initiative, judgment and tenacity in the resolution of difficult problems, the respect in which he is held, and the exceptionally high quality of his work are in keeping with the highest traditions of the Army, and reflect great credit on himself and the military service.
>
> Entered military service from the state of Oklahoma. (Citation, Army Commendation Medal, 9-30-60)

Then General Oakes and I shook hands for the photographer, and my Army career of 20 years and one month was over.

As I left General Oakes's office, I paused briefly and looked to my left down the "E" Ring passageway toward the nearby offices of the Army Chief of Staff,

General Lyman L. Lemnitzer, in Room 3E668. General Lemnitzer was being elevated that same day to the position of Chairman of the Joint Chiefs of Staff and would be succeeded as Army Chief of Staff by the Vice Chief of Staff, General George H. Decker. A short distance beyond the Chief's office was the office of the Secretary of the Army, Wilbur M. Brucker, in Room 3E718. Secretary of Defense Thomas B. Gates's office, in Room 3E880, was around the "corner" from there and beyond the 8th Corridor. The corner was one of five in the "E" Ring where, in this case, the 700 and 800 blocks converged at an internal angle of 108 degrees.

Lt. Col. Major Clark on the occasion of his retirement from the Pentagon, 1960.

I recalled that the key actions I had "initiated, coordinated, and obtained approval of" had required me to have some contact with the highest Army officials, including the DCSOPS (Deputy Chief of Staff for Operations and Plans), the Vice Chief of Staff, and in a few cases, the Chief of Staff, and the Secretary of the Army. I had to deal with Congressional Committees and individual congressmen; other executive agencies such as the Bureau of the Budget and the State Department; military missions and military attaches; other Department of Defense agencies including Joint and Specified Commands, the Air Force, Navy, and Marine Corps; the other Army general staff agencies such as the Deputy Chief of Staff for Personnel, the Deputy Chief of Staff for Logistics, and the Chief of Research and Development; the major special staff agencies such as the Adjutant General, the Chief Signal Officer, the Chief of Ordnance, and the Chief of Transportation; and the missile contractors and their civilian personnel accredited to the Department of Defense.

Before I could leave the Pentagon, I had to stop by my former office in Room 3C400 to clean out my desk and select the personal items that I would save and carry out of the Pentagon. So I turned to my right, followed the "E" Ring around the corner made by the convergence of the 500 and 600 blocks, and continued down the long straight passageway that served the 400 and 500 blocks of the "E" Ring. These blocks contained the offices of the five directors in ODCSOPS (Office of the DCSOPS)—Air Defense and Special Weapons, Army Aviation, Organization and Training (O&T), Operations, and Plans—and in addition the office of the Chief of Research and Development.

During the more than two years that I was "the only general staff officer available to the Missile Training Section," I had spent most of my time coordinating with agencies other than my own directorate (O&T). As a matter of fact, my career had been significantly affected by two specific events that had involved the Director of Plans, on the first occasion, when I gained a great deal of attention and extra work; and the Director of Operations, on the other occasion, when I received a mid-term assessment of my performance and a directive for continuation of the extra work.

The first of these events occurred on October 15, 1956, when Major General Earle G. Wheeler, then Director of Army Plans, was giving a preview of a presentation he was to make later that day to General Maxwell Taylor, U.S. Army Chief of Staff, concerning the U.S. Army's plan for providing advanced weapons systems to NATO countries. The preview was being given to selected action officers who had worked on the plan. I was there because I had developed the training concept for the plan.

When General Wheeler displayed his charts of the proposed schedule of deployment dates for the NATO units, I noticed that a significant error had been made. The error stemmed from the fact that the action officer, who prepared the schedule, had not taken into consideration the incompressibility of certain long lead time training requirements for foreign military personnel. The foreign military personnel had to be trained in U.S. Army schools before their missile units could become operational. That training could not begin until the plans were approved and qualified personnel selected, brought to the United States, and enrolled in appropriate courses of instruction. Therefore, to arrive at the deployment objective dates, the training times should have been added to the projected training start date, and that was still several weeks into the future. The action officer had computed the deployment dates by adding the training times to the date we started planning six months before, and had not revised the dates to reflect the "slippage."

At the time of General Wheeler's briefing, I was still a major, the only black and the lowest-ranking officer in the group. In spite of my reluctance to tell a major general that his charts were wrong, I realized that a lot of confusion would result if the approved NATO missile plan contained such a gross error. So I spoke up and pointed out the error. I thereby attracted a great deal of attention to myself and caused an immediate increase in my workload.

The second event occurred a little less than two years later and was a direct outgrowth of the first. The plans for furnishing missile systems to NATO had been approved by the Chief of Staff late in 1956. From the outset, although the Chief, Foreign Military Training Branch was responsible for coordination of the foreign missile training programs, he did not have a missile-trained officer assigned to his branch. Accordingly, he had defaulted to me for coordination of the technical requirements associated with the program, and I had accepted the requirement on a voluntary basis. By mid-1958, implementation of the plans had proceeded well beyond the initial stages. Coordination requirements had increased significantly, both in scope and magnitude, to the point where the U.S. program and the concurrent foreign programs each deserved the full-time attention of the agency responsible for the specific program. I had reached the point where a 16-hour day was not unusual, and was concerned that continuation of the situation would cause me to be less effective.

In order to resolve the problem, the Acting Director of O&T accompanied me, on August 4, 1958, to a meeting in the office of the newly promoted Director of Operations, Major General Francis T. Pachler. In essence, we hoped that General Pachler would recognize the enormity of my task and would agree for the Foreign Military Training Branch to assume the responsibilities assigned to his office so that I could concentrate on the requirements of the programs for which I had primary responsibility.

After listening briefly to our discussion, General Pachler stated that, since he did not yet have a missile-trained officer in his organization, the situation should remain unchanged for the time being. The Foreign Military Training Branch would continue to fulfill the administrative effort required to process foreign military personnel as individuals, but I should continue to coordinate all the technical requirements associated with the programs.

I was naturally disappointed at the outcome of the meeting. Not only had my workload not been reduced, but the increase in workload that I had accepted on a voluntary basis had been confirmed as an official requirement. However, I was reminded of one positive aspect of the situation: General Pachler had confirmed, beyond a shadow of doubt, that the Army had abandoned the myth that blacks were inherently inferior in technical matters. He had officially expressed his confidence in my ability to handle the technical requirements for which his office was responsible in addition to the workload of my primary responsibility. This was an unmistakable confirmation that things had changed in the 50 years since the publication of the minority conclusion in a 1907 Army War College Study which, at that time, expressed an opinion held by a large and influential group of staff officers that "the Negro, from his evident inferiority ... is not fitted for the modern artillery service."

It also invalidated the comments included in a memo written during World War I to the Army Chief of Staff by Major General Frank McIntyre, former artillery officer for the American Expeditionary Forces. He had written that "it would seem advisable not to commission colored men in the Field Artillery as the number of men of that race who have the mental qualifications to come up to the standards of efficiency of the Field Artillery officers is so small that the few isolated cases might be better handled in other branches."

I turned left and followed Corridor 4 until I reached the "C" Ring, and then turned right and followed the passageway until I reached Room 3C400. I recalled that, during John Eisenhower's tour of duty in the Pentagon in 1957 and 1958, he had been assigned to Joint War Plans, and his office in 3C460 had also been along the "C" Ring. My office was between Corridor 3 and Corridor 4 and his was between

Corridor 4 and Corridor 5. We had passed each other many times in Corridor 4 on the way to our respective director's offices in the "E" Ring.

John was a major when he was first assigned to the Pentagon during the late summer of 1957, and by that time I had been promoted to lieutenant colonel. I recalled that my morale had improved significantly when I realized I lived in a country where I could outrank the president's son; a son who visited the White House frequently and saw his father at all White House functions.

I reached my former office at about 1430 hours, but could not complete my business until my successor returned from a meeting that he was attending elsewhere in the building. During my tour of duty in the Pentagon, I had accumulated a large file of classified documents, consisting primarily of copies of actions I had initiated or coordinated, which I needed to refer to from time to time. Since we had decided to transfer the documents to my successor instead of turning them in for destruction, it was necessary for my successor to sign our joint inventory to relieve me of responsibility. I hoped that he would return soon because I wanted to get through the Washington traffic before the weekend "bug-out" began.

While waiting for my successor to return, I used the top of my desk to organize the personal items that I was going to carry with me out of the Pentagon, beginning with the citation and certificates that had just been given to me by General Oakes. I opened all of the drawers of my desk and began to sort the material contained in the folders.

One drawer contained a letter from the Chief of the Artillery Branch of the Officers Division that I had received in May 1956, about two months after I arrived in the Pentagon. I had been told, informally, that I was the first black field artillery officer to be assigned to ODCSOPS. The letter welcomed me to duty in the Washington area and stated: "The quality of officers required for assignment here ensures that you have been selected on the basis of your record thus far in the service."

In addition to the letter, the drawer contained several mementos of my most significant assignments as an officer. The next item was a list of my assignments during the four school years, 1947–48 through 1950–51, when I was an Assistant PMS&T at Hampton Institute, Virginia. My primary responsibility during that period was to give artillery instruction to Advanced ROTC students. However, during that period, I had additional assignments as Executive Officer, Adjutant, Intelligence Officer, Information and Education Officer, Recreation Officer, Plans and Training Officer, Officer in Charge of First Year Basic Course, Officer in Charge of First Year Advanced Course, Officer in Charge of Second Year Advanced Course, Officer in Charge of Pershing Rifles, and Officer in Charles of Ladies of the Faculty Rifle Team.

The next items included a Certificate of Proficiency reflecting completion of the Field Artillery Field Officers Refresher Course at Fort Sill, Oklahoma in 1951, immediately after leaving Hampton Institute; and citations for the Oak Leaf Cluster to the Bronze Star Medal and for the Chung Mu Medal with Gold Star (in Korean, without English translation), for services as Senior Artillery Advisor to the 3rd ROK Division during the Korean War in 1951 and 1952.

There were several items reflecting my assignment as Executive Officer to the 595th Field Artillery Battalion at Fort Sill, Oklahoma, after I returned from Korea. One was a note to me dated January 15, 1953 from the battalion commander:

> ... I shall be transferred from the Bn next Monday, 19 January. Until then I remain in command; my successor has not been chosen yet.
>
> You will familiarize yourself with Bn operations so that you will be prepared fully to take command if no officer senior to you is assigned on 19 January.
>
> That I expect Major Jules Savan to take command should not deter you in complying with these instructions.

Major Savan did indeed take command and was immediately promoted to lieutenant colonel. Our professional relationship was outstanding, as indicated by the next item, DA AGO Form 68. Recommendation for Promotion of Officer. Four months after he assumed command, Savan had initiated a special recommendation for my promotion to lieutenant colonel, noting on the form that "This superior officer is considered fully qualified for promotion to lieutenant colonel."

The recommendation was approved by the 77th Field Artillery Group, The Artillery Center at Fort Sill and Headquarters Fourth Army at Fort Sam Houston, Texas. However, since it was not approved at the Pentagon, four more years went by before I was promoted.

There was also a clipping from the *Los Angeles Times* dated March 18, 1953, headlined "Times Man Eyewitness to Destruction," an account of the March 17, 1953 atomic test in Nevada. I had been there and had witnessed the same test as an observer for the Artillery Center. The account stated that 1,000 troops and 20 newsmen were closer to atomic detonation than any human being in history except the Japanese at Hiroshima and Nagasaki.

Following that clipping was a diploma reflecting my graduation from the 1953–54 Artillery Officer Advanced Course at Fort Sill, Oklahoma and Fort Bliss, Texas.

Next was a list of duties reflecting my assignment as Executive Officer of the 69th Antiaircraft Artillery Battalion in New York City from mid-1954 until mid-1955. In addition to the tactical duties, there were 38 non-tactical staff duties for which I had direct or supervisory responsibility.

There was also a clipping from the *New York Post* dated September 2, 1954, headlined "Caissons Went Rolling Along to Aqueduct." It was an account of the situation at Aqueduct race track after Hurricane Carol had knocked out the 270,000-volt high tension cable which supplied the race track with power. Battery D of the 69th was emplaced in the corner of property adjacent to and belonging to Aqueduct. On the day following the hurricane, I received a request from the steward at Aqueduct for the use of one of our portable generators during the emergency. After receiving permission from the defense headquarters, I directed the battery commander to comply with the steward's request. However, in making the request, the steward had not explained that their most significant emergency was an inoperative tote board, which required much more power than our portable generator could deliver. Accordingly, I am not sure that the generator was used at all. The article in the *Post* had been written by a reporter who saw the generator being towed to the race track.

Then there were items reflecting my attendance at the Command and General Staff College at Fort Leavenworth, Kansas during 1955 and 1956. One item was a short memorandum to me from the Secretary of the Command and General Staff College dated October 3, 1955 notifying me of my score on the Pre-selection Test for the Special Weapons Course:

1. Your score ... was 46 [out of 50]. The Associate Class average was 27.
2. You were included in the list of those nominated to attend the Special Weapons Course, commencing 4 January 1956 and terminating 11 February 1956.

I clearly recalled the circumstances surrounding the test because it was administered on September 28, 1955, just as the first game of the 1955 World Series was beginning between the Brooklyn Dodgers and New York Yankees. The Yankees won the first game by a score of six to five, but the Dodgers won the series four games to three.

There were also diplomas reflecting my graduation from the Associate Command and General Staff Officer Course in 1955 and the Special Weapons Course in 1956.

The next drawer contained the unclassified portions of the Trip Reports I had made while assigned to the Pentagon. These reflected the trips I had made in dealing with major subordinate commands within the United States, including United States Continental Army Command at Fort Monroe, Virginia; The United States Air Defense Command at Colorado Springs, Colorado; The Air Defense Center at Fort Bliss, Texas; the Field Artillery and Missile Center at Fort Sill, Oklahoma; the Ordnance Missile Command at Redstone Arsenal, Alabama; and the major missile contractors.

Only a few of the trips had been made in the period 1956–58 when I was the only missile-trained officer available to the directorate and could not spare the time. Six trips, for a total of 27 days, had been made to the U.S. Army Air Defense at Fort Bliss, Texas. These included attendance at an Atomic Weapons and Guided Missiles Orientation Course, an Air Defense Instructors Conference, and a side trip to visit the Artillery and Missile Center at Fort Sill, Oklahoma. Six trips, for a total of 24 days, had been made to visit Headquarters, Continental Army Command, at Fort Monroe, Virginia. Two trips, for a total of six days, had been made to visit the Army Ballistic Missile Agency and the Ordnance Missile Command at Redstone Arsenal, Alabama. Two trips, for a total of nine days, had been made to visit Bell Telephone Laboratories at Whippany, New Jersey. Two one-day trips had been made to Philadelphia, Pa., the first to visit a demonstration of a training device by General Electric Missile and Space Division, and the second to attend a DOD Aerial Target Symposium.

One five-day trip was made to Boston and Andover, Mass., to visit Raytheon and attend the HAWK missile Engineering Concept Review. One 15-day trip had been made to Fort Leavenworth, Kansas, to attend the Senior Officers Nuclear Weapons Employment Course. A one-day trip had been made to New York City for a conference on contractor training for the Nike Zeus missile (grandfather of the proposed "Star Wars" missile defense system), and a two-day trip was made to Fort Belvior, Virginia, to attend a conference on "Atoms for Nike."

Reports of both trips to Redstone Arsenal had some additional information attached. The first trip was made on August 30, 1956 to attend an Army Ballistic Missile Agency Orientation Program. Attached to that trip report was a room reservation for me at Russell Erskine Hotel in nearby Huntsville. The reservation had been made for me, along with those for the other attendees, by the officer-in-charge of the orientation program before he knew that I was black. Since Alabama continued to enforce laws requiring the segregation of the races, he changed my reservations to the Goddard House (the place where VIPs stayed) at Redstone Arsenal when he found out I was black.

The second trip to Redstone Arsenal was made in January 1958 to attend an Army-Air Force planning conference in connection with the transfer of the Jupiter missile from the Army to the Air Force. A C-47 had been furnished by the Air Force to carry us to Huntsville, but after taking off from Boling Air Force Base, it had crash landed at Anacostia Naval Station "next door." There were 17 of us passengers on board, all colonels and lieutenant colonels assigned to the Army and Air Force staffs in the Pentagon. Attached to the trip report was a clipping from the *Huntsville Times* dated January 7, 1953 with a short account of our airplane accident, which described the passengers as "mostly low-ranking officers."

Although none of us were hurt, our trials were not over for the day. We changed to a commercial carrier, with a stop in Atlanta, where we arrived late in the afternoon and went immediately to the airport dining room. Although we were all in uniform, the lady in charge stood in the door and stopped us from going in as a group. She stated that she could admit the 16 white officers, but she could not admit me because of Georgia's segregation laws. Without saying anything, an Air Force colonel in our group stepped forward and gave a signal. The other officers surrounded me, and we went into the dining room together. The lady realized that she could not stop us without creating an incident, so she scurried around and directed the diners seated at two long tables to move elsewhere in the dining room. Then she seated us at the tables they had left and placed a large portable screen between us and the other diners before we were served.

There was some additional information attached to the report of the trip made to New York on October 21, 1957 to discuss Nike Zeus training with the contractor. Our meeting was held at the Western Electric Company's building at 120 Broadway, in a company executive's office "with a view," on one of the upper floors. Since the building was along the route of the ticker tape parade for Queen Elizabeth II, the meeting was interrupted when she approached our position. The executive took enough field glasses from his desk to supply all of the individuals attending the meeting, and we were all able to get an outstanding view of the parade.

The next folder contained information concerning the Ad Hoc Study Group on Guided Missile Training, which had been appointed by the DOD Director of Guided Missiles in 1958. Included in the folder was a list of the members, the liaison personnel from the DOD (including Army, Navy, and Air Force officers), and the times and places of the Study Group meetings. The members included college administrators, college professors, a corporation president, and some other corporation executives. Seven of the eight members were PhDs. I was the liaison representative from the Department of the Army, and had attended the four meetings held in the Pentagon between June 1958 and January 1959. A report of the study group had been made in March 1959, but since it was still classified, it was among the files I had transferred to my successor.

The next folder contained an unclassified summary of every conference I had conducted in the Pentagon, with the sign-in rosters of the conferees. I decided to save the rosters because among the signatures they contained were those of several who were general officers when they attended the conferences, many who had become general officers since the conferences, and many more who, undoubtedly, would become generals in the future.

The next item was a booklet I had obtained when I made my last visit earlier in the day to the office of Mr. James C. Evans, Civilian Assistant to the Assistant Secretary of Defense (Manpower, Personnel and Reserve), where my long-time friend and Washington neighbor, Lieutenant Colonel John T. Martin, was the Executive. The booklet had been published by that office on July 4, 1960 and was titled "The Negro Officer in the Armed Forces of the United States of America." The booklet contained the current assignments of more than 200 black officers in the Armed Forces of the United Sates, which according to the memorandum of transmittal "while broadly representative, is not in any sense a complete listing of Negro officer personnel."

It reminded me of the significant changes that had occurred in the status of black military personnel during the 20-year period since I began my career, in 1940, as a field artillery trainee. When I enlisted in the U.S. Army for assignment to the 349th Field Artillery on August 31, 1940, there was not even one black artillery officer in the U.S. Army. As a matter of fact, there were only five black officers on active duty in the Regular Army—and three of them were chaplains—and no black officer had ever served on the Army General Staff. I glanced through the booklet to find the current assignments of some of my friends and former associates:

Lieutenant Colonel Lester F. McCants had been a fellow battery commander and staff officer in the 597th Field Artillery Battalion during World War II. He was assigned as Aviation Officer, 24th Infantry Division, Germany.

Major John H. Gayles had been a fellow staff officer in the 597th. He was assigned as Assistant G-4, Military Training Mission, Saudi Arabia.

Major James Mundy had also been a fellow staff officer in the 597th. He was assigned to the Operations Section, Headquarters Military District of Washington.

Lieutenant Colonel C. M. Davenport, a 1943 graduate of the U.S. Military Academy, had been assigned to an antiaircraft artillery battalion in the Pacific theater during World War II. During the 1947–48 school year, we had served together as Assistant PMS&Ts at Hampton Institute, Virginia, before he was reassigned as PMS&T at Florida A&M College, Tallahassee. His current assignment was to the Artillery Section, Headquarters Eighth U.S. Army, Korea.

Freddie Davidson and I had been promoted to major on the same order in 1950. We had met in February 1944 when I had visited the headquarters of the 1st Bn., 366th, where he was a staff officer. Lieutenant Colonel Davidson was assigned to the G1 Division, Headquarters, Second Army, Fort Meade, Maryland.

Roscoe Cartwright had graduated from FA OCS in November 1942, four weeks after me. During World War II, he had been assigned to the 599th Field Artillery of the 92nd Division. Major Cartwright was currently assigned as Assistant Chief, Supply Division, Post S-4, Presidio of San Francisco, California.

Henry Minton Francis graduated from the U.S. Military Academy in 1944, the eighth black graduate in history and the first black graduate to be assigned to the field artillery. I first met Lieutenant Francis in 1945 while he was assigned to the 349th Field Artillery Battalion in Grafenwohr, Germany. Major Francis was assigned to the Office of the Comptroller, Headquarters, Sixth Army, Presidio of San Francisco, California.

Steve Davis had served in the 600th Field Artillery Battalion of the 92nd Division during World War II, and had been assigned briefly to the 597th when personnel of the 600th were reassigned before return to the United States. His next assignment was to the office of the Assistant Chief of Staff for Personnel in the Pentagon, which gave him the distinction of being the first black officer to be assigned to the Army General Staff. Lieutenant Colonel Davis was still assigned to the same office, now designated as the Office of the Deputy Chief of Staff for Personnel, Department of the Army, Pentagon.

Also listed in the booklet were the current assignments of the other two black officers who had helped me to desegregate ODCSOPS in the 1956–58 period. In the summer of 1958, both officers had been reassigned and, after they left, I was the only black officer in ODCSOPS for the next several months:

Lieutenant Colonel Arthur Booth had apparently served in an antiaircraft artillery battalion in the Pacific theater during World War II. During his tour of duty in the Pentagon, he had been assigned to the Operations Directorate of ODCSOPS. In the summer of 1958, he had been reassigned as PMS&T at Prairie View.

Lieutenant Colonel James Carr had served in the 614th Tank Destroyer Bn. in Central Europe during World War II. During his tour of duty in the Pentagon, he had been assigned to the Plans Directorate of ODCSOPS. In the summer of 1958, he was reassigned as PMS&T at Hampton Institute, Virginia, where we had served together a few years before.

By the summer of 1960, there were again two other black officers in ODCSOPS: Major James Buchanan, assigned to the Operations Directorate, and Lieutenant Colonel Luther Evans, assigned to the Training Support Branch of the O&T Directorate.

When my successor returned to the office at about 1500 hours, we rechecked our joint inventory of classified documents and he signed my copy of the inventory, relieving me of responsibility. In the meantime, several officers and civilians had come into the office or were standing outside to express their best wishes to me. I was surprised to see among them a major general, who was an Assistant Deputy Chief of Staff for Military Operations.

Finally, the goodbyes were all said and, without looking back, I picked up my personal items and began the long walk to the River entrance on the north side of the Pentagon. From there, it was another long walk to my car, which I had parked in the visitors' area. I had not parked in the more convenient N-2 area because I had turned in my N-2 parking permit earlier that day as part of the clearance procedure.

I unlocked my car door, but before opening it, I took one more look toward the Pentagon. I had to pause a moment as I was almost overwhelmed by a flood of memories of the 1,679 days that had passed since I had reported there to serve on the Army General Staff. During that period, I had spent more than a thousand 10-hour work days, dozens of 16-hour work days, and many 24-hour work days. I had walked thousands of miles along the 17½ miles of corridors and up and down the 150 stairways. But most importantly, I had been a participant-observer in the making of a great deal of history.

As I started my car and drove away from the Pentagon and into retirement from active duty, I realized that although we had made a good beginning, the struggle for progress was not finished. Many more obstacles had to be overcome before black military personnel would have an equal opportunity to compete in the mainstream. In spite of the significant advances we had made since 1940:

- Only one black officer had ever been promoted to brigadier general in the Regular Army, and that had occurred 20 years ago, in 1940, when Benjamin O. Davis, Sr., was promoted to brigadier general a week before I was promoted to private first class. Prospects for another such promotion in the near future did not seem favorable, because recent retirements had reduced to three the number of black Army colonels on active duty.
- No black officer had yet attended the Army War College, although my 1956 efficiency report had included the statement: "Recommend early attendance at the Army War College."
- No black Army full colonel had yet been permitted to command Army troops in combat.
- Thirteen years had passed since the last black officer, Lt. Col. Wendell T. Derricks, had commanded a field artillery battalion. However, there were two occasions during that period when I would have assumed command, if events had been permitted to take their normal course. But in each case, the Army took extraordinary action and found an officer senior to me to prevent me from doing so.

Within a short time after I retired, the white lieutenant colonels and colonels with whom I had worked began to rise through the ranks to became one-, two-, and three-star generals. General Wheeler, whose charts I had criticized in 1956, became a four-star general and served as Army Chief of Staff from October 1962 until June 1964. Then he served as Chairman of the Joint Chiefs of Staff from July 1964 until July 1970, longer than any other man had been in that position.

Many of the restrictions that had barred blacks from participation in certain areas of the mainstream were progressively removed, and especially after the beginning of the Vietnam War, the rate of black progress in the Armed Forces began to accelerate.

Accordingly, by the mid-1970s, the Army had gained the distinction of being considered a showcase of equal opportunity compared to other phases of society.

Now, over a quarter of a century after I retired, most of the changes that I anticipated concerning black progress have occurred. Many of those changes can be attributed to officers with whom I had served at some time during the 1940–60 period. These officers achieved the additional "firsts" and reached the additional milestones, after 1960, that made it possible for the Army to develop a "color blind" policy toward military personnel.

In 1962, Lieutenant Colonel Freddie Davidson became the first black officer to attend the Army War College. Five years after that, Davidson made more history as the first black full colonel to command U.S. Army troops in combat; and a few months later, in 1963, he was the second black to become a brigadier general in the Regular Army. In 1972, Davidson, by then the Army's first black major general, again made history, this time as the first black officer to command an infantry division.

Roscoe C. Cartwright was promoted to lieutenant colonel in 1961, and in 1962 became the first black officer in 13 years to be assigned to command a field artillery battalion. On July 30, 1971, I had the pleasure of returning to the Pentagon, at his invitation, to witness his "pinning" as he was promoted to brigadier general, the first black artillery officer to become a general officer in the Regular Army.

Charles Rogers was one of my students at the 1950 Fort Bragg ROTC Field Artillery Summer Camp. At the time of my retirement, Captain Rogers was assigned to the 1st Howitzer Battalion, 76th Artillery, at Fort Devans, Massachusetts. In 1968, Rogers earned the Congressional Medal of Honor for services as a battalion commander in Vietnam, and in 1973 he became the first black corps artillery commander. He would retire in 1983 as a major general.

Henry Minton Francis retired in July 1965 as a lieutenant colonel. In July 1973, Secretary of Defense James R. Schlesinger appointed Francis to be Deputy Assistant Secretary of Defense (Equal Opportunity). Francis served in that capacity until June 1977. The period of his service is considered by many to be the most productive four-year span ever for the progress of equal opportunity for blacks in the Armed Forces.

Epilogue: A Distinguished Journey

Before working at the Pentagon, Major Clark also fought in the Korean War. During his career, Clark earned 12 medals and citations:

Bronze Star & Oak Leaf Cluster
Presidential Unit Citation
Defense Meritorious Service Medal
Army Commendation Medal
American Defense Service Medal
American Campaign
European–African–Middle Eastern Campaign Medal
World War II Victory Medal
Army of Occupation Medal & Germany Clasp
Korean Service Medal
Armed Forces Reserve Medal
United Nations Service Medal

As a retired officer, Lt. Col. Major Clark moved his family first to Haskell in 1960 and then to Tulsa in 1961. He was employed by McDonnell-Douglas and was active in the Tulsa community, working with the Carver Freedom School, Junior Achievement, and the McDonnell-Douglas management club.

Clark continued his efforts to recognize and reward black military achievements. He confronted the Department of Defense (DoD) regarding the omission and/or negative depiction of African-American soldiers and their performance in war. This resulted in changes in DoD-published materials. Clark also successfully worked on the campaign to designate Flipper's Ditch—named after the first black graduate of West Point, Henry O. Flipper—as a national Black Historic Site. One of Clark's greatest achievements was working behind the scenes for decades to bring about the awarding of Medals of Honor to seven African-American World War II veterans, including Oklahoman Reuban Rivers. Clark was invited to a White House ceremony by President Bill Clinton for his efforts, but was unable to attend for health reasons.

Major Clark passed away on December 22, 1999, at the age of 82. He was buried with full military honors and a 21-gun salute at the Haskell Cemetery. He is survived

THE WHITE HOUSE

Lieutenant Colonel Major Clark, USA(Ret.)
503 East 29th Place North
Tulsa, Oklahoma
74106

74106/2313

The President and Mrs. Clinton

request the pleasure of your company at

a ceremony to be held at

The White House

on Monday morning, January 13, 1997

at ten-thirty o'clock

Reception to follow

Invitation to the White House for Medal of Honor Ceremony for seven African-American World War II veterans, January 1997.

Funeral of Lt. Col. Major Clark, Haskell Cemetery, Oklahoma, December 1999.

Major's children, from left to right: Gregory Clark (wife Felecia), William Clark (wife Deborah), Vivian Clark-Adams (husband Carl), and Leonard Moody (wife Gloria).

Family reunion in Lafayette, Louisiana, August 2018.

and loved by four children—Leonard Charles Moody (and wife Gloria), William Marcus Clark (and wife Deborah), Vivian Noreen Clark-Adams (and husband Carl), and Gregory Lewis Clark (and wife Felecia); nine grandchildren—Leonard Moody, Jr. (and Tangie), Maya Moody, Nathan Turner (and Jerrie), Monica Moody (and Malygin), Lael Clark (and Deon), Wenona Clark, Letoia Clark, Marcus Clark, and Franklin Clark; 10 great grandchildren—Leonard Moody, III (and Ashley), Christopher Lacy, Preston Nykyrain Williams, Silas Moody, Lael Clark, Jr., Amiran Clark, Ashlyn Clark, Jackson Rogers, Rylan Gunter, and Maleah Clark; and two great great grandchildren—John John Moody and Natalie Moody.

Lineage and Battle Honors for 597th Field Artillery Battalion

When the 597th Field Artillery Battalion was activated in 1942, it had no history and was not entitled to battle honors. Under the command of Colonel Derricks, the 597th earned a combat history and was thereafter entitled to battle honors, as indicated by the following official statement of lineage and battle honors from the US Army:

Lineage

Constituted 5 May 1942 in the Army of the United States as 597th Field Artillery Battalion

Activated at Camp Atterbury, Indiana, 15 October 1942 as an element of the 92nd Infantry Division

Inactivated 24 November 1945 at Camp Myles Standish, Mass.

Campaign Streamers

World War II

North Apennines
Po Valley

Decorations

Streamer in the colors of the Italian Cross for Merit of War (Croce al Merita de Guerra) embroidered Italy

Names Mentioned in the Diary

Almond, Edward M., Maj. Gen.—92nd Div. CG

Beasley, Louis J., Let. Col.—Senior 92nd Div. Chaplain

Bell, Phineas, Pvt—assigned to Btry A; wounded in action by enemy artillery. Dec. 11, 1944

Briggs, Albert A., First Lt. (later Capt.)—Bn. Intelligence Off. (S-2); later Btry A CO

Brock, Charles—one of Colonel Derricks' close friends and a fellow veteran of World War I

Buchanan, Otis, Capt.—Btry A CO

Campbell, Ralph, WOJG—had served in the 930th FA Bn. when Derricks was Bn. CO; Campbell had remained in the Bn. when it was converted and re-designated as the 1699th Engr. Comb. Bn.

Cel—see Davidson, Celia

Clark, Major, Capt.—newly assigned Bn. Intelligence Off. (S-2); had been Btry A CO

Colbern, William H., Brig. Gen.—CO, 92nd Div. Artillery

Curry, Robert, Pfc—assigned to Btry A; killed in action Feb. 17, 1945;. awarded Silver Star posthumously

Davidson, Celia—Mrs. Celia Davidson. Mr and Mrs. Davidson, who had a daughter also named Celia, taught in the Durham City School System. Colonel and Mrs. Derricks stayed with the Davidsons while the 930th FA Bn. was stationed in nearby Camp Butner.

Derricks, Elvira Mayfield—Colonel Derricks' wife; in his diary, Derricks used "Ma" and "Vi" when referring to his wife

Diggs, Franklin, First Lt. (later Capt.)—Asst. Chaplain, 92nd Div. Artillery

Doctor—see Shorter, Henry F.

Dunston, Alfred G., Capt.—Senior Chaplain, 92nd Div. Artillery

Freeman, Nat, Maj.—had served with Derricks in the 184th FA

Gayles, John, First Lt.—Bn. Ren. and Surv. Off.

Gibson, Truman K.—Civilian Aide to the Secretary of War

Hargrove, Hondon B., Capt.—Btry C CO; later LnO

Harris, Hugh, First Lt—assigned to Sv. Btry but detailed to special duty as Div. Px. Off.

Jackson, Leonard L., First Lt.—Btry B Exec. Off.

Jacobs, Norman, First Lt.—Btry A Exec. Off.

Johnson, Errington, Capt.—officer in 366th Inf.

Johnson, Marion I., First Lt.—Btry A FO

Johnson, Wesley B., Capt.—LnO with 365th Regt. HQ

Jones, Ann—wife of William B. Jones

Jones, Donald, T/5—assigned to HQ Btry; wounded in action by enemy artillery fire Dec. 11, 1944

Jones, William B., First Lt.—Battery Officer in Service Battery

Junior—daughter of Celia Davidson; see Cel

Ma—see Derricks, Elvira Mayfield

Maxwell, (first name unknown), Brigadier (British Army)—Commanding Officer, 10th Army Group, Royal Artillery (AGRA)

Mayo, Priscilla—one of Colonel Derricks' friends who had worked with him in the Chicago Post Office

McCants, Lester, Capt.—HQ Btry CO, Bn. Comm. O

Meconi—the name of the family in whose home Derricks and some members of his staff stayed during the period Nov. 15 – Dec. 1, 1944; included Mario, Maria, Lina, and Sandra

Nelson, Otto, Maj. Gen.—Deputy CG, MTOUSA

Page, Orion, Maj.—Bn. Exec. Off.

Pickett, Charles, Capt.—LnO with front-line Inf. Bn.

Quis—see Quisenberry

Quisenberry, James A., Capt.—Sv. Btry CO

Randall, Oscar, Lt. Col.—3rd Bn. CO, 366th Inf.

Rita—one of Colonel Derricks' nieces

Robinson, James, Lt. Col.—2nd Bn. CO, 366th Inf.

Rochelle, Herman E., Pfc.—Btry A FO party; killed in action Feb. 17, 1945; awarded Silver Star posthumously

Shorter, Henry F., First Lt. (later Capt.)—Bn. Surgeon

Theresa—one of Colonel Derricks' nieces

Truscott, Lucian K., Lt. Gen.—CG Fifth Army

Turnley, Percy R., Maj.—Bn. Operations and Training Off., S-3

Vi—see Derricks, Elvira Mayfield

Vicky—Colonel Robinson's sister; a close friend of Colonel Derricks' wife

Watkins, Raymond, Maj.—detailed to special duty with 92nd Div. Staff; served with Derricks in 184th FA

White, Charles, Capt.—LnO to 2nd Bn., 365th

Wood, John E., Brig. Gen.—92nd Div. Asst. Div. CG

Wyatt, Willie, S/Sgt.—Btry B, Chief of Section; wounded in action by enemy artillery, Dec. 11, 1944

Abbreviations

Am:	Ammunition
Arty:	Artillery
Asst:	Assistant
BC:	Battery Commander
Btry Comdr:	See BC
Bn:	Battalion
BP:	Base Point
Btry:	Battery
Ch:	Chaplain
CG:	Commanding General
Can Co/Cn Co:	Cannon Company
CO:	Commanding Officer
Comb:	Combat
Comdg:	Commanding
CP:	Command Post
CPH:	Camp Patrick Henry
Depty:	Deputy
Div:	Division
Div Arty:	Division Artillery
D/S:	Direct Support
EM:	Enlisted man/men
Engr:	Engineer
Ex/Exec:	Executive
FA:	Field Artillery
FO/Fwd Obsr:	Forward Observer
Frag:	Fragment
Ft:	Fort
G-2:	Division Intelligence Officer
GCM:	General Court Martial
Gen/Gen'l:	General
G/S:	General Support
Hosp:	Hospital

HQ/Hq:	Headquarters
Hrs:	Hours
Hwy:	Highway
Inf:	Infantry
Info:	Information
Int:	Intelligence
LnO:	Liaison Officer
mm:	millimeter
MTOUSA:	Mediterranean Theater of Operations, USA
OP:	Observation Post
PX:	Post Exchange
Ren/Recon:	Reconnaissance
Rec'd:	Received
Regt:	Regiment
RJ:	Road Junction
RO:	Reconnaissance Officer
SA:	Small arms
SS:	Steam Ship
Surv:	Survey
Sv:	Service
S-2:	Battalion Intelligence Officer
S-3:	Battalion Operations and Training Officer
T/5:	Technician Fifth Grade
USAT:	United States Army Transport
w/:	With
WOJG:	Warrant Officer Junior Grade

Glossary

Adjustment—the determination of corrections by firing to obtain the correct bearing and range as data for use in subsequent accurate engagement of enemy targets.

Air strip—an unimproved surface, with minimum facilities, which had been adapted for take-off or landing of aircraft.

Ammunition dump—a place where ammunition is stored in the field, dispersed as much as possible for safety, and protected as much as possible from mud, sand, dirt, water, high temperatures, weather, and enemy fire.

Assembly area—an area in which a unit is assembled preparatory to further action.

Attached—the placement of units or personnel in an organization where such placement is relatively temporary.

Battery—A unit in the artillery that is organizationally the same as an infantry company.

Battle Indoctrination—the attachment of newly arrived troops, usually individually or in small groups, to units already in combat to permit them to gain their initial battlefield experience alongside battle-wise troops.

Big doings—term used by Colonel Derricks (interchangeably with big show and push) when referring to the Allies' plan to break out of the mountains and into the Po Valley before bad weather set in. The plan was postponed several times and finally rescheduled for spring 1945.

Big show—see Big doings.

Bivouac—a temporary encampment, usually in the open.

Booby hatch—a slang term for an insane asylum.

C-ration—an individual combat ration consisting of three cans of "B" unit and three cans of "M" unit. The "B" unit contained biscuits, confections, cigarettes, and a beverage. The meat components of the "M" unit were more acceptable when heated, but could be consumed cold if the situation warranted.

California—code name for one of the numerous hills in the coastal sector occupied by enemy troops.

Command Inspection—an inspection conducted by commanders, as required by Army Regulations, of all motor vehicles assigned to their jurisdiction to verify the functioning of maintenance and operating personnel and to ensure that subordinate commanders comply with regulations and procedures.

Command Post—a unit's headquarters where the commander and staff perform their activities.

Concentration—fire from a number of weapons directed at a single point or area.

Counterattack—attack by a part or all of the defending force against an enemy attacking force, usually for the purpose of regaining ground that had been lost.

Counterbattery—artillery fire directed at the enemy's artillery positions.

Crack troops—a highly functional, smooth-running team.

Defensive Fires—those specific prearranged fires which covered the most dangerous approaches to positions.

"Dictate"—code name assigned by Signal Operations Instructions to identify 365th.

Direct Support (DS)—a mission guaranteeing support to a specific unit, though assets would also be available as directed by Div. Arty when the priority right was not being exercised.

Division Intelligence Officer—division general staff officer responsible for keeping the Div. CG, Div. staff, and subordinate units informed of the enemy situation and for issuing a periodic (daily) intelligence report.

Field Artillery—Field artillery includes surface to surface cannon, rocket, and missile systems which are light and mobile enough to move with ground combat units. This excludes fixed fortifications (e.g. coastal artillery, fortress cannons), surface-to-air artillery, and indirect fire systems so large that they are not mobile enough to move with troops. Field Artillery is separated into three main parts: light (105mm or less) medium (106–155mm) and heavy (greater than 155mm).

Fire Mission—a specific assignment given to an artillery unit to fire at an enemy target.

Fire Plan—a tactical plan for using the weapons of a unit or formation so that their fire will be coordinated.

Forward Observer—artillery personnel operating with front-line troops trained to adjust artillery fire on enemy targets and to pass battlefield information back to their units.

G-2—see Division Intelligence Officer.

General Court-Martial (GCM)—the highest of three types of courts-martial convened by military commanders. It consisted of five or more officers plus a trial judge advocate, a defense counsel, and their assistants. It was authorized to try men who had committed serious crimes, including capital offenses.

General Support—an artillery mission that required a battalion to support the division as a whole, to answer calls for fire from Division Artillery, to move as ordered by Division Artillery but did not require the furnishing of LnOs or FOs to the supported infantry.

General Support—Reinforcing—an artillery mission that required the battalion to support the division as a whole and the provision of reinforcing fire to another artillery unit.

Gun Pits—emplacements constructed to provide protection for howitzers and crews from small arms, mortar, and artillery fire. They were usually circular pits about 24ft in diameter and 2ft deep, with a sloping ramp to the rear to permit moving the piece out of the emplacement. Additional protection was afforded by surrounding the emplacements, except to the rear, with a parapet (an earth mound, or sandbags, about 1½ft high).

Gunnery—the practical handling of artillery to place accurate fire on selected targets. It consists of two phases: preparation of firing data and conduct of fire.

Ingles—Italian term for English.

Jerry—slang term for German military units or individuals.

Kraut—see Jerry.

La Bombe—slang expression used by American soldiers to describe enemy artillery fire.

Liaison Officer (LnO)—artillery officer who represented the battalion commander at the CP of the supported unit, maintaining intercommunication to ensure mutual understanding and unity of purpose. A direct support field artillery battalion furnished a liaison officer to the supported infantry regimental CP, the CPs of each of the supported front-line infantry battalions, and, when reinforcing another artillery battalion, to the CP of that battalion.

Massa Front—term used frequently to describe the coastal sector of the 92nd Division.

Mess—in the Army, a place where a group of people have their meals together.

Mission—a task given to the commander together with its purpose, thereby clearly indicating the action to be taken and the reason therefore.

Niente Bono—slang expression used by American military personnel to describe something unpleasant.

Observation Post (OP)—a position from which military observations were made or fire directed and adjusted, and which possessed appropriate communications.

Occupation of Position—movement into and proper organization of an area to use as a battle position.

Organic—assigned to and forming an essential part of a military organization.

Push—see big doings.

Rear Echelon—those administrative, supply, and maintenance elements not required in the forward areas. In the 597th, it was the area controlled by the Service Battery.

Reconnaissance—a mission undertaken by commanders and their staffs to obtain by visual observation the geographic characteristics of an area to permit selection of the most suitable positions from which the various elements of their organizations can accomplish their assigned missions.

Registration—see adjusting.

Rendezvous—a place designated for a meeting or assembly of troops.

Smoked—artillery smoke shells containing white phosphorous, fired to mask the movement of U.S. troops from enemy observation.

Staging—to process, in a specified area, troops which are in transit from one place to another.

Staging Area—a general locality, containing accommodation for troops, established for the concentration of troop units and transient personnel between moves.

Supply Agencies—see Technical Service Agencies.

Technical Service Agencies—those agencies within the division (Engr., Med., Ord., QM. and Sig.) responsible for supply and support functions peculiar to their specialties, throughout the division area, including in or near the front lines. However, most of their work was done in the division service area to the rear of the bulk of the combat troops.

Tedesche—see Jerry.

Volley—a simultaneous discharge of a number of weapons.

Bibliography

Books

Barbeau, Arthur and Henri, Florette. *The Unknown Soldiers: Black American Troops in World War I.* Philadelphia: Temple University Press, 1974.

Clark, Mark W. *Calculated Risk.* New York: Harper & Brothers, 1950.

Coakley, Robert W. and Leighton, Richard M. *Global Logistics and Strategy 1943–1945.* Washington, D.C.: Office of the Chief of Military History, 1968.

De Moraes, Mascarenhas. *The Brazilian Expeditionary Force.* Washington, D.C.: Government Printing Office, 1966.

Fisher, Ernest F. Jr. *Cassino to the Alps.* Washington: Center of Military History, U.S. Army, 1977.

Fletcher, Marvin. *The Black Soldier and Officer in the U.S. Army 1891–1917.* Columbia: University of Missouri Press, 1974.

Franklin, John Hope. From Slavery to Freedom. New York: Alfred A. Knopf, 1974.

Goodman, Paul. *A Fragment of Victory: In Italy During World War II, 1942–1945.* Carlisle Barracks, Pennsylvania: Army War College, 1952.

Greene, Robert Ewell. *Black Defenders of America 1775–1973.* Chicago: Johnson Publishing Company, 1974.

Gropman, Alan L. *The Air Force Integrates 1945–1964.* Washington, D.C.: Office of Air Force History, 1978.

Hargrove, Hondon B. *Buffalo Soldiers in Italy: Black Americans in World War II.* Jefferson: McFarland and Company, 1985.

Hunter, Jehu and Clark, Major. *The Buffalo Division in World War II.* (Unpublished).

Huston, James A. *The Sinews of War: Army Logistics 1775–1953.* Washington, D.C.: Center of Military History, U.S. Army, 1966.

Lee, Ulysses. *The Employment of Negro Troops in World War II.* Washington: Office of the Chief of Military History, 1966.

Lottinville, Savoie. *The Rhetoric of History.* Oklahoma: University of Oklahoma Press, 1976.

McGregor, Morris J., Jr. *Integration of the Armed Forces 1940–1965.* Washington, D.C.: Center of Military History, 1981.

McGregor, Morris J., Jr. and Nalty, Bernard. *Blacks in the United States Armed Forces: Basic Documents, Volume III, Freedom and Jim Crow 1865–1917.* Delaware: Scholarly Resources, Inc., 1977.

McGuire, Phillip. *Taps for a Jim Crow Army.* California: ABC-Clio, 1983.

Miller, Kelley. *Kelley Miller's History of the World War for Human Rights.* Washington, D.C.: Austin Jenkins Co., 1918.

Motley, Mary P. *The Invisible Soldier.* Michigan: Wayne State University Press, 1975.

Nichols, Lee. *Breakthrough on the Color Front.* New York: Random House, 1954.

Osur, Alan M. *Blacks in the Army Air Forces During World War II*. Washington, D.C.: Office of Air Force History, 1977.

Sawicki, James A. *Field Artillery Battalions of the U.S. Army, Volume 1*. Virginia: Centaur Publication, 1977.

Sawicki, James A. *Field Artillery Battalions of the U.S. Army, Volume 2*. Virginia: Centaur Publication, 1978.

Scott, Emmett J. *History of the American Negro in the World War*. Chicago: Homewood, 1919. Reprinted as *Scott's Official History of the American Negro in the World War*. New York: Arno Press and the New York Times, 1969.

Truscott, L.K., Jr. *Command Missions: A Personal Story*. New York: E. P. Dutton, 1954.

Magazines

"Defense Dept. Refuses To Award Late Black Colonel Army's High Commendation," *Jet Magazine* (August 27, 1984): 19.

"Negro Artillery in World War II," *The Field Artillery Journal* (April 1946): 228.

"Push Still On For Laurels Due Black WWII Colonel," *Jet Magazine* (October 22, 1984): 30.

"Urge Military Honor For Late Black Army Colonel," *Jet Magazine* (May 21, 1984): 30.

Newspapers

The Afro-American, March 11, 1944.

The Oklahoma Eagle, February 24, 1982.

The Oklahoma Eagle, October 25, 1984.

The Pittsburgh Courier, March 4, 1944.

The Pittsburgh Courier, March 11, 1944.

The Pittsburgh Courier, March 18, 1944.

The Washington Afro-American, June 9, 1984.

U.S. Army Publications

Newspapers

The Buffalo, 92nd Infantry Division newspaper during World War II, 1942–1945.

The Stars and Stripes (February 6, 1945).

The Stars and Stripes (February 14, 1945).

The Stars and Stripes (November 6, 1945).

Unit Histories

Allied Forces. 15th Army Group. *Finito! The Po Valley Campaign*, 1945.

History of the 77th Field Artillery Group. Atlanta: Army Press, 1942.

History of the 349th Field Artillery. Atlanta: Army Press, 1942.

Fifth Army. *19 Days from the Apennines to the Alps: The Story of the Po Valley Campaign*. Milan: Pizzi & Pizzio, 1945.

U.S. Army. 92nd Infantry Division. Historical Committee. *With the 92nd Infantry Division, October 1942–June 1945*. MTOUSA, 1945.

Books

Matloff, Maurice (General Editor), *American Military History*. Office of the Chief of Military History, United States Army, Washington D.C., 1969, revised 1973.

Public Documents

Published Records

Congressional Record. "Appendix to the Congressional Record." Extension of remarks of Honorable Hamilton Fish, February 9, 1944: A659, A660.

Congressional Record–House. "Speech by Hamilton Fish, Colored Troops in Combat Units." February, 1944: 2007–2008.

Evans, James C. Summary prepared for the Secretary of the Army, Subject: "The Negro in the Army, Policy and Practice." Washington, D.C.: Department of the Army. July 31, 1948.

Marshall, George C. "Biennial report of the Chief of Staff of the United States Army," July 1, 1943, to June 30, 1945, to the Secretary of War. Washington, D.C.: War Department, 1945.

Martin, John T. Memo for Civilian Assistant, Office of the Assistant Secretary of Defense (Manpower, Personnel and Reserve), Subject: "The Negro Officer in the Armed Forces of the United States of America." Washington, D.C.: Office of the Assistant Secretary of Defense, 1960.

Office of Deputy Assistant Secretary of Defense for Equal Opportunity and Safety Policy. "Black Americans in Defense of Our Nation." 1982.

Unpublished Documents

Ketchum, D. W. Memo for the Chief, Subject: "Personnel of the 167th Brigade," April 20, 1920, NA RG 165, item 8142–125.

McIntyre, Frank. Memo for Chief of Staff, Subject: "Colored Officers for Labor Battalions," July 16, 1918, NA RG 165, item 8142–179.

Scott, Emmett J. "Letter to President Theodore Roosevelt" requesting the organization of colored artillery units, dated March 8, 1907. NA RG 164, file WCD 4483.

Snow, William J. Memo for the Chief of Staff, Subject: "Colored officers in the 167th Field Artillery Brigade, 92nd Division," NA RG 165, item 8142–152.

Wilcox, De W. Memo for the Chief of Staff, Subject: "Negroes for Artillery Service," dated April 16, 1907.

Unit Historical Records

88th Division Artillery History, December 1933 and January 1945. NA RG 407, 388 – ART – 0.3, file 9775.

597th Battalion History, October 1942–November 1944. NA RG 407, 392 – FA (597) – 0.2, file 45582.

597th Battalion History, December 1944–October 1945. NA RG 407, 392 – FA (597) – 0.2, file 19012.

92nd Division Artillery History, October 1944–July 1945. NA RG 407, 392 – ART – 0.3, file 18305.

92nd Division Artillery Operations Report, 15 August 1954. NA RG 407, 392 – ART – 0.3, file 45623.

Miscellaneous

Interviews

Baber, Mrs. Elvira M. Telephone interviews with author, 1974–85.

Baber, Mrs. Elvira M. Tape recordings made by Mrs. Baber and furnished for author's files.

Derricks, Wendell T. Conversation with author, January 1, 1945.

McCants, Lester H. Telephone interviews with author, 1974–85.

Letters

Derricks, Wendell T. Personal letter to author, January 27, 1949.
di Ruffano, Marchesa Virginia Ferrante. Personal letter to author, August 20, 1945.

Unpublished Manuscripts

Clark, Major. "History of the 597th Field Artillery Battalion." Expansion and revision of the October 15, 1945 edition.

Endnotes

Author's Preface

1. The World War II 369th Coast Artillery, formerly the World War I 369th Infantry, was the parent unit of the 870th.

Introduction

1. In a general sense, psychological warfare is the use of any means to influence the thought, morale, or behavior of any group of people. In its restricted sense, it is defined as a dissemination of propaganda to undermine the opponents' will to resist, to demoralize the opponents' forces, and to undermine the morale of the supporters. Propaganda is an organized effort to spread particular doctrines or information. It is information disseminated for a purpose and has no relation to the truth or falsity of facts.
2. "Documents of War," collected by William E. B. Dubois, *The Crisis*, XVIII (May, 1919).
3. Field artillery is that arm of the military service which, by means of maneuverable devices placed on the ground (cannon), propels missiles that are beyond the weight capabilities of hand weapons. See Glossary.
4. Survey: the determination and delineation of the form, content, and position of a tract of land by taking linear and angular measurements and by applying the principles of geometry and trigonometry.

Chapter 1. A Limited Opportunity

1. The 349th had served as part of the National Army (forerunner of the Army Reserve) during World War I. Since it was not yet a Regular Army unit, it was demobilized within a few months after that war ended. (349A Hist)
2. Although the rate of pay was $21.00 per month, small amounts were deducted each month for Old Soldiers Home and for personal laundry, leaving a little more than $19.00.
3. The parent unit of the 8th Infantry, Illinois National Guard was organized in 1895 at Chicago. During World War I, it was temporarily re-designated as the 370th Infantry and assigned to the 93rd Division. It was deployed overseas and served in the Oisne and Lorraine sectors of the Western Front.
4. These barracks were located east of Gate 1, and separated from the main post by two railroads (Rock Island and Frisco) and Highway 277/281.
5. As used here, service practice is a part of the field training of artillery officers with special emphasis on the preparation, execution and conduct of fire with service ammunition. The modern expression for this is gunnery training tables.
6. Congressman Fish, who had commanded black troops during World War I as a captain in Company K of the 369th Infantry, was outstanding in his efforts in a reluctant Congress to prevent discrimination against black military personnel during World War II. In 1944, his efforts

had a significant impact on the reorganization of the 597th and 600th Field Artillery Battalions of the 92nd Division (see Chapter 6).

7. Each of these medium howitzers weighed over 28,000 pounds and could fire a 95-pound projectile a distance of 18,000 yards. The guns were classified as medium artillery and each was towed by a 10-ton International Harvester Diesel tractor. (349 Hist)

8. The battery detail section was responsible for battery communications, reconnaissance, survey, and the establishment of the battery observation post.

9. Thereafter, until I had been in the Army four months, my rate of pay would be increased to $36.00 per month ($21.00 as a private first class plus $15.00 as a specialist 4th class).

10. A review is a formal inspection of troops on parade by a high-ranking officer.

Chapter 2. The Opportunity Expands

1. Most of the black officer candidates for the Field Artillery Officer Candidate School (FA OCS) at Fort Sill, Oklahoma were provided by the 184th, 349th, and the three field artillery regiments (350th, 351st, and 353rd) of the 46th Field Artillery Brigade (personal observation).

2. Documents cited in the text are identified by initials as follows: WTD/D—Colonel Derricks' Diary; HBH/D—Captain Hargrove's diary; MC/FDC—my letters to my wife; FDC/MC—my wife's letters to me; MC/NB—entry from one of my notebooks; MC/EC—my letters to my mother; MC/POR – my letters to?; MC/OCS – my letter to Officer Candidate School; HWE/MC—letter from Harry Elkins to me; Tanner/MC—Tanner (a soldier) to me; MC/WTD—note from me to Derricks; RFR/MC/1-2-86—?; WJC/MC—letter from brother William Clark to me?

3. The major elements of the 46th Field Artillery Brigade were the 46th Brigade Headquarters Battery and the 350th, 351st, and 353rd Field Artillery Regiments.

4. Field artillery was divided into three (weight) classes—light, medium, and heavy—and grouped tactically into division, corps, Army, and General Headquarters (GHQ) reserve artillery. All classes were contained in GHQ reserve artillery and were used to support various armies, corps, and divisions for specific periods and definite missions in accordance with the general plan of operations. (Sawicki, Volume II, 1,228)

5. These were men whose Army General Classification Test (ACT) scores were 110 or higher.

6. Figures compiled Army-wide after World War II indicated that only one out of 10 eligible blacks applied for OCS, compared to four out of 10 eligible whites. (MacGregor, 1981, 36)

7. The two black line officers on active duty in August 1940 were Colonel B. O. Davis and First Lieutenant B. O. Davis, Jr. The two black officers who had graduated from West Point since 1889 were B. O. Davis, Jr. (Infantry, 1936) and James D. Fowler (Infantry, 1941). Davis transferred to the Air Corps in May 1942.

8. Orders dated July 7, 1942, Headquarters IV Army Corps, Camp Beauregard, Louisiana.

Chapter 3. Camp Atterbury, Indiana

1. The 597th was the third black field artillery unit in which Major Workizer had served. He had previously served in the 349th Field Artillery and in the 596th Field Artillery Battalion of the 93rd Division.

2. The mission of direct support requires the battalion to ensure coordination and cooperation of effort with the supported infantry by means of command liaison, liaison officers (LNOs), and forward observers (FOs). (See Glossary)

3. In February 1943, Truman Gibson became Civilian Aide to the Secretary of War after William H. Hastie resigned. Hastie resigned because, after trying unsuccessfully for two years within the

government to bring about changes in the Army's policy concerning black military personnel, he concluded that he would be more useful as a private citizen who could express his views freely and publicly.

4. Familiarization with overhead artillery fire was a part of the training of combat arms soldiers. After the troops were positioned between the guns and the target, the guns were fired in the direction of the target and the trajectory of the shells passed directly overhead, but a considerable distance above the troops. However, the shells were close enough that the troops could hear their characteristic whine.

5. Indirect fire was used when the target could not be seen through the sight of the guns. Under those circumstances, an observer positioned where he could see the target and who had communication with the guns or a fire direction center would "adjust" the fire on the target. (See Glossary)

Chapter 4. Camp Robinson, Arkansas

1. On December 1, 1974, Brigadier General and Mrs. Cartwright were killed in an airplane accident near Washington, D.C.

2. O = Officers, WO = Warrant Officers, EM = Enlisted Men.

Chapter 5. Fort Huachuca, Arizona

1. Draft letter, "Morale of Negro Officers and Troops, 365th Infantry, 92nd Infantry Division," dated May 24, 1943, to the President of the United States.

2. General Davis had previously visited the separate elements of the division when they were located at four different posts.

3. Bracket: the interval in range between two rounds of artillery fire, one over and one short of the target, used to find the correct range.

4. The purpose of the field artillery survey was to determine the horizontal and vertical locations of points on the ground so that they could be plotted on a firing chart, and to provide a means of orienting the howitzers on the ground.

5. The guidon is a small distinctive flag issued to and carried by a battery or company for unit identification in formations, marches, and parades.

6. Hook area of Fry: a wire-enclosed area outside the post's fencing, with tents and shanties, inhabited by prostitutes.

7. Major Clement W. Crockett relieved Major Daniel Workzier as 597th FA Battalion Commander, April 3, 1943.

8. A picture of the buffalo was normally included on division newspaper *The Buffalo* and on all division special publications.

Chapter 6. Maneuvers in Louisiana

1. 184th, 333rd, 349th, 350th, 351st, 353rd, and 597th Field Artillery Regiments. (Sawicki, 1977/1978, 1279–80)

2. The 930th was re-designated as the 1699th Engineer Combat Battalion; the 931st was re-designated as the 1698th Engineer Combat Battalion.

3. I wrote numerous letters to my fiancée during the period from March to June 1944 concerning the change in command of the 597th. Many of these letters covered several different subjects related to the change, and subsequent letters covered different aspects of the same subjects. Accordingly, in Chapters 6 and 7, some of the excerpts covering a particular subject have been taken out of chronological order and have been included with other excerpts covering the same subject.

Chapter 8. The Tide Turns

1. A letter written by me to my fiancée (FDP) who became my wife (FDC), reflecting my impressions of what happened, contemporaneous with the events.
2. First Lieutenants Hondon B. Hargrove, Walter L. Macklin, Lester McCants, and James W. Quisenberry were promoted to captain; and Second Lieutenants James R. Munday, Leonard L. Jackson, Frank J. Boutte, and William G. Dix were promoted to first lieutenant.
3. After we arrived overseas, the recommendation for my promotion was resubmitted and I was promoted three months later. However, that was four months after my initial date of eligibility.
4. Transmitted to Lieutenant Colonel W. T. Derricks, subject: Commendation.

Chapter 9. Going Over

1. Camp Patrick Henry (CPH) had a capacity of 24,100 troops, and was one of four major staging areas on the east coast of the United States where units were assembled for final checks of personnel and equipment before embarking for overseas movement during World War II.
2. The *Colombie* was a former French luxury liner which had been in service between Le Havre and the West Indies.
3. Brazil was the only Latin American country to send an expeditionary force to take part in the European conflict during World War II. (Clark, 1950, 389) The Brazilian Expeditionary Force, consisting of an infantry division, with an artillery and liaison squadron employing light aircraft, entered combat at about the same time and in the same general area as the 92nd Division.
4. The disembarkation was documented on motion picture film now filed in the National Archives as ADC 2451 and 2452.
5. This required them to leave the battalion for short periods, during which they were attached to units already in combat, permitting them to gain their initial battlefield experience alongside battle-wise troops.
6. Colonel Derricks was pleasantly surprised to find Colonel Ketchum, the 91st Division Artillery Executive Officer, who had been one of his classmates in the Field Officers course at the Artillery School, Fort Sill, Oklahoma, during the period August 25–November 14, 1941.
7. I was told that civilians were not usually evacuated from the forward areas unless they hampered combat operations or were a menace to security.

Chapter 10. By the Sea

1. Initial registration by the center battery of the battalion was in accordance with standard procedure and was made to obtain the correct bearing and range for use in subsequent accurate engagement of enemy targets.
2. The permanently assigned liaison pilots for the 597th were Lieutenants Chauncey Eskridge and James Christian.
3. The cannon company was armed with a short-barreled 105mm howitzer with a maximum range of about 7,200 yards, some 60 percent of the approximately 12,200-yard maximum range of the regular 105mm howitzers with which the 597th was armed.
4. Colonel Derricks and some members of his staff, including First Lieutenant Henry F. Shorter, Battalion Surgeon, and Chaplain (First Lieutenant) Franklin B. Diggs, one of the two chaplains assigned to Division Artillery, were lodged in the home of the Meconi family, consisting of Signor Mario Meconi, Signora Maria Meconi, Lina, and Sandra.
5. Lieutenant Colonel Oscar Robinson was Commanding Officer, 3rd Battalion, 366th Infantry. He and Captain Errington Johnson had served with Colonel Derricks in the 184th before they transferred to the 366th.

6. The battery was armed with four 3.7in. guns which, because of our air supremacy in the area, were being used in the secondary mission of furnishing artillery support for ground troops.

7. Early in November, Truman Gibson had asked Major Magee, then about to depart on a mission to Italy, to bring back factual data on the 92nd Division.

8. Colonel Marston did not return to duty in the 92nd Division, and, in accordance with special orders from the 33rd Hospital dated January 9, 1945, was transferred out of the division.

9. For several months, Derricks even outranked the Acting Division Chief of Staff, Lieutenant Colonel William J. McCaffrey. McCaffrey had been appointed to the position after Colonel Barber's death in October 1944, but he was not promoted to full colonel until early in 1945.

10. Colonel Robinson's sister Victoria (Vicky) was a friend of Colonel Derricks's wife.

11. Our main source of printed news came from *The Stars and Stripes*, the Army newspaper, delivered each day with the perishable rations. In addition, some of us were fortunate to receive, periodically, from our correspondents back home, copies of black newspapers such as the *Chicago Defender*, *Pittsburgh Courier*, *Afro-American*, *Kansas City Call*, and *Norfolk Journal and Guide*.

12. In the coastal sector, the liaison officer with 365th Regimental Headquarters was Captain Wesley B. Johnson. Liaison officers with the infantry battalions were Captains Walter Macklin and Charles Pickett, while forward observers and observers at the battalion Ops were Lieutenants Jackson, Millner, Burton, McFadden, Lee, Cordwell, Richardson, Connor, Dix, and Rose.

13. Within a few days of Fifth Army entering Rome in June 1944, facilities were prepared there for a Fifth Army Rest Center where personnel from combat units could return for a period of approximately one week. Facilities for the enlisted men were located in the Foro Mussolini, which had served as a military school for the Fascist Youth Movement. Facilities for the officers were provided in various hotels in Rome, including the Excelsior. Similar facilities for leave for combat unit personnel were provided in other selected cities such as Florence.

14. Available documentation does not contain a satisfactory explanation of the reason why the 92nd Division, after it received an addition of a not-quite-ready-for-combat infantry unit of approximately 3,200 officers and men because the division was considered understrength for its mission, then released a combat-ready combat team of over 3,700 officers and men for use in other parts of the Fifth Army line. In doing so, the division sustained a net loss of over 500 men, in addition to a significant net loss in the combat-readiness of the units involved.

Chapter 13. A New Year and a New Assignment

1. He confirmed that evaluation by giving me such a high rating on my next efficiency report that the 92nd Division Artillery Commander, with whom I had very little contact during the period, deemed it necessary to reduce it by several points to prevent my ratings from exceeding those of his most outstanding white officers.

2. Quotations involving WTD and MC in this chapter are a reconstruction of part of a private conversation with Colonel Derricks based upon notes taken shortly thereafter and my memory of the event.

3. Undoubtedly, the exacerbation of Derricks' condition by the rigors of combat contributed to his vulnerability to subsequent illnesses which eventually caused his untimely death in 1949 at the age of 53.

4. Colonel Queen, in his letter requesting relief from command of the 366th, had stated: "The treatment the regiment and myself have received during the period of attachment to the 92nd Division has been such as to disturb me mentally and has not been such as is usually given an officer of my grade and service … I am physically and mentally exhausted." (Letter CO 366th Inf Regt to CG Fifth Army, Dec. 11, 1944, 92nd Div Files)

Chapter 14. In the Valley

1. 10 AGRA controlled all of the artillery in the Serchio Valley and was under the operational control of the 92nd Division.
2. 3rd Battalion, 366th, was in the coastal sector.
3. Derricks's diary does not contain any further explanation of the situation indicated in this diary entry. It is possible Derricks had encountered the racially biased attitude indicated in the response made by the regimental commander to a questionnaire from the division commander concerning the performance of his regiment during Operation *Fourth Term* (see Chapter 16).
4. Although all of the 92nd Division's air operations were conducted initially from the air strip near Viareggio, some of them were moved later to an air strip near Lucca and a forward air strip near Ghivizzano to support units in the Serchio Valley.

Chapter 15. Operation Fourth Term

1. 3rd Battalion, 365th, as part of Task Force 1, participated in the attack in the coastal sector beginning on February 8.

Chapter 16. The Aftermath

1. Battery A of the 600th was in the Serchio Valley supporting the diversionary operation.
2. Task Force 1 was commanded by Lieutenant Colonel Edward R. Rowny, who had commanded the 317th Engineer Bn.
3. The comments of the 365th regimental commander were contained in 1st Ind to CG 92nd Inf Div, 21 Feb 45, on Ltr, CG 92nd Inf Div to CO 365th Inf, 3 Feb 45, copy in WDSSP RG 113 (MTO) (see app. II).
4. General Marshall's visit to the 92nd Division is documented on combat films titled "General Marshall Visits Fifth Army Front" which are filed in the National Archives as ADC 3338, ADC 3339, and ADC 3369.
5. The 473rd Infantry had been activated on January 14, 1945 from veterans of the 434th, 435th, and 900th Antiaircraft Artillery Battalions, many of whom had already fought as infantry for several months. Following activation, the new infantry regiment engaged in an intensive training program that lasted from mid-January until mid-February. The 442nd Infantry was in France but would be returned to Italy for the forthcoming spring offensive. (Goodman, 1952, 115–17)
6. A small number of 366th personnel were transferred to 92nd Division units. The remainder were transferred to the 224th and 226th Engineer General Service Regiments which had been organized for that purpose. The 366th was disbanded on March 28, 1945.

Chapter 17. On the Move

1. Locust was among the former members of the 366th who had been transferred to one of the Engineer General Service Regiments.
2. Which was driving on Massa.
3. A descriptive field artillery term for the large oval symbol drawn on a map by artillery commanders after a reconnaissance. The "goose egg" is used to designate a general area in which subordinate commanders are authorized to select specific positions for their units.
4. Procedure used in the field artillery to cause all the pieces (howitzers or guns) in the battery to be pointed in the prescribed initial direction.

Chapter 18. *The Enemy Withdrawal Becomes a Rout*

1. In general, a trail was a beam-like part of the howitzer carriage used to attach the howitzer to the prime mover for towing and to form a rear brace on the ground in the firing position. The 105mm howitzer had two trails, one on each side, which were locked together when attached to the prime mover for towing. "Dropped trails" referred to the action of disconnecting the trails from the prime mover, lowering them to the ground, and spreading them apart to form a brace in preparation for firing.

Chapter 19. *Two Down and One to Go*

1. The 92nd Division parade and ceremony on May 2 was documented on films filed in the National Archives as ADC 4327 and ADC 4329.
2. In addition, Bronze Star Medals were presented to General Colbern, Colonels Virgil R. Miller and William P. Yarborough, and Lieutenant Colonels Philo M. Baumgartner and Marcus H. Ray. These officers were commanders of the 92nd Div Arty, 442nd and 473rd Inf., and 539th and 600th FA Bns., respectively.
3. Decorations and awards earned by 597th personnel during combat operations included two Silver Stars (posthumous), one Soldier's Medal, 20 Bronze Star Medals, six Air Medals, four Oak Leaf Clusters to Air Medals, 17 Purple Hearts, and 11 Division Commander's Commendations.
4. The Christopher Columbus Memorial Ceremony in Genoa was documented on film, which is filed in the National Archives as ADC 4703.

Chapter 20. *A Special Mission Carried out From Varazze*

1. I did meet Giovanni several weeks later. On August 3, about six weeks after we had moved from Varazze back to the Viareggio area, I returned to the area west of Varazze and visited the Ferrania camera and film factory. There I met Giovanni, who had not been at home during my first visit to the old farmhouse in June.
2. Letter from Marchesa Ferrante di Ruffano to Captain Major Clark, 597th Field Artillery Battalion, dated Aug. 20, 1945. (597A Hist)

Chapter 21. *Preparing for Redeployment*

1. With the 92nd Infantry Division, October 1942–June 1945. Published by Information – Education Section, MTOUSA.
2. Colonel Davis, the former commander of the 332nd, had returned to the United States to assume command of the 477th Composite Group at Goodman Field, Kentucky; Colonel Spanky Roberts was the Commanding Officer of the 332nd at the time of Colonel Derricks's visit.
3. Before the awards orientation program could be fully implemented, the war ended.

Chapter 22. *Three Down and It's Over*

1. The exception was Lieutenant Colonel Marcus H. Ray, former Commanding Officer of the 600th, who was transferred to 92nd Division Artillery Headquarters.